'THEY ARE NOT DEAD'

Also by the author

St Augustine's Church, Norwich, Norfolk
(Churches Conservation Trust, 2004)

*Somewhere in Flanders: Letters of a Norfolk Padre
in the Great War*
(Larks Press, 2005)

Editorial Note

Due to the special nature of this book, many people may read the text piecemeal rather than continuously. It has therefore been appropriate to repeat certain information in several articles so that each serviceman's story is complete.

Those seeking information about a deceased relative should be aware that the biographies presented here may contain information they will find distressing or which does not agree in every detail with their family's memories. Nothing has been invented, no fact deliberately suppressed.

'THEY ARE NOT DEAD'

A Norwich Parish in the First World War
Remembering a Lost Generation

With a revised and expanded biographical
roll of honour of the Norwich parish of
St Augustine with St Mary Coslany
1914–1921

To the memory of Rosemary Taylor,
churchwarden of St Augustine's, who started me on this journey,
and to the heroes I discovered on the way.

Stuart John McLaren

Larks Press

Published by the Larks Press
Ordnance Farmhouse, Guist Bottom
Dereham NR20 5PF   Tel.01328 829207
Larks.Press@xlnmail.com
Website: www.booksatlarkspress.co.uk

Printed by Short Run Press, Exeter, July 2014

British Library Cataloguing-in-Publication Data
A catalogue record for this book is available from the British Library

Acknowledgements

Thanks are due to Paul and Helen Abigail; Richard Abigail; Roy Abigail; The Churches Conservation Trust; Pam Davenport; Margaret Hall; Babette Mann Huber (Victor Town Archives, New York, USA); Frank Meeres; John Munson; Norfolk Record Office; Norfolk Studies Library; Norwich Central Baptist Church; John Sayer; Sue Stead; Anna Stone (Aviva Group Archive, Norwich); Kate Thaxton (Royal Norfolk Regimental Museum, Norwich); Peter Turner; the Revd Nicholas Vesey and St Augustine's District Church Council, Norwich; Mike Wilkinson; Commander Dan Williams (American Legion, James Cooke Post 931, Victor, New York, USA); Nick Williams; Major B. G. Woodfield (Grenadier Guards Archive, London).

The author acknowledges the financial support of Norwich Heart and the Harry Watson Bursary.

Picture credits

Images used courtesy of American Legion, Victor, New York, pp.216, 219; Archant (Norfolk Studies Library) pp.48, 168, 252, 255, 267; Aviva Group Archive, pp.65, 198; Churches Conservation Trust, pp.11, 75, 131; Commonwealth War Graves Commission, p.288; Pam Davenport, p.211 Robert Maguire, p.140; Norfolk Libraries (Picture Norfolk), front cover, & pp. 34, 38, 53, 59, 641, 69, 109, 116, 128, 137, 142, 146, 158, 224, 234; Northampton Museum & Art Gallery, pp.260, 262; Ordnance Survey, p.6; John Sayer, pp. 67, 768; Other images are from the author's collection.

Contents

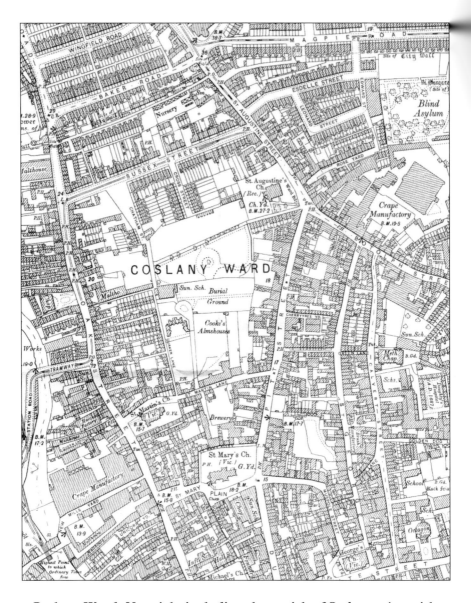

Coslany Ward, Norwich, including the parish of St Augustine with St Mary, from Ordnance Survey's 1:2,500 inch plan of Norwich published in 1907.

Introduction

On 11 November 1914 the headmistress of St Augustine's Infants School noted in the school log book that owing to the great increase in noise from the passing military and their wagons, timetables and arrangements had been revised to minimise the hindrance to school work. A century later the First World War still resonates powerfully in the nation's collective consciousness. It is impossible to exaggerate its impact. There can have been very few whose lives were not altered in ways they could hardly have imagined before the war. At its end more than eight million men had served in the British Empire's armed forces, almost a million of whom had lost their lives, around 12,000 of them from Norfolk alone. Millions more were left scarred and maimed both physically and emotionally.

Soldiers passing through St Augustine's early in the war

The scale of suffering and loss is almost too big to comprehend. We need to find a more human scope. Local war memorials and rolls of honour can help once we have learned to unravel the stories behind the names they contain; names that once had poignant meaning for a bereaved relative or friend but are now, for the most part, remembered only by ghosts. The revised and expanded roll of honour for the Norwich parish of St Augustine with St Mary Coslany presented here includes detailed biographical information on 104 servicemen and former servicemen associated with the parish who died between 1914 and 1921. This is 25 more than on St Augustine's war memorial and 44 more than are listed in *Norfolk Roll of Honour*. The roll has been arranged chronologically by the date of the serviceman's death so that readers can see the unfolding toll of life caused by particular campaigns and battles in the various theatres of war. In addition, there is a separate section telling the story of an executed soldier, Private John Henry Abigail, and another on four local men who survived the conflict.

When this research began, more than a decade ago, much of the material on which it is based (see 'Primary sources') was either unavailable for public scrutiny or difficult to access. Increasing openness in the public sphere, digitisation and the World Wide Web have transformed the process of research, making it possible to discover much more about the personal life and military record of First World War servicemen, including when and where they were born; who their parents were and what they did for a living; the names of their siblings; where they went to school; what work they did; whom they married and where they lived; whether they had children; where and when they enlisted; their movements in the military; their promotions, demotions, medical and disciplinary records; where and how they died; where and how they are commemorated and what medals they were awarded. In addition private family documents have helped round out some of the lives and the author is grateful to those who so generously allowed access to these invaluable resources.

St Augustine's lies in the north-west quarter of Norwich within its medieval boundary. People have lived and worked here for more than a thousand years. The parish church with its distinctive red brick tower, which earned its parishioners the nickname 'Red Steeplers', is the most northerly of the city's 32 surviving medieval churches. From the 15th to the 19th century the local economy was dominated by Norwich's textile trade, invigorated by waves of migrants from northern France and Flanders, known as the 'Strangers', who settled here in the 16th and 17th centuries. It is one of history's ironies that hundreds of years later their descendants would return to their ancestral home to fight and some to die in the world's first truly global conflict.

St Augustine's church

By the early 20th century weaving had been replaced by shoemaking as the area's main industry. It is estimated that 7,500 people were employed in this trade in Norwich by 1900, 15 per cent of the city's entire workforce. Few of the soldiers commemorated on the parish's war memorial had no connection with this industry, either through his own civilian employment or his relatives. Before the war the parish still had something of the character of a small, self-contained village. The majority of adults who lived here also worked here and most of their children went to St Augustine's School, which included mixed infants, junior and senior girls, and junior boys. There were shops here to cater for almost every requirement from cradle to grave (there were indeed two monumental masons) as well as scores of pubs. Most of the families were poor. Their living conditions, particularly in the area's 'yards', were often insanitary and over-crowding was also a serious problem, with families of ten or more children not uncommon. Infant mortality was high, often accounting for a third or even half of a family's offspring.

St Augustine's School

The parish of St Mary's Coslany lies to the south-west of St Augustine's, closer to the River Wensum than St Augustine's and separated from it by the parish of St Martin at Oak. Coslany is the name of an area north of the river which includes the parishes of St Mary, St Miles or Michael Coslany and St Martin at Oak. It was if anything even more tightly packed and industrialised than St Augustine's except at its heart where the early medieval church of St Mary Coslany with its distinctive Saxon round tower still stands on one side of a broad plain facing St Mary's Baptist church.

During the early 20th century St Augustine's was a united Church of England benefice with St Mary Coslany, sharing a minister, the Revd John Herbert Griffiths, who had been appointed in 1906. Originally from Shropshire, he was unusual for an Anglican clergyman of that era in having a science background. A trained chemist, until 1896 he had run his own pharmacy business on the Wirral until he gave it up to study Divinity at Cambridge.

John Griffiths was a hard-working, compassionate, pragmatic and conscientious priest and was evidently well loved and respected in the parish where he was frequently turned to for help in moments of family crisis, particularly during the war. Letters and official forms signed by him found among the Army Service papers of deceased soldiers from the parish are witness to his duels with military bureaucracy on behalf of grieving parents and widows, sometimes in dire financial hardship, to obtain personal possessions, allowances, awards and pensions due to them as next-of-kin. His eldest son, Vernon Griffiths, served in the Army during the War: first as a private in the Artists Rifles before receiving a commission as a second lieutenant in the Sherwood Foresters. Badly wounded by a gas shell in France in 1918 he spent the end of the War in hospital in England. Vernon was a talented musician. He had been taught to play the piano and organ as a youth by St Augustine's organist and choirmaster, R. W. Wilkinson. In the 1920s, after having been an organ scholar at Cambridge University, he emigrated to New Zealand where he became a celebrated composer and music teacher. An unpublished thesis on his life and work (Hawkey, 1993) provides valuable insights into the character of his father and his work in the parish. Poverty and hunger were significant problems in the area and the Revd J. H. Griffiths set up breakfast kitchens to feed the poor at St Mary's Coslany, while the nearby Baptist church supported a dispensary for the poor run by a nursing sister. Talking to a journalist decades later about his boyhood and youth in St Augustine's Vernon Griffiths recalled 'those women in Norwich's pre-1914 slums who with love and pity battled for their families in circumstances hardly imaginable today':

He shared his parents anguish at the lot of the poor. A beggar woman crying out on a Norwich street in the early 1900s spurred [him] to emigrate to New Zealand. The impotence he felt as a child, that such misery could become endemic in a so-called Christian nation was to have a significant impact. [Hawkey, p. 50.]

The Revd J. H. Griffiths also helped raise funds to build a community hall on land adjacent to St Augustine's churchyard, later dedicated to the memory of the parishes' war dead. St Augustine's Hall, known for many years as St Augustine's Memorial Hall, contains a framed scroll on which the parish's First and Second World War rolls of honour are inscribed. This notes that 'The Hall was built in 1920 as a Memorial using money given by parishioners and friends', although work seems to have begun as early as 1915. The parish's other war memorial takes the form of a roll of honour carved into a great oak screen inside the main parish church. On Sunday 25 January 1920 people of the parish of St Augustine with St Mary Coslany gathered in St Augustine's church to remember sons, brothers, fathers, husbands, friends and neighbours who had lost their lives in the Great War. During the service the bishop of Norwich, the Right Revd Bertram Pollock, dedicated the parish's new war memorial to 'The Glory of God and in the Memory of the Fallen'. Made by Norfolk craftsman and elaborately carved in the Gothic style, the memorial had been installed under the tall, central arch between the chancel and the nave. A more prominent position could hardly have been found, and for those among the congregation who knew about ecclesiastical architecture, its design and location where a painted rood screen had once stood before the Reformation could hardly have failed to suggest to them that an unspoken parallel was being drawn here between the martyrdom of the saints and Christ's Sacrifice on the Cross (or 'rood' in Old English) and the sacrifice of the fallen in the war.

Immediately after the war there had been something like a national collective will to gather together the names of the dead by parish, village, town, city, regiment, profession, workplace, school, sporting club and so on. The UK National Inventory of War Memorials estimates that there are around 54,000 extant war memorials in the United Kingdom. Many hundreds, possibly thousands, have been

Contemporary photograph of the newly installed memorial screen in St Augustine's

lost. Before the First World War it was uncommon to commemorate ordinary soldiers and sailors publicly by name. Norwich's Boer War memorial is a rare example. The vast majority of Britain's servicemen in the First World War were not full-time Regulars but civilians temporarily in uniform and thus with closer links to their local communities than long-service soldiers and sailors, who tended to live overseas for much of their careers. Additionally, the British military authorities refused to allow the remains of the dead to be brought home for burial, partly for practical reasons but also because it was thought that so many funerals might sap the public morale.

With no funeral service, closure was sought by grieving relatives and friends by other means. Almost from the beginning of the war improvised street shrines with casualty lists, photographs, flowers and patriotic flags and ribbons began to appear. Later, more permanent memorials to individual servicemen were installed in churches and other public places. In St Augustine's a stained glass window in memory of Rifleman Leonard Pert was commissioned by his parents within weeks of his death in France in May 1917 and in place before the war had ended. Considering that the process of installing a permanent memorial was both difficult and expensive, the number and quality of the memorials in St Augustine's is all the more remarkable and one cannot help wondering whether competitive memorialising was being engaged in here among the slightly better off families.

Filling seven panels across the base of the west-facing side of St Augustine's chancel screen, facing the nave, are carved the names of 79 servicemen, arranged from left to right by rank and name. A few names, out of alphabetical order, were clearly added after the screen was installed. Above the panels are carved the words 'IN MEMORY OF BRAVE MEN 1914–1919'. All such permanent structures in a Church of England church required the permission of the Diocese, a legal process known as a Faculty. Among the documents supporting the Faculty for St Augustine's war memorial is this note:

> *At a well-attended meeting of the churchwardens, sidesmen, and parishioners of St Augustine's held on Tuesday September 16, 1919, it was agreed unanimously that the memorial should take the form of an oak chancel screen. The working class Parishioners have subscribed the needed funds [about £90] and the design, which is in keeping with the architectural features of the church, has been prepared by Mr F. Varney of Messrs Morgan & Buckingham of Norwich. The work will be entrusted to Howard & Sons, the Norwich Ecclesiastical Wood Carvers.*

The emphasis on the parishioners' class was clearly considered noteworthy. This was one of the poorest parishes in the city and yet the parish church contains the finest collection of First World War memorials of any church in Norwich other than the cathedral, with no less than six local soldiers commemorated individually in addition to the main roll of honour.

It is difficult to determine a definitive figure for the proportion of St Augustine's men of service age who lost their lives on active service in the war; it is unlikely, however, to have been very different from Norwich or Norfolk as a whole, which are reckoned to have lost above the national average. According to *Norfolk Roll of Honour*, published in 1920, St Augustine's had the 11th highest number of casualties in Norwich. Its casualty total for the whole city was 2,200. By an odd coincidence 2,200 was the exact population of St Augustine in the 1911 Census. Looked at this way, Norwich's loss was the equivalent of the entire population of one of its medium-sized parishes. In fact, the total losses for both parish and city were significantly higher. *Norwich Roll of Honour*, published in 1924, lists 3,544 citizens who died. The male population of Norwich in 1911 was 56,171, which means the city lost between 4 and 7 per cent of its male population due to the war. The percentage is, however, much higher if one only counts those males aged between 10 and 30 in 1911, that is, those most likely to have been of an age to have served in the armed forces between 1914 and 1918. It is not known precisely how many Norwich men served in the war, but out of this cohort of 20,351, the loss of up to 3,544 men amounts to something like 17 per cent of those who served. The national percentage is around 12 per cent. The close knit nature of the area meant that most of those who died would have been known within the community as a relative, school friend, workmate or neighbour, and with an attrition rate of around two deaths per month throughout the war there would have been little respite from shock, grief and mourning.

Across a darkly stained oak beam at the top of St Augustine's war memorial the words 'THEY ARE NOT DEAD WHO LIVE FOREVER IN OUR HEARTS' have been carved and gilded on its east-facing side. No literary source for this phrase has been found. It is not from Scripture and appears to derive more from folklore and Romantic poetry than Christian theology, as for example in the poem 'Hallowed Ground' by Scottish poet Thomas Campbell: 'To live in hearts we leave behind is not to die'. The words clearly inspired one local family who had them inscribed on the headstone of their son Private George Bridges of the Royal Norfolk Regiment who died in 1942, aged 22, while a prisoner of war in the Far East. For decades

after the First World War it was the tradition to read out the names
on the roll of honour on Remembrance Sunday. As the years passed

St Augustine's Boys Football Club, *c.* 1910
How many of these boys survived the war?

fewer and fewer of the congregation would have had any personal
connection with these men. Slum clearances in the 1920s moved
many families away from the parish and gradually death took those
who remained. Now, few if any local families are even related to the
people listed on the parish's Second World War memorial let alone
its First. It is hoped this work will in some small measure stand in
place for those hearts now gone.

The Toll of the Years

A biographical roll of honour of the Norwich parish of St Augustine with St Mary Coslany arranged chronologically by date of death.

1914 – The Old Contemptibles

Corporal 9439 Robert Henry Carriage, 2nd Battalion, Essex Regiment

Robert Henry Carriage was born in Norwich in 1891, the second child of George Carriage, a hawker and fish dealer, and Eliza Jane Carriage née Frost, a shoe-binder. The Carriage family lived at a number of addresses in the parish of St Mary Coslany from the 1880s onward. In the 1891 Census they are recorded at 13 Buck's Yard off Oak Street. By 1901 they had moved a short distance to 7 Unicorn Yard, where the growing family shared a home with Mrs Carriage's 74-year-old father, Henry Frost, who was still working as a jobbing blacksmith. The Census that year recorded Mrs Carriage as the head of the household with Mr Carriage nowhere to be found. He reappeared in the 1911 Census, by which time the family had moved again, to 19 St Mary's Plain. Robert, who seems to have been known as Bobby, had at least nine brothers and sisters: Percy, his elder, and George, Violet, William, Christopher (who died in infancy), Jonas Mafeking (so named, presumably, because of the siege and relief of Mafeking during the Boer War in the year of his birth, 1900), Clara, Elsie and Ivy.

Robert enlisted as a Regular in Great Yarmouth some time before the war and was posted to the 2nd Battalion, Essex Regiment. His Army Service papers have not survived though his regimental number suggests he joined up sometime around 1908. He married Elizabeth Emily Scotter in St Augustine's church on 5 November 1912, at which time his occupation was given as 'Corporal' in the register. At the outbreak of war in August 1914 the 2nd Essex were garrisoned at Chatham in Kent. On 7 August they entrained for Cromer in north Norfolk. They had hardly arrived before being ordered to proceed to Norwich on the 10th. They remained there until the 18th. It is not known whether Robert got a chance to visit his wife and parents during this period. If he did it would be the last time they would ever see him. On 24 August the 2nd Essex Regiment disembarked at Le Havre with other reinforcements for the British Expeditionary Force (BEF). Corporal Robert Carriage, 23, was killed in action just two days later, on 26 August 1914, during the Battle of Le Cateau. It was here II Corps under General Smith-Dorrien made its famous stand during the Retreat from Mons, giving the BEF more time to regroup before the advancing German forces could overwhelm them. During the battle the 2nd Essex came under attack at Longsart Ridge, losing more than 90 men. Robert Carriage was almost certainly the first St Augustine's man to die on active service during the war. He has no known grave and is commemorated at La Ferté-sous-Jouarre Memorial, Seine-et-Marne, France, and on the St Augustine's roll of honour. He was awarded the 1914 Star with Bar (indicating that he was under fire in France between 5 August and 23 November) and the British War and Victory medals.

Several of Robert's relatives served in the military during the war. His father, Private 28180 George Carriage, served on the Home Front in the Royal Defence Corps, an early form of Home Guard formation established in 1917, made up of men deemed too old or medically unfit for front line service. His uncle, Private 6476 William Carriage, a railway labourer who had lodged with the family in 1911, served in the 1st Battalion, Norfolk Regiment, and later in the Liverpool Regiment before being discharged in February 1916. His brothers Percy and George, like Robert himself, went overseas at the beginning of the war and were also awarded the 1914 'Mons' Star. Older brother, Private 7600 Percy George Carriage, served in the 2nd Battalion, Norfolk Regiment, in Mesopotamia until discharged in June 1916, after which he returned to labouring, marrying in St Augustine's church on 10 November 1917. Younger brother, Sapper 23793 George Carriage, served in the 38th Field Company, Corps of Royal Engineers. He also married in St Augustine's church, on 1 February 1917. Another of Robert's younger brothers, William, enlisted, underage, in August 1914, aged 16, and was posted first to the Norfolk Regiment's 3rd (Reserve) Battalion then to its 10th (Reserve) Battalion. He does not seem to have been mature enough at this age to buckle down to the discipline of Army life and was in more-or-less constant trouble: not complying with an order, being dirty on parade, creating a disturbance after lights out and being absent without leave or absent from parade on three occasions. He was eventually discharged in December 1914, having been found to have misrepresented his age on enlistment. He appears to have rejoined the Norfolk Regiment as a conscripted private (Service No. 43121), possibly as early as 1916 when he became 18, and survived the war.

Private 11521 William Alfred Hudson, 2nd Battalion, King's Own Scottish Borderers

William Alfred Hudson was born in Norwich in 1895, the eldest child of William John Hudson, a bricklayer, and Maria Hudson née Ward. In 1901 the family, including William's 2-year-old sister Ivy, was living at 5 Reads Court in the parish of St Mark, Lakenham, a southern suburb of Norwich. By 1911 the family had moved to 35 Trafalgar Opening off Trafalgar Street, Lakenham. William's siblings now also included Gertrude, Thomas, Violet and Alfred. He, however, lived with his aunt and uncle, Thomas and Louisa Hudson, in the village of Rockland St Mary south of Norwich where, aged 16, he was working as a farm labourer 'tendering sheep'.

William enlisted in Norwich. His Army Service papers have not survived but he seems to have enlisted as a Regular before the war. He joined the BEF in France with the 2nd Battalion, King's Own Scottish Borderers (known as the 'Kosbies'), on 15 August 1914. When war was declared on 4 August the Battalion had been garrisoned in Dublin. It sailed for Le Havre on SS *Gloucestershire* on the 14th, arriving in Le Havre on the 15th as part of 13th Brigade, 5th Division. Its first duty was to defend the Mons-Condé Canal, and its first encounter with the enemy came in the shape of the Brandenburg Grenadiers on 23 August during the Battle of Mons. Over the next three weeks the Battalion was in almost constant motion during the retreat from Mons, fighting rearguard actions at Le Cateau on 26 August; at Campiègne on 1 September; at Doue, Mauroy and St Cyr during the Battle of the Marne on 8 September; and during the Battle of the Aisne on 13 September. Private William Hudson, 19, was killed in action during the Battle of the Aisne on 13

September 1914, probably at Sermoise. He is commemorated at La Ferté-sous-Jouarre Memorial, Seine-et-Marne, France, and on the St Augustine's roll of honour. He was awarded the 1914 Star with Bar and the British War and Victory medals.

Private 8906 Robert Mitchell, 1st Battalion, Norfolk Regiment

Robert Mitchell was born in the parish of St Augustine, Norwich, in 1897, the eighth child of Robert Mitchell, a brush-maker, and Elizabeth Mitchell née Gooch, who had married in Norwich in 1877. By 1901 the family was living at 68 Aylsham Road, just north of St Augustine's. Robert's older siblings sharing the family home at this date were, in descending order of age, Louisa, Rosa and Gertrude, all employed in the local shoe-making industry; William, an errand boy, and Thomas, Ernest and Ivy, all still at school. Their father died in 1906, aged 50, and by 1911 Louisa, Gertrude and William had left home. Thomas and Ivy were now also in the shoe trade, while Ernest was a grocer's delivery boy. Robert, 14, had left school and was also an errand boy, for a jeweller.

Robert enlisted in Norwich before the war as a Regular in the Norfolk Regiment. His Service number suggests he enlisted in 1913 aged 16 or 17. At the declaration of war on 4 August 1914, the 1st Battalion, Norfolk Regiment, was in Belfast. Ten days later they sailed for Le Havre on SS *Anthony* to join the BEF. Robert first set foot in France on the 16th. On 24 August the 1st Norfolks took part in the Battle of Mons, the first major battle of the war, suffering more than 250 casualties, killed and wounded, mainly from shell fire. Over the next two days the remnants of the Battalion helped General Smith-Dorrien's II Corps cover the retreat of the BEF, making its famous stand at Le Cateau. After retreating almost to the outskirts of Paris, the British and French armies were finally able to turn back the German advance in early September, first at the Marne and then at the Aisne. Private Robert Mitchell was killed in action here on 14 September 1914 near the village of Missy, probably on the Chivry Spur where the 1st Norfolks suffered more than 100 casualties while attacking the Condé fort, which overlooked the River Aisne from the top of a narrow, steep ravine. On this confined battleground there was much confusion and several casualties from 'friendly fire' as a result. Another St Augustine's man, Frederick Simpson, also died here. Robert is commemorated at La Ferté-sous-Jouarre Memorial, Seine-et-Maine, France. Although born in the parish, his name does not appear on St Augustine's roll of honour. He is commemorated on St Luke's roll of honour in Aylsham Road. He was awarded the 1914 Star with Bar, and the British War and Victory medals.

Private 6704 Frederick Simpson, 1st Battalion, Norfolk Regiment, formerly in the 2nd Battalion

Frederick (known as Freddy) Simpson was born in 1887 in the parish of St Margaret, Norwich, the third son of Henry Simpson, a house painter, and Eliza Simpson née Edwards. In 1891 the family, including Freddy's older siblings Henry, William, Eliza and Ellen, and younger sister Caroline, was living at 21 Neale's Square off Pottergate in the parish of St Benedict. By 1901 the family had moved to 174 Armes Street, Heigham, a western suburb of Norwich, which Freddy shared with his mother and siblings William, Eliza and Ellen, all three now employed in the shoe-making industry; Caroline, still at school; and new additions to the growing household, Arthur and Rose. Freddy's eldest brother Henry, however, cannot be located. His father was also absent at this date: in lodgings in Bournemouth with a small band of East Anglian jobbing carpenters and decorators. Freddy, now 14, had left school and was a labourer in the rope-making trade.

Freddy enlisted as a full-time Regular soldier in the Norfolk Regiment on 2 November 1903. His civilian trade: pressman in the shoe trade. Although his Army Service papers state his age on enlisting as 18, he was in fact 16. Despite his youth he had already served a total of 76 days in the Regiment's 3rd Battalion; a Special Reserve unit formerly known as the Norfolk Militia, which he had joined on 2 March 1903, aged 15. After three weeks at the Norfolk Regiment's Depot (Britannia Barracks) Freddy was transferred to the 2nd Battalion. On 19 July 1905 he voluntarily extended his period of service with the colours to eight years. Less than four months later he was in South Africa where he remained until 11 September 1908, serving tours of duty in Bloemfontein, Standerton and Johannesburg before returning to England via a spell in Gibraltar. On 5 November 1910 he was posted to the Regiment's 1st Battalion. On 1 September 1911, his eight-year commitment almost over, he was transferred into the Army Reserve and discharged with an exemplary record, two good conduct badges and a reference for being 'thoroughly honest, sober and trustworthy'. In addition, he had served as a waiter in the officers' mess for six months. By 1911 Freddy's family had moved again, this time to 92 Calvert Street in the parish of St George Colegate, and it was to this address that he returned after leaving the Army. His father by now was back home and still a house painter, employed in a horticultural department in Bowthorpe village to the west of Norwich. Also at home at this date were Freddy's mother and siblings Eliza, Caroline, Arthur, Rosa and new sister Florrie, born 1905. Eldest brother Henry was still absent, while William and Ellen had left home.

Freddy was mobilised from the Army Reserve in Norwich on 5 August 1914, the day after Britain declared war, and posted immediately to the 1st Battalion, Norfolk Regiment. He arrived in France on 16 August 1914 with the other Reservists and proceeded to join the bulk of the 1st Battalion, which had sailed from Belfast two days earlier and was now being prepared for action at Le Cateau. In the week or so that had elapsed since he left Norwich no news had reached his loved ones of his whereabouts. His Army Service papers include a poignant letter written on 15 August 1914 by a Miss Ada Leggett of 4 Lily Terrace, Norwich, perhaps his fiancée, 'anxious about him' and 'very pleased to hear anything'. By the time the Army dealt with her enquiry, Freddy, 26, was dead, killed in action on 14 September 1914 in the fighting around Missy during the Battle of Aisne, almost certainly on the Chivry Spur where the 1st Norfolks suffered heavy losses on a confined and confused battlefield, a number of their casualties, according to the regimental history, resulting from 'friendly fire'. He had served with the Norfolk Regiment for a total of 11 years since the age of 15 and not seen a shot fired in anger until the last month of his life. As his body was not identified, he was posted missing in action and was not finally regarded officially as having died in service until 11 October 1915. Another St Augustine's soldier, Robert Mitchell, was also killed in this battle. Freddy is commemorated at La Ferté-sous-Jouarre

Memorial, Seine-et-Marne, France, and on the St Augustine's roll of honour. He was awarded the 1914 Star with Bar and the British War and Victory medals.

Private 6248 Arthur Grady, 1st Battalion, Norfolk Regiment

Arthur Grady was born in the parish of St Martin at Oak, Norwich, in 1884, the seventh child of Michael Grady, a general labourer, and Mary Ann Grady née Moore, a silk winder. In 1881 his parents were living in Angel Yard off Oak Street. By 1891 they had moved to 2 Cattermoul's Yard off Pitt Street, St Augustine's. Arthur's older siblings were Charles, John, Martha, Ann, James and Louisa; his younger, Maggie and Mike. By 1901, Arthur, 17, was a domestic servant doing general labouring work in the household of Henry Murrell, a coach-builder in Yarmouth Road, Thorpe next Norwich. By 1911 he was a boarder in the household of Samuel Greenhough, a railway worker, at Eyam Woodlands, Nether Padley, Derbyshire. His occupation railway drayman: driving a horse-drawn or possibly a steam or petrol-powered wagon for the station yard.

Arthur enlisted as a Regular in Norwich before the war. Though his Army Service papers have not survived, his regimental number indicates he enlisted in the 1st Battalion, Norfolk Regiment, sometime between 1902 and 1903. At the outbreak of war in August 1914, aged 30, he was called up from the Reserves. He arrived in France on 22 August 1914, six days after the bulk of the 1st Norfolks had landed at Le Havre to join the BEF. He may have caught up with them just in time to take part in the aftermath of the Battle of Mons, when on the 25th the 1st Norfolks, together with the 1st Cheshires, fought a rear guard action near Elouges, covering the retreat of the remainder of 15th Brigade, losing more than 250 killed, wounded or missing. Over the next three months, the BEF fought backwards and forwards over the same few square kilometres of French and Belgian soil, at Le Cateau, the Marne, the Aisne, the La Bassée Canal and Ypres. Arthur, 30, died of wounds on 27 November 1914. Given the date and his place of burial, it is likely he was wounded either in the fighting around Ypres or when the 1st Norfolks were briefly entrenched in the Kemmel sector of Belgian Flanders in mid-

November. Arthur is buried at the Bailleul Communal Cemetery, Nord, France, grave no. A.10, and is commemorated also on the St Augustine's roll of honour. He was awarded the 1914 Star with Bar, and the British War and Victory medals.

Private 1263 Albert James Lundy, 1st Battalion, Northumberland Fusiliers

Albert James Lundy was born in Norwich in 1887, the fifth surviving child of Frederick Lundy, a horsehair-sorter and gasworks labourer, and Harriet Lundy née Hayhoe, a silk-warper. *(For more on Albert's family background see Frederick Lundy, p.55.)* In 1901, Albert, 14, was employed as a brick-maker.

Albert enlisted in Norwich as a Regular before the war. His Army Service papers have not survived but the 1911 Census locates him in Westridge Canton garrison in Rawalpindi, Punjab (now part of Pakistan), a private in the 1st Battalion, Northumberland Fusiliers. By August 1914, the 1st Battalion was back in England, at Cambridge Barracks, Portsmouth. On 13 August it sailed from Southampton on SS *Norman*, part of the 9th Brigade, 3rd Division, to join the BEF in France. Ten days later it was engaged in the first major battle of the war, near the Belgian town of Mons. Unable to stem the tide of the invading Germans, the BEF fought a series of holding actions, most notably at Le Cateau, before beginning to push back alongside the French Army at the Battle of the Marne. On 14 September the 1st Battalion re-crossed the River Aisne in support of the 4th Royal Fusiliers and took up positions at Rouge Maison, where they held off wave after wave of German attacks for a week until finally relieved on 21st by the 4th Middlesex Regiment. Private Albert Lundy, 27, was one of four men of the 1st Battalion who died near Rouge Maison on 19 September 1914. He has no known grave.

Albert Lundy is commemorated at La Ferté-sous-Jouarre Memorial, Seine-et-Marne, France, and on St Augustine's roll of honour. He was awarded the 1914 Star with Bar, and the British War and Victory medals. The Lundys suffered grievously in the war, not only losing sons Albert and Frederick but also youngest daughter Gladys's husband Ralph Gant and his brother, Frederick Gant. *(See p. 168.)*

1915 – Ypres, Gallipoli, Loos, Mesopotamia

Private 3921 Arthur Lake, 2nd Battalion,
Northumberland Fusiliers

Arthur Lake was born in Norwich in 1893, the fifth child of Walter Lake, a labourer, and Eliza Harriet Lake née Mace, a silk weaver. The family was recorded in Priory Yard off Cowgate in the parish of St James Pockthorpe in the 1891 and 1901 censuses, so it is probable this was where Arthur was born. His older siblings were Walter, a wicker worker; George, an errand boy and later a gardener; and Eliza and Lily, both still at school in 1901. By 1911 the family, minus Walter and Eliza who had left home, had moved to 1 Cremer Court off Old Cat and Fiddle Yard, Botolph Street. Arthur, 18, was employed as a shoemaker's riveter.

Arthur enlisted in Norwich, possibly before the war. The 2nd Battalion, Northumberland Fusiliers, was a Regular Army battalion garrisoned at Sabathu, India, before the war. On returning to England they encamped in Wiltshire and in December 1914 were placed in the 84th Brigade, 28th Division. Arthur first went over to France on 6 March 1915. He was killed in action in Belgian Flanders just six days later, on 12 March 1915, aged 22. A death notice placed in the *Eastern Daily Press* by his mother and siblings, includes a verse that was to become a frequent lament of loved ones:

If I had but seen him at the last
And watched his dying bed,
Or heard the last sigh of his heart,
Or held his drooping head,
My heart, I think, would not have felt
Such bitterness and grief;
But God has ordered otherwise,
And now he rests in peace.

On the first anniversary of his death, his mother placed an 'In Memoriam' notice in the same paper, with the verse:

Oft-times I sit and think of him
When I am all alone,
But memory is the only friend
That grief can call its own.

Arthur Lake is commemorated at the Ploegsteert Memorial, Comines-Warneton, Hainaut, Belgium, and on the St Augustine's roll of honour. He was awarded the 1914 Star and the British War and Victory medals.

Private 3/7239 Herbert Cartwright, 'C' Company, 1st Battalion, Norfolk Regiment

Herbert Cartwright was born in the parish of St Augustine, Norwich, in 1889, the second child of John Cartwright, a shoe-finisher, and Eliza Cartwright née Willis, a horsehair-weaver. In the 1891 Census the family, including older brother George, were recorded at 4 Chapel Yard off Botolph Street, St Augustine's. By 1901 they had moved to 61 Rose Yard off St Augustine's Street. They were still there in 1911, when Herbert, 22, was a porter in a pianoforte works, almost certainly W. Howlett & Son of Pottergate, Norwich. Brother George meanwhile had followed his father's footsteps into the shoemaking trade as a riveter.

Herbert enlisted in the 3rd Battalion, Norfolk Regiment, on 9 February 1912. The 3rd was a reserve militia unit where soldiers received drill and musketry training for several months before returning to their civilian life, attending weekend drills and annual, month-long summer camps, in Herbert's case over May and June 1913 and 1914. Oddly, his Army Service papers give his age on enlistment as 18 years and 9 months, when he was in fact 22. His civilian occupation was now shoe-presser. In 1913 he married Hannah Buttolph. The couple lived at 4 Kings Buildings, Union Street near Chapel Field Road and had one child, Dorothy Florence, born shortly before the outbreak of war in August 1914. She lived only a few months, dying, according to the Coroner, of 'Natural causes, to wit Sickness and diarrhoea' on 23 September 1914.

Herbert Cartwright was mobilised from the Army Reserve for immediate active service on 8 August 1914 and was posted to the 1st

Battalion, Norfolk Regiment. He disembarked in France on 22 September, the day before his daughter's death, and was plunged straightaway into the thick of action on the Festubert Front before the Battalion went into winter quarters. The ranks of the 1st Norfolk had been severely depleted in 1914. During February 1915, while he was enduring winter in the trenches, Herbert's wife Hannah was required by the Army Record Office at Warley to provide proof that their baby daughter had died, presumably for pay and allowance calculations. Unable to afford the 3s.7d needed to obtain a certified copy of her death certificate she sent instead a copy of the Coroner's inquest statement.

On 15 March 1915 Herbert was wounded during fighting around the village of St Eloi just south of Ypres, near a much-disputed topographical feature known as the Mound. The Norfolk Regiment's Wound Book records that he was taken to No. 13 General Hospital in Boulogne, suffering from a gun-shot wound to the chest. On 21 March he was taken over the English Channel and admitted to the Charing Cross Hospital, London, on the 23rd. He died there ten days later, on 2 April 1915 at 12.45 a.m. He was 26. His body was returned to his family in Norwich for burial. Herbert is buried at Norwich Cemetery, Bowthorpe Road, Norwich, Commonwealth War Grave no. 26/309 (located in a detached portion of the cemetery near the South Africa War memorial), and is commemorated also on the St Augustine's roll of honour. He was awarded the 1914 Star with Bar, and the British War and Victory medals.

Lance Corporal 8863 Alfred Lince, 1st Battalion, Norfolk Regiment

Alfred Lince was born in the parish of St Paul, Norwich, in 1894, the second surviving child of Walter Lince, a shoe-finisher, and Laura Lince née Warman, who worked at home as a shoe-machinist. Alfred was baptised at St Saviour's, Magdalen Street, on 19 December 1899. In 1901 the family was at 6 Little White Horse Yard off Botolph Street. Alfred, 7, had two sisters at this date, Laura, 8, and Charlotte, 2. By 1911 the family had moved to 17 Catherine Wheel Opening off St Augustine's Street. There were now six children: Laura, working at home as a shoe-fitter; Alfred, 17, a shoe-finisher like his father; Beatrice and Walter, still at school; and infants Albert and Charlotte (this was the second Charlotte, the first had died aged 5 in 1905). The family later moved to 18 Gildencroft near St Augustine's churchyard. Later in 1911 Alfred married Selina Gilbert, a charwoman from Baldwin's Yard off Oak Street who was ten years his senior.

Alfred enlisted in Norwich, probably before the war as he was already serving in a Regular Army battalion in August 1914. His Army Service papers have not survived. The 1st Battalion, Norfolk Regiment, was in Belfast when war was declared. They sailed for France on SS *Anthony* on 14 August and disembarked at Le Havre on 16 August as part of the 15th Brigade, 5th Division. Their first major action was at Mons, following which they fought at Le Cateau, the Marne and the Aisne. The Norfolk Regiment's Wound Book records that Private Lince reported sick on 27 September. On this day the 1st Norfolks moved into billets at Vasseny, having been on the move and fighting continually for over five weeks, suffering particularly heavy casualties on 24 August during the Retreat from Mons, and on 14 September at Chivry Spur. Further severe fighting took place along the La Bassée Canal in October and during the 1st Battle of Ypres in November.

That winter in the trenches there occurred the famous 'Christmas Truce' in which British and German soldiers met in no man's land and exchanged gifts and festive greetings. Alfred would almost certainly have witnessed this extraordinary display of decent humanity in the midst of war. According to the 15th Brigade's War Diary, it was the 1st Norfolks who first left their trenches to challenge a party of German officers walking towards the front line on Christmas morning, an act which led to general fraternising along the Front, including communal hymn singing.

Lance Corporal Alfred Lince, 21, was killed in action during the 2nd Battle of Ypres on 18 April 1915. The 1st Norfolks were in the St Eloi sector south of Ypres at this date, engaged in heavy fighting in and around a series of prominent topographical features: man-made spoil heaps alongside the Ypres–Comines Railway referred to in the British Army's maps as the Mound, the Caterpillar, the Dump and Hill 60. According to the Battalion's War Diary the German Army exploded gas shells at the last of these positions on the 18th. Gas was a new weapon of war and masks had not yet been issued, so casualties were high.

Alfred is buried at Perth Cemetery (China Wall), Ieper, Belgium, grave no. VI.L.13, and commemorated on the St Augustine's roll of honour. Alfred is also included in *Ireland's Memorial Records*, a list of Ireland's citizens who died in the war; possibly due to his having been resident in Belfast in 1914. One other St Augustine's soldier, William Mutton *(p.115)*, is also included. Alfred was awarded the 1914 Star with Bar and the British War and Victory medals. His Medal Roll Index card notes that on 27 April 1919, Alfred's father applied for his late son's 1914 Star, which presumably had not yet been issued. His address at this time was 5 New Yard, Magdalen Street, Norwich.

Private 11244 George William Howell, 4th Battalion (Central Ontario), Canadian Expeditionary Force, formerly Private, 11th Infantry Regiment (Irish Fusiliers of Canada) and 36th (Peel) Regiment, Canadian Militia

George William Howell was born in Norwich on 22 March 1893, the second child of Arthur James Howell, a stone mason, and Charlotte Howell née Chilvers. He was baptised at St Augustine's church by the Revd W. Elder on 3 September. *(For more on George's background see p.180.)* In 1911 George, 18, was an apprentice plumber. In 1912, like his brother Arthur before him, George emigrated to Canada, sailing from Liverpool on SS *Empress of India*, arriving at St John,

New Brunswick, on 21 December. Although he is recorded in the purser's ledger as 20, he was in fact 19. His final destination, like Arthur's eight months earlier, was the town of Brampton, Ontario. As a plumber he would have found plenty of work there – the Flower Town of Canada – in its many steam-heated hot houses.

Despite being the younger brother, George was the first to enlist. He signed Attestation papers, joining the

Canadian Overseas Expeditionary Force (CEF) in Valcartier, Quebec, on 22 September 1914. Valcartier Camp, about 15 miles from Quebec, was the largest army camp in Canada and living conditions there were Spartan. Prior to enlisting, George had served in the 36th Peel Regiment, a small Militia unit based in Brampton. His Army papers record he was still a plumber, unmarried and a member of the Church of England. He was 5ft 4½ in height, and had a fair complexion, blue eyes and brown hair. After enlisting he was briefly placed in the 11th Regiment (Irish Fusiliers of Canada) before being transferred to the 4th Canadian Infantry Battalion, also known as the Central Ontario Regiment (the Canadian Army did not follow the British Army pattern of a number of battalions within a regiment).

On 24 September 1914 the 4th Infantry Battalion or 4th Canadians sailed from Quebec on SS *Tyrolia*, one part of a grand flotilla that bore the First Canadian Contingent 500 miles from the St Lawrence River to England. As the ship departed, friends and relatives on the dockside sang 'It's a long way to Tipperary'. The convoy luckily escaped the attentions of U-boats on the crossing though rumours of one in the English Channel forced the ships to switch from Southampton to Plymouth, where the 4th Canadians disembarked on 23 October. The raw recruits now spent a cold, damp autumn and winter on Salisbury Plain in training. Then on 8 February 1915 they finally embarked for France, on board SS *Atlantian*, landing at St Nazaire on the 12th.

Private George Howell, 22, was killed in action on 23 April 1915, during the Battle of Gravenstafel Ridge; an early action in the 2nd Battle of Ypres. The 4th Canadians had been moved up to the village of Vlamertinghe in Belgian Flanders on 22 April in readiness for an assault across the Yser Canal towards Pilckem. From their trenches only 400 yards from the enemy's front line, the 4th went over the top at Hill Top Ridge at 5.25 a.m. into a withering hail of machine-gun and rifle fire. At 7.00 a.m. their commanding officer, Lieutenant-Colonel Birchall was killed. Two hours later the attack was called off. The 4th had lost 18 officers and more than 430 other ranks in less than four hours for no material gain. George is commemorated at the Ypres (Menin Gate) Memorial, Ieper, Belgium, and also on the St Augustine's roll of honour. His name is inscribed in the book of remembrance placed in the Brampton Great War Memorial, Ontario, and on a brass plaque in Christ Church (an Anglican church), Brampton. His photograph appeared in the *Eastern Daily Press* one month after his death. In 1935 his photograph in uniform appeared in a commemorative volume on the military men of Peel District in southern Ontario. He was awarded the 1915 Star and the British War and Victory medals. His older brother, Arthur Howell, was killed in action in 1918.

Private 9610 William Tidd, 1st Battalion, York and Lancaster Regiment

William Tidd was born in the parish of St Mary Coslany, Norwich, in 1889, the second child of John Tidd, a maltster's labourer, and Elizabeth Tidd née Mountain, a silk-winder. In 1891 the family was living at 1 Buck's Yard, St Mary Coslany. They were still there in 1901 when the household included William and his five siblings: older brother John, a 14-year-old shoe-worker, Florence, Elizabeth, Emma and baby Eliza. By 1911 the family had moved to New Mills Yard in the same parish. A seventh child, Ann Maud, was born there in 1903.

William enlisted in Norwich as a Regular soldier before the war. Although his Army Service papers have not survived, his regimental number indicates that he probably enlisted in 1909 or early 1910. The 1st Battalion, York and Lancaster Regiment, was garrisoned in Jubbulpore, India, when war as declared in August 1914. It returned to England on 23 December and was sent to France in January as part of the 83rd Brigade, 28th Division. William disembarked in France on 15 January 1915.

Private William Tidd was killed in action in Belgian Flanders on 23 April 1915, almost certainly during an early action in the 2nd Battle of Ypres known as the Battle of Gravenstafel Ridge. The 22 April had seen the first use of poison gas (chlorine) by the German Army as a battlefield weapon of mass destruction. This had caused terror and confusion, opening up large gaps in the Allies' defensive line around the Ypres Salient. The following day the British Army put together a makeshift brigade under Colonel Geddes in order to help plug some of the gaps. One of the four battalions that formed what became known as Geddes' Detachment was the 1st York and Lancs, which was pulled from its rest billets in Ypres late on the evening of the 22nd. On the late afternoon of 23rd the Battalion was assembled on Hill Top Ridge ready to take part in a daylight attack, the ultimate aim of which was to capture the village of Pilckem about 4 miles north of Ypres. Crossing open ground with barely a hedge for cover, the Battalion was mowed down by machine-gun fire, suffering over 400 casualties. William is commemorated at the Ypres (Menin Gate) Memorial, Ieper, Belgium, and on the St Augustine's roll of honour. He was awarded the 1915 Star and the British War and Victory medals.

Private 3/7422 John Hardy, 2nd Battalion, Bedfordshire Regiment

John Hardy was born in the parish of St Mary Coslany, Norwich, in 1895, the second surviving child of George Hardy, a shoemaker, and Ellen Hardy née Starling. In 1901, aged 5, he was living at 23 St Mary's Plain with his older sister Ellen and younger sisters Lydia and Hilda. Two more sisters, Priscilla and Ethel, were born in 1902 and 1908. In 1908 his father died, aged 38. The following year his mother married William Harvey, originally from County Cork, who was employed in Norwich as a machine operator. By 1911 the family had moved to 2 Playford's Court off Pottergate. John's mother and stepfather now had a baby daughter, May. The 1911 Census records that Mrs Harvey had 12 children born alive, of whom seven were still living. John, 16, was now a maker of turnshoes (a soft pump or slipper).

John enlisted in Norwich. Given that he was in France by November 1914 with the 2nd Bedfordshire Regiment, a Regular Army battalion, it seems likely he had enlisted before the war. His Army Service papers have not survived though the prefix 3 to his regimental number indicates that he was initially held in the Regiment's 3rd (Reserve) Battalion, which carried out Home Defence duties on the Essex and Suffolk coasts as well as providing battle training for batches of troops ear-marked for the Front. The 2nd Bedfordshires had been on garrison duty in South Africa when war was declared in August 1914. They were immediately recalled to

England, arriving on 19 September. After being re-equipped for European duty, they embarked for France on 5 October, where they formed part of the 21st Brigade, 7th Division. Known as 'The Immortal Seventh', the Division was composed entirely of pre-war Regular Army battalions and was regarded as one of the finest British Army Divisions of the BEF. By the time John arrived in France on 8 November, the 2nd Bedfordshires were rebuilding their strength after heavy losses in October during the 1st Battle of Ypres. The Battalion's War Diary notes that 119 other ranks joined the Battalion, then in billets near a lunatic asylum at Bailleul, on 12 November. A further 100 arrived three days later. In December 1914, the 2nd Bedfordshires had first-hand experience of the famous 'Christmas Truce' while they were in trenches near Fleurbaix. Its War Diary notes that singing was heard from the German trenches on Christmas Eve and an informal truce was arranged in order that both sides might bury their dead left lying in no man's land. At this section of the front line, direct face-to-face contact between the two sides seems to have been limited to a few officers and senior NCOs, at least that was the official version, though rumours of impromptu football matches being played between British and German sides were told and there were rumours that the Bedfordshires must be facing a 'millionaires' battalion' as every German soldier they encountered was smoking a big fat cigar, a Christmas present, in fact, from the Kaiser, which many German soldiers exchanged for British chocolate and cigarettes.

Private John Hardy, 20, was killed in action on 16 June 1915, probably during a battle known as the Second Action at Givenchy. He has no known grave. This battle was designed to provide a flanking attack in support of the French Army's push in Artois. The 21st Brigade was chosen to spearhead the assault, which by any account proved to be a costly and futile failure with wave after wave of troops mowed down by machine gun fire as they struggled to pass through their own barbed wire. The attack was supposed to have started under cover of night but was postponed again and again, and did not finally get going until the afternoon. The 2nd Bedfordshires' War Diary notes they managed to occupy a large crater from where they were able to inflict heavy losses on the enemy; however, they were not able to advance beyond here or defend themselves against counter attacks, and those who survived the day here crawled back to their trenches under cover of darkness. The 2nd Battalion's losses were five officers and 45 other ranks with another 70 wounded. John's Medal Roll Index card notes he died of wounds rather than was killed in action. Presumably, he was alive but badly wounded when last seen alive in the crater by the survivors who escaped during the night. It would be 11 months before he was officially confirmed dead and his mother could finally place a death notice in the *Eastern Daily Press.* Her address at this time was Greenland Fishery Yard off Oak Street. John is commemorated at Le Touret Memorial, Pas de Calais, France, and on the St Augustine's roll of honour. He was awarded the 1915 Star, and the British War and Victory medals.

Private 1591 Bertie Cecil Cushion, 1/4th Battalion, Norfolk Regiment

Bertie Cecil Cushion was born in Norwich on 13 July 1894, the second surviving child of Edward Ernest Cushion, a shoemaker, and

Amelia Cushion née Ryder. He had an older brother, Albert, born 1891. Their mother died in 1895, aged 23. The following year, their father married Catherine Hardiman, a horsehair-weaver in the brush-making trade. By 1901 the family was at 22 Pye's Yard in the parish of St Martin at Palace in the shadow of Norwich cathedral's spire. Bertie now had two young stepsisters, Elsie and Maud. Jessie Hardiman, 16, boarded with them. Bertie was a pupil at Bull Close School until 26 March 1907 when he was admitted to Quay Side

School. His address at this time was 23 Quay Side, only a few steps from Pye's Yard. By 1911 the family had moved to 8 Calvert Street in the parish of St George Colegate. *Soldiers Died in the Great War* gives this as his place of birth, though St Mary Coslany, where his parents were living in 1891, would be more likely.

According to information with a photograph of Bertie in uniform given to Norwich Library by his family after the war, he enlisted in Norwich in July 1911, aged 17. This is possibly inaccurate. What survives of his badly burnt Army Service papers indicates he went through a rather drawn-out recruitment process, beginning on 6 February 1912 when he enlisted with no previous military experience in the 4th Battalion (Territorial Force), Norfolk Regiment. This was followed by Attestation on 1 March, when he swore an oath to be 'faithful and bear true Allegiance to His Majesty The King' and to defend him 'against all enemies'. His medical board examination took place nearly a year later, on 14 February 1913, and final approval for his enlistment was granted on behalf of the Battalion's CO by the Adjutant on 18 July 1913, by which time Bertie was 19.

Among Bertie's Army papers is a fragment of a form he signed on 9 September 1914, agreeing to serve overseas. Pre-war Territorials were under no obligation, unlike Regulars, to serve outside the UK. He is described here as a lance corporal, possibly only a temporary, unpaid appointment; subsequent records give his rank as private. In July 1915, the 4th Battalion, Norfolk Regiment, or more properly 1/4th (first-fourth), as there was also a 2/4th (second-fourth) training Battalion that remained in England throughout the war, was transferred to the 163rd Brigade, 54th (East Anglian) Division, which was then being assembled at Watford for engagement in the Dardanelles. On the 30 June the 163rd Brigade, which included the 1/4th and 1/5th Norfolks and the 1/5th Suffolks, embarked at Liverpool on RMS *Aquitania* for the eastern Mediterranean. The *Aquitania* was the flagship of the Cunard Line and had only been in commission, plying the transatlantic route, since 1913. She was one of the largest and the longest ship in the world at that time and regarded by many as the most beautiful. She was requisitioned by the British Government in May 1915 and briefly operated as a battle cruiser before being converted to a troop carrier. She would have presented a truly awe-inspiring, if bizarre, spectacle to the young East

Anglians who lined the docks at Liverpool waiting to embark, her immensely long hull and four funnels painted in an Art Deco-style dazzle pattern of black, white and grey diamonds. St Augustine's Parish Magazine of November 1915 had an extract from a letter written by a St Augustine's man named 'W. Johnson' of the 'Mediterranean Exped. Force'. It is full of his sense of wonder at sailing, probably for the first time, in a large ship to foreign climes:

> *You* [i.e. the Revd J. H. Griffiths] *know what it is to travel on the sea, but I think the wonders of this boat will amaze you. She is one of the largest afloat, but of course I cannot mention her name or that Censor fellow will destroy the letter. It is grand how she is fitted out with contrivances I never dreamed of ashore. We are favoured with cabins, which in ordinary times would cost £120. A very large percentage of the troops were down with sea sickness, but I escaped.*
>
> *We have indeed something to be thankful for, as we were chased by a Submarine, but owing to our superior speed and the clever manoeuvring of the officers we, thanks to God, escaped. So sorry I cannot tell you where we are, etc., etc., but shall be able to lecture on the wonders of such a voyage upon seeing England again.*

On 6 August the *Aquitania* dropped anchor in Mudros Bay, the British supply depot on the Greek island of Lemnos. Four days later, the Brigade was transported to Sulva Bay on the Dardanelles Peninsula, where it had to disembark from row boats under enemy fire. From this moment, they were under almost continuous attack until early December, their bloodiest day being 12 August, only two days after landing, when they attacked the Turkish front line on the plain of Kuchak Anafarta. This was the battle in which virtually the entire King's Company from the Sandringham Estate in Norfolk disappeared never to be seen again, giving rise to the legend that they had been spirited away in a cloud like mythological heroes.

Bertie, 21, was killed in action one week later on 19 August 1915, while the 1/4th Norfolks were holding an exposed position known as Jephson's Post along a ridge that straddled the Sulva Bay front line. He has no known grave. The Battalion's War Diary has no entry for this date; the regimental history, however, includes an entry transcribed from the diary of Captain (later Lieutenant Colonel)

E. W. Montgomerie, who was in temporary command of the 1/4th Battalion. His entry for the 19th reads: 'All quiet during day, worked hard at night fetching food, water, etc. and improving the trenches.' A photograph of Bertie in Norfolk Libraries' collection shows him with a signaller's proficiency badge on his lower left sleeve. Laying or repairing telegraph wire was a signaller's job, a dangerous enough task on the front line with the added danger of sometimes having to crawl out into no man's land at night. Another job was running with hand-written messages, an activity which tended to attract a sniper's attention who would calculate when the running man would pass the next exposed position.

On the first anniversary of his death Bertie's family placed an In Memoriam notice in the *Eastern Daily Press*. It included the patriotic verse:

> *He proudly answered to his country's call;*
> *He has paid his price to try and save us all.*
> *His heart was good, his spirits brave;*
> *We have laid him at rest in a soldier's grave.*
> *Oh God above, in Your loving grace,*
> *Find in Your heart, for him a place.*

Bertie is commemorated at the Helles Memorial, Gallipoli, Turkey, and on the St Augustine's roll of honour. He was awarded the 1914-15 Star and the British War and Victory medals.

During the war Bertie's father, Edward Ernest Cushion, served as a private (No. 302557) in the Labour Corps. His older brother, Albert, was also a private (No. 7983) in the 2nd Battalion, Norfolk Regiment. An article in the *Eastern Daily Press* published in August 1916 mentions that Albert's family had received a postcard from him telling them he was a prisoner of war following the surrender of the British forces at Kut in Mesopotamia. The only other St Augustine's soldier to die at Gallipoli was Edward Wiseman. *(See p.53.)* Given they were in the same battalion, the proximity of their home addresses and the closeness of their ages, it is very likely they knew one another.

Rifleman R/11880 William Spooner, 7th Battalion, King's Royal Rifle Corps

William Spooner was born on 6 August 1898 at 61 Adelaide Street, Heigham, a suburb to the west of Norwich, the third child of Fred Spooner and Annie Spooner née Cooke. His father, who had grown up in Rose Yard off St Augustine's Street, worked as a brewer's labourer. His mother came from the village of Buxton, to the north of Norwich. After marriage his parents lived first at 8 Eagle Opening, a narrow yard off Sussex Street, St Augustine's, near the Spread Eagle pub. By 1901 they had moved to Adelaide Street outside the parish. At this date there were four children: Elma, Frederick, William and Stephen. By 1911, still at Adelaide Street, the family also included Alice and Lottie. The two eldest had left home: Elma to domestic

service with the family of a surgeon in Deal in Kent and Frederick to domestic service in London with the family of the Honourable Robert Ward, a stock broker and former Conservative MP and soldier. By 1915 William's parents and younger siblings, Stephen, Alice and Lottie, had moved to 41 Bakers Road, which lies parallel to the line of the old city wall that bounded St Augustine's parish on its north.

William enlisted in London on 17 April 1915 and was posted to No.2 Company, 6th Battalion, King's Royal Rifle Corps (KRRC). Although he gave his age as 19 he was still only 16. The legal minimum age for enlistment into most of the British Army was 18 (the Territorials could take youths from 17). Soldiers could not be sent overseas until they were 19 but the rules were frequently flouted and blind eyes cynically or indulgently turned to eager lads presenting themselves for enlistment who were clearly under-age. The 6th KRRC was a Reserve unit, based for most of the war at Sheerness on the Isle of Sheppey in Kent. After four months training there, William was transferred to the 7th KRRC, a 'Kitchener' Service battalion, which had been established in Winchester in August 1914.

Among William's Army Service papers is a rare survival, a page torn from his pay book itemising his journey from Queenborough in Kent to Watou in France, written in what appears to be his own handwriting. It was against Army Regulations to keep a diary, so perhaps this was confiscated. Leaving England on 24 August 1915, 18 days after his 17th birthday, William disembarked at Boulogne the following morning and spent his first night in France at the St Martin's Army Rest Camp just outside the town. The next day he was moved on to the vast Army base at Étaples and then, two days later, to the beleaguered town of Poperinghe, one of only two unoccupied Belgian towns, arriving there at 4.30 p.m. on 28 August. On the 31st he finally joined his new battalion, newly camped in rest bivouacs to the east of the village of Watou, having just completed an 18-day tour of duty in front line trenches about a mile east of Ypres, a period described in the 7th KRRC's War Diary, without apparent irony, as 'quiet and marked by no particular incident'; a period in which the Diary further notes it lost three men killed and 38 wounded.

William's first taste of action came on 6 September when the 7th KRRC was moved by motor bus to the Kaaie Salient defences near Ypres, where it remained until the 21st, losing three more men killed in action. After three days in rest bivouacs at Poperinghe, the Battalion was ordered to a position known as White Chateau on the Menin Road, a mile east of Ypres. Here, starting on 25 September, it took part in an action known as the 2nd Attack on Bellewaarde, a diversionary feint intended to draw the German Army's attention from the major offensive being launched simultaneously at Loos. Private William Spooner, 17, was killed in action on 27 September 1915. The 7th KRRC's War Diary notes that on this day 'B' and 'D'

Companies were shelled in their dugouts, losing four killed and 26 wounded. Presumably, William was among those who died here.

On the first anniversary of his death his parents and his sister Elma, who had emigrated to the United States in May 1916 to work as a domestic maid, each placed an 'In Memoriam' notice in the *Eastern Daily Press*. His sister's contained the following lines:

> *When the battle's roar is silent, and the field is lost and won,*
> *There are still some faithful watchers – praying, praying*
> *for the dead.*

Elma settled in Wayne, Michigan, and married there in 1921. William is buried at the Bedford House Cemetery, Ieper, Belgium, enclosure no. VI.A.6-8, and commemorated also on both St Luke's and St Augustine's rolls of honour. He is the youngest serviceman commemorated on the St Augustine's war memorial whose age is known. He was awarded the 1915 Star and the British War and Victory medals.

Private 3/10605 William Wilson, 9th Battalion, Norfolk Regiment

William Wilson was born in the Norwich suburb of New Sprowston in 1887, probably at his parents' home in St Clement's Row. His father, John Wilson, was from Stockton on Tees and worked in Norwich as a brick-maker and general labourer. His mother, Emma, was from Norwich and is described in the Census as a 'mangling woman' in a laundry. By 1891 the family had moved to 5 Hartley's Yard off Cowgate in the parish of St James Pockthorpe. William's siblings at this date were older sisters Emily and Martha and younger Ellen and Edith. By 1901 the family, with new additions John and Harry, had moved a short distance away to 48 Peacock Street in the parish of St Saviour. In 1907 William married Ellen (known as Nellie) Bridget Spaul of Pimlico, London, and by 1911 the couple were living at 4 Cherry Tree Yard off Pitt Street, St Augustine's, with their children: Nellie, Flora and Robert. At this date William was a general labourer for the Great Eastern Railway.

William enlisted in Norwich and was posted to the 9th Battalion,

Norfolk Regiment, one of Lord Kitchener's Service battalions, formed in Norwich on 9 September 1914. The 9th Battalion spent the following 11 months training, first at Shoreham in Kent, where the 24th Division, part of Kitchener's Third New Army (known as K3), was being readied to go to France. On 30 August 1915 William disembarked at Boulogne with the 9th Norfolks. Less than four weeks later the Battalion took part in its first major engagement of the war, the Battle of Loos. Between the 25 and 27 September, near a spot known as Lonely Tree Hill, they fought a costly and confusing battle across an industrial terrain of wrecked factories and quarries. When the roll was called after the battle they had lost more than 200 casualties, including 34 reported missing in action, Private William Wilson, 28, among them.

It is not known whether William's family harboured any hope that he might have been taken prisoner, but it would be the end of January 1916 before they placed a death notice in the *Eastern Daily Press*. It included the words 'He has done his duty towards home and country'. Three days later his photograph in uniform was published in the paper. Strangely, his death was officially said to have occurred on 30 September 1915, though the exhausted remnants of the 9th Norfolks were out of the front line in a rest camp by this date. On the first anniversary of his death his family placed three 'In Memoriam' notices with verses in the *Eastern Daily Press*, one each from his married sisters and brothers-in-law, his widow and children, and parents, unmarried sister and younger brothers. His widow's choice of verse was particularly poignant, evoking her loneliness and grief:

Oft times I sit and think of him
When I am all alone;
For memory is the only friend
That grief may call its own.
I think of thee in silence
No eye may see me weep,
Yet deep within my heart
Thy memory I will keep.

On the second anniversary of his death his family's 'In Memoriam' notice included a patriotic verse that seems to suggest William had been a sportsman, perhaps a footballer:

It was on the field he did his best – his best he always tried,
And as a soldier, on the field for his king and country died.

William Wilson is commemorated on the Loos Memorial, Pas de Calais, France, and on the St Augustine's roll of honour. He was awarded the 1914–15 Star and the British War and Victory medals.

Private 13431 Walter Alfred Brightwell, 'B' Company, 8th Battalion, Norfolk Regiment

Walter Alfred Brightwell was born in St Augustine's, Norwich, in 1894, the fourth child of Alfred Brightwell, a shoemaker, and Hannah Brightwell née Johnson. In 1901 the family was at 48 Leonards Street, St Augustine's. By 1911 it had moved to a slightly larger house nearby at 85 Magpie Road. At this date there were nine in the household. Besides his parents, Walter shared home with older sisters Helen and Florence (both shoe-machinists), Alice (a chocolate-maker), and younger siblings Harriet, Harry and May, all still at school. Walter himself was also a shoemaker.

Walter enlisted in Norwich and was posted to the 8th Battalion, Norfolk Regiment. On 25 July 1915 he went to France. The Battalion was then encamped in an area north of Amiens where it received trench warfare training throughout August. After a fortnight in the trenches near the Mametz–Carnoy road on the Somme, the Battalion had a week's rest in billets in Albert before relieving the 6th Berkshires in the front line near La Boisselle on the Albert–Bapaume road on 27 September. The regimental history notes that it was here 'subjected to a good deal of bombardment by aerial torpedoes and other annoyances of trench warfare'. A letter published in the *Eastern Daily Press* in January 1916, written by Private Stanley Pfob, of the 8th Norfolks, describes a bomb the Tommies called 'the sausage' (a type of mortar): 'The noise it makes is terrific. It can be discerned in flight, consequently we are all expert dodgers by this time.' It was possibly in such circumstances that Private Walter Brightwell, 21, was killed, on 6 October 1915.

On the second anniversary of his death Walter's family placed an In Memoriam notice in the *Eastern Daily Press* with the words 'As time goes by we miss him more'. On 12 December 1919 the newspaper published a letter by Corporal Hart, who was searching for his brother's grave in France, probably that of Private Gilbert Hart, 8th Norfolks, who was killed in action on the first day of the Battle of Somme. While searching the battlefield Corporal Hart had come across a group of 8th Norfolks graves, including that of Walter. They were, he noted, 'all in good condition'. At this period the Imperial War Graves Commission was still in the process of 'bringing in' isolated, battlefield internments to larger military cemeteries.

Walter Brightwell is buried at the Norfolk Cemetery, Becordel-Becourt, Somme, France, grave no. I.A.86. The cemetery had originally been used to bury men of the 1st Norfolks in 1915. Walter's name does not appear on St Augustine's roll of honour. He was awarded the 1915 Star and the British War and Victory medals.

Private 9168 Clare Edward Carey, 7th Battalion, Norfolk Regiment, formerly 3rd Battalion, Norfolk Regiment

Clare Edward Carey was born in the parish of St Augustine, Norwich, on 6 December 1894, the fifth child of Henry Ellis Carey, a brush-maker, and Maria Carey née Harris. The 1911 Census records that Mr and Mrs Carey had 13 children of whom eight survived infancy: Donald, William, Henry (or Harry), Sidney, Clare, May, Martha and Nellie. Although their mother is named Mrs Carey in the 1911 Census and in Clare's Army Service papers, she and Mr Carey were not in fact married. Henry Carey already had a wife, Eliza Carey née Scales, described in the Census as a tailoress, whom he had married in St Augustine's church in December 1878. The marriage seems have been a troubled one, almost from the start. By 1881 they were living in separate dwellings: Eliza with her sister and brother-in-law in Old Crown Yard off St Martin at Oak Street, Henry with his parents, both weavers, in St Augustine's; he is described in the Census that year as unmarried. By 1891 Henry had set up home at 1 Adelaide Yard off Pitt Street with Maria Harris, who was described in the Census that year as his housekeeper. (They finally married in 1928 when both were in their late sixties). By 1901 they and their expanding family had moved to 7 Rose Yard off St Augustine's Street and by 1911 they had moved again, to 133 Churchill Road. Clare, 16, was now a shoemaker; his brother Henry made wooden boxes for a local timber merchant and his father continued to make brushes for a well-known Norwich firm, Cooks.

Clare enlisted in Norwich on 10 August 1914, six days after the declaration of war against Germany. His Army Service papers record he had been in the 3rd Battalion, Norfolk Regiment (a reserve, training battalion) in 1912 but had bought his discharge. His medical report noted that was just a quarter of an inch short of six foot in height, which was notably tall for an era when the average British male height was 5ft 6. He went over to France with the 7th Battalion, Norfolk Regiment, on 30 May 1915, sailing from Folkestone to Boulogne on *Invicta*. The Battalion spent the summer training and trench digging on the St Eloi and Ploegsteert (known to the Tommies as 'Plug Street') Fronts, losing here a steady stream of men from enemy shelling. On 13 October 1915 the 7th Battalion went over the top into a shattered industrial wasteland of quarries, factories and slag heaps during the final phase of the Battle of Loos in an attempt to capture the formidably defended Hohenzollern Redoubt. Their advance across no man's land was supposed to be covered by a smoke screen, which, in the understated language of the regimental history 'went wrong', exposing them to machine gun fire. Casualties were appalling, with over 70 confirmed dead, 166 wounded and 196 missing.

Private Clare Carey, 20, was reported missing in action on 13 October 1915. His family had to wait ten months for official confirmation that he had been killed. His body was never identified and he has no known grave. On the first anniversary of his death, one of Clare's older brothers, William, placed an 'In Memoriam' notice in the *Eastern Daily Press*, with the words 'Death divides but memory clings'. Poignantly, his parents' own 'In Memoriam' notice gave Clare's age as 21, perhaps thereby preserving their faith that he may still have been alive on his 21st birthday in December. Another St Augustine's man in the 7th Norfolks, Lance Corporal Gayton, was also reported missing (though presumed dead) on this day.

Clare Carey is commemorated on the Loos Memorial, Pas de Calais, France. His name does not appear on the St Augustine's roll of honour and he is listed in *Norfolk Roll of Honour* under the neighbouring parish of St Martin-at-Oak. He was awarded the 1915 Star and the British War and Victory medals.

Lance Corporal 17278 Frederick Gayton,
7th Battalion, Norfolk Regiment

Frederick Gayton was born in the parish of St Augustine, Norwich, in 1879, the second child of Alfred Gayton, a shoemaker, and Mary Ann Gayton née Rickwood. Frederick had an older sister, Amelia, and nine younger siblings, Alice, Ada, Beatrice, Alfred, Gertrude, Donald, Claude, Oscar and Clarence. In the 1881 Census Frederick is recorded with his mother, an upholsterer, and his sister Amelia in Gilling's Yard off Magdalen Street in the parish of St Paul. His father, however, is recorded still living with his parents and siblings in Tubby's Yard off Muspole Street in the parish of St Mary Coslany. Curiously, despite having married Frederick's mother in 1878 he is listed as unmarried. His place of birth is given as St Augustine's, as are his siblings'. By 1891 the Gayton family seem to have reassembled and was living at 77 Mill Hill off Constitution Hill in the suburb of New Catton, north of St Augustine's. Frederick's father is now described as a shoe-finisher and general shopkeeper, his mother a shopkeeper's assistant. Frederick, 12, was an errand boy for a shoemaker. At this date the school-leaving age was 11. By 1901 the family had relocated a few streets away to 77 Millers Lane, New Catton. Frederick, 22, was still at home with his parents and was now working as a clicker (a skilled cutter of leather in the shoemaking trade). His father and sisters Amelia and Alice where also employed in the local shoemaking industry. Later that year, Frederick married Hannah Brown. By 1911 they were living at 18 Stone Masons Square in St George's parish with their four children: Frederick, John, Evril and Rose. Frederick senior was still a clicker.

Frederick enlisted in Norwich and was posted to the 7th Battalion, Norfolk Regiment, the first of the Regiment's new 'Kitchener' Service battalions. His Army Service papers have not survived. Aged 35, he would have been one of the older volunteers. The 7th Norfolks went over to France for the first time on 31 May 1915. Frederick's Medal Roll Index card notes that he arrived in France three weeks later, on 23 June. After being moving around French Flanders for just over a week, the Battalion finally settled into billets in Armentières close to the Belgian border and this is presumably where Frederick joined them. Over the next four months the Battalion alternated between rest billets here and front line duty near Ploegsteert Wood at the southern end of the Ypres Salient, a position of ill-fame known to the Tommies as 'Plug Street'. The trenches here were more than usually exposed and over that summer the Battalion lost a steady stream of men killed or wounded from snipers and bombing.

Lance Corporal Frederick Gayton was killed in action during the final phase of the Battle of Loos on 13 October 1915. He has no known grave. On this date the 7th Norfolks went over the top at 2 p.m. following a bombardment of the German lines. The Battalion's War Diary notes they had been told they would be advancing under cover of a smoke screen laid down by the Coldstream Guards. For some reason the smoke stopped 20 minutes before they went over the top in full view of the German's machine guns, which mowed scores of them down before they had even got past their own barbed wire. The few remnants of the Battalion that reached the German's trenches couldn't hold on to them due to lack of ammunition and reinforcements. Casualties were appalling, with over 70 confirmed dead, 196 missing and 166 wounded. Another St Augustine's man, Private Carey, was also killed in this action on this day.

Like Private Carey *(see p.43)*, Lance Corporal Gayton was among those reported missing in action and it would be two years before his death was officially confirmed. Meanwhile, poignant evidence of his demise did arise in a curious fashion. The archives of the Royal Norfolk Regimental Museum in Norwich contains an undated press clipping from an unidentified newspaper. Its editor had received 'a rumpled and discoloured scrap of paper … torn from a small notebook'. On it was written in pencil: 'R.I.P. / No. 17278 / Lance-Corporal Gayton, F. / Norfolk Regiment'. The note had been found in a mess tin beside the corpse of a Norfolk Regiment soldier, presumably Frederick's, which had lain out in no man's land all winter. After moralising over the inhumanity of the Germans in not allowing the wounded to be recovered from the battlefield, the editor concluded that Lance Corporal Gayton must have written the note himself as he lay dying and unable to reach his own lines in order that his body might be identified. While possible, this would seem unlikely. More likely, a comrade left the note and was then killed before he could report Frederick as dead. British soldiers at this period were issued with a single identity disk made of vulcanised asbestos, which disintegrated in wet ground. The finder of the note, Lieutenant Jack Read, is reported as saying 'Last night [i.e. Friday night of the previous week] was dark enough to get out to them. There were several Norfolks but this is the only indication of who they were.' Subsequent correspondence about the press report between the War Office and Frederick Gayton's widow, dated 5 March and 10 April 1916, suggests the discovery probably occurred in February. Unfortunately, it has not been possible to identify Lieutenant Read, whose regiment (following censorship rules then in force) was not identified in the press.

A letter from the War Office to Mrs Gayton noted that the officer commanding the 7th Battalion, Norfolk Regiment, was unable to confirm his death 'although it is feared that he can no longer be alive'. His status remained 'missing, believed killed' until the second anniversary of his death, when his widow placed an 'In Memoriam' notice in the *Eastern Daily Press*. It included a verse, which in its reference to a 'little token' recalls perhaps the note left with his body:

> *Although his hands we cannot clasp,*
> *His face we cannot see,*
> *Just let this little token tell*
> *That we remember thee.*

Frederick Gayton is commemorated at the Loos Memorial, Pas de Calais, France. His name does not appear on St Augustine's roll of honour screen. He was awarded the 1915 Star and the British War and Victory medals.

Private 3/8058 George Hardy, 1st Battalion, Norfolk Regiment

George Hardy was born in Rampant Horse Yard in the parish of St Edmund, Norwich, in 1880, the fifth child of Tom Hardy, a coal porter, and Sarah Ann Hardy née Havers, described as a 'washer woman'. His older siblings were Sarah, Sophia, Mary and Thomas; his younger, Herbert and Lucy. Their mother died in 1890 and by 1891 the family had moved to Cross Lane in the parish of St George Colegate. Eldest daughter Sarah was now running the household, while Mary was employed as a starch hand (a job in the confectionery trade) and Thomas, like his father, was a general labourer. What had happened to Sophia is unexplained. The youngest children, George, Herbert and Lucy, aged 11, 9 and 3 respectively, were still at home. By 1901 their father had also died and the household had dispersed. Mary had married in 1895 and Sarah and Herbert had gone to live with her in-laws, the Attoes, in Old Catton. Thomas had also married, in 1899, while Lucy, 13, was an 'inmate' at the Chapel Field East Orphans Home. George himself, 21, had married Laura Beatrice Corder in Norwich before the Census was taken in March 1901, although there's no record of them living together at this date. While Laura was lodging on her own at an address in Waterloo Road, George was possibly the George Hardy recorded as a private at Colchester barracks. They had two children, Cecil, born 1906, and another, name unknown, who died in infancy. By 1911, George, Laura and Cecil were living at 33 Bishopgate Street. George was now a labourer at an iron foundry while Laura ran a fish shop.

George enlisted in Norwich. His Army Service papers have not survived. George enlisted in Norwich. If he had in fact been an old

soldier, possibly in the Norfolk Regiment, as the 1901 Census may show, George could well have been called up as a Reservist in August 1914, and the prefix to his Service number, 3, does indeed indicate he was drawn from the Regiment's 3rd (Reserve) Battalion. He was posted to the 1st Battalion and first went over to France on 3 December 1914. At this date the 1st Norfolks were in trenches in the Wulverghem sector of Flanders, enduring bitterly cold, wet, muddy conditions under constant shelling; conditions described in the usually understated regimental history as 'supreme misery'. George's younger brother Herbert, a lance corporal in the 1st

Norfolks, had been here before him and had perished just over five weeks earlier under intense shell fire on the Festubert Front while defending the La Bassée Canal. Some respite from the discomfort was experienced on Christmas Day when the famous 'Christmas Truce' took place as hundreds of men from Norfolk and Saxony met peacefully in no man's land to recover their dead, shake hands, sing carols, exchange gifts and, most famously, kick a football.

During the spring of 1915 the 1st Norfolks were engaged in front line duties defending the Ypres Salient. In July they were entrained to the Albert Front on the Somme. Private George Hardy, 35, was killed here on 20 October 1915. At this date the Battalion was entrenched between Carnoy and Mametz to the east of Albert. There was no major battle going on at this period so it seems likely that his death was the result of an accident. On the first, second and third anniversaries of his death, family members placed 'In Memoriam' notices in the *Eastern Daily Press*. Interestingly, they do say he was accidentally killed rather than killed in action (the latter term was necessarily elastic). The Norfolk Regiment's Wound Book confirm this, noting he was killed by the 'premature explosion of a bomb'. The regimental history remarks that at this time the 1st Battalion was experimenting with all sorts of weird and wonderful improvised trench weapons, including one based on the ancient catapult. By an unhappy coincidence George died exactly a year after his brother Herbert. An 'In Memoriam' notice placed by his family included a verse commemorating both brothers:

> *Memories, with sad recollections, we'll cherish,*
> *Fond thoughts of our brothers, now cold in the clay.*
> *Their image is stamped where it never will perish,*
> *Nor pass from the memory in silence away.*

Seventeen days after his death George's photograph appeared in the *Eastern Daily Press*, along with five other local men who had recently died on active service. According to the caption, he was 'Late of 37, Esdelle Street, Norwich', which is his only known connection with the St Augustine's area. His widow later lived at 25 Silver Street in the parish of St James Pockthorpe, before remarrying and moving to Sheerness on the Isle of Sheppey in Kent. George is buried at Villers-Bretonneux Military Cemetery, Somme, France, grave no. XVIII.F.7.

He is not commemorated on the St Augustine's roll of honour and is listed in *Norfolk Roll of Honour* under the parish of St James Pockthorpe. He was awarded the 1915 Star and the British War and Victory medals.

Private 7638 Archie Fulcher, 2nd Battalion, Norfolk Regiment, formerly Private 6055 1st City of Norwich (Volunteer) Battalion and 4th (Territorial) Battalion, Norfolk Regiment

Archie Fulcher was born in the parish of St Mary Coslany, Norwich, in 1891, the sixth child of Thomas Fulcher, a brewer's labourer, and Elizabeth Fulcher née Pleasants. His older siblings were Thomas, Elizabeth, Beatrice, Walter and William; he had a younger brother, Bertie. In 1891 the Fulcher family was living at 2 Catermoul's Yard off Pitt Street, and this is presumably where Archie was born. By 1901 the family had moved to 31 Muspole Street, just across the road from St Mary's church. The household now consisted of Archie (mistakenly named Arthur in the Census), his mother and his three remaining unmarried siblings, Walter, Beatrice and Bertie. Their father, however, was absent, listed as an inmate at Norwich Lunatic Asylum in Hellesdon and mistakenly described as a widower. He died a few months later, aged 42. Archie's mother remarried in 1904, to Henry Burman, a basket-maker 17 years her senior with whom she had two children, Daisy and Henry, described in Archie's Army Service papers as his half-sister and half-brother. On leaving school in around 1905, Archie was employed by a Norwich brush-maker, S. D. Page & Sons, working in the finishing room as a pressman. His foreman described him as 'Hard working & steady & satisfactory'.

In 1907, Archie, 16, enlisted in the Norfolk Regiment's 1st Volunteer (City of Norwich) Battalion. County-organised volunteer rifle and artillery corps had first come into existence in 1859 as a patriotic movement to defend the homeland while the professional standing army was largely occupied in defending and policing the British Empire overseas. This arrangement lasted until the Haldane reforms of 1907 amalgamated the county volunteer and the yeomanry regiments into the new Territorial Force. On 3 December 1907

Archie transferred to the Norfolk Regiment's new 4th (Territorial) Battalion, having completed 49 days' drill with the Norwich Volunteers. Although his age was given on enlisting as 18 and half, he was in fact barely 17.

On 5 July 1908, Archie, 18, ascended the next rung in his military career, enlisting as a Regular in the 2nd Battalion, Norfolk Regiment. He remained in Norwich until May when he was posted to Warley Camp near Brentwood, Essex, remaining there until the end of 1909. In September 1909 the bulk of the 2nd Norfolks sailed to Gibraltar to take up garrison duties. Archie, however, did not join them immediately, being confined at this time to Warley Hospital for seven weeks while receiving treatment for syphilis. Venereal disease among members of the armed forces at this period was very common and the cure, before the discovery of Salvarsan and penicillin, principally involved the use of the poison mercury and a lengthy, painful and often ineffective course of treatment. Concealment rather than contraction of the disease was an offence under Military Law, but a system of 'hospital stoppages' in which pay was docked while in hospital led many soldiers and sailors to try quack cures before owning up to the Medical Officer. Archie's VD was diagnosed as 'severe with secondaries', these often presented as a rash on the palms of the hands and feet, which means he had probably had primary symptoms, such as ulcerated fingers or toes for four to ten weeks before entering hospital. As if this weren't enough, Archie's treatment was carried out at Warley Hospital, also known as Essex Lunatic Asylum. Remembrance of his father's confinement at Norwich Asylum would presumably have occupied his thoughts.

After being discharged from hospital Archie Fulcher belatedly joined the 2nd Norfolks in Gibraltar. In 1911, the Battalion sailed to India to join the garrison at Belgaum in the south-west of the sub-continent. Arriving on 7 February 1911, Archie's period of service with the colours expired and he was transferred to the Reserves. Despite this he seems to have remained with the Regiment in India right up to the outbreak of war in 1914 and to have been employed by the Army as a signaller. On 2 April 1911, the Census of overseas military recorded him still at Belgaum garrison. In January 1913 he was hospitalised for a couple of days after having been struck in the jaw by a falling boulder while on manoeuvres.

Following the outbreak of war in August 1914, Reservists were recalled to the colours. Archie's call-up came on 5 November, the delay at least partly accounted for by a spell in hospital in India in October where he was receiving treatment for malaria, which, ironically, was known to have a curative effect on syphilis sufferers. On 15 November the 2nd Battalion disembarked from the transport ship HMT *Elephantia* in Mesopotamia (part of modern-day Iraq) with the 18th Indian Brigade, part of the 6th Indian Division. For the remainder of the year, the Battalion moved up and down the River Tigris between Basra and Qurna, fighting a series of skirmishes with the Turkish Army and Arab insurgents. In April 1915 the 2nd Norfolks took part in the Battle of Shaiba, fought to secure the western approaches to Basra. During a decisive charge towards the Turkish trenches, undertaken by companies of the 2nd Norfolks and 2nd Dorsets, officers carried drawn swords, said to be the last occasion when British officers did this in battle.

Through the stifling hot summer months of 1915, the 2nd Norfolks sailed up and down the Tigris, occupying Amara in early June. Here on 14 August Archie was placed on a charge for drunkenness. Pushing on to Azizieh in October the Battalion began to succumb to fatigue, malnutrition and sickness. Over 100 men reported sick or had to be hospitalised, including Archie who spent two days in hospital being treated for dysentery. A week later he was readmitted suffering from beriberi, a debilitating illness now known to be caused by a vitamin B deficiency, partly the result, it is thought, of eating bread made from refined flour. Significantly, the native Indian troops, who mainly ate chapattis made from unrefined whole wheat flour, did not get the illness as often as the white troops. According to the regimental history about 35 cases of beriberi were reported at this period. As his condition worsened, Archie was transferred to hospital at Kut, where he died on 2 November 1915.

Archie is buried at Kut War Cemetery, Iraq, grave no. B.17, and is commemorated also on the St Augustine's roll of honour. He was awarded the 1915 Star and the British War and Victory medals. Archie's younger brother, Bertie, a postman, enlisted in the Norfolk Yeomanry in September 1914 and was later transferred to the Machine Gun Corps as a transport driver. He served in Salonika in September 1916 and survived the war. After the war Archie's surviving siblings in England, Walter, Elizabeth, William and Beatrice, had a long and ultimately fruitless struggle with the War Office to receive his medals. Their parents having died, eldest brother Thomas was regarded by the authorities as Archie's next-of-kin. His stepfather did not qualify because he was not a blood relation. Thomas, however, had emigrated to Canada and seems to have lost touch with his relatives in Norwich. Archie's medals finally came to him in London, Ontario, in 1922.

Private 4494 Edward Percival Wiseman, 1/4th Battalion, Norfolk Regiment

Edward Percival Wiseman (known as Percy) was born in the parish of St Augustine, Norwich, on 2 June 1896, the youngest surviving child of John Wiseman, a shoemaker, and Rosina Wiseman née Read. *(For more on Percy's family background see the entry on his brother George Wiseman, p.233.)* In 1911 Percy, 14, was working as an assistant in a grindery store, part of the shoe-making process, mainly involved in making heels.

Percy enlisted as a Territorial in the 4th Battalion, Norfolk Regiment, in Norwich in May 1915. A photograph of him in uniform shows him wearing the Imperial Service badge, indicating he had volunteered to undertake overseas service should it be required, an obligation which at this stage of the war was not mandatory for Terriers. Within two months he found himself in Liverpool boarding RMS *Aquitania*, Cunard's newest passenger liner – it had only made its maiden voyage in 1914 – now converted to a troopship. One of the largest and most luxurious ships in the world, the *Aquitania* would have made a memorable impression on the troops as they queued on the dockside, her hugely long hull painted in the Art Deco-style 'dazzle' design of the Navy's anti-U-boat camouflage. They were bound for the Dardanelles, the Turkish peninsula where the ill-fated Gallipoli campaign would be fought, arriving at the British base at Mudros on the Greek island of Lemnos on 6 August. Four days later, under intense fire, they landed from rowing boats at Sulva Bay and were thereafter in almost continuous action until early December. For most of this time they were pinned down by sniper fire and shelling in overcrowded, insanitary, fly-infested trenches.

Having survived nearly four months of these conditions Percy, 19, died of heart disease at Mudros base hospital on Sunday 28 November 1915. The vast majority of the casualties suffered by the Allies at Gallipoli were due to disease. One other St Augustine's soldier, Bertie Cushion, died at Gallipoli. St Augustine's Parish Magazine for November 1915 included an extract from a letter written by one of their comrades, 'Private E. M.':

> *I have been to the Dardanelles, and I am sorry to say I am back again wounded. I am progressing very favourably, and I will come and see you the first Sunday night after I come back to Norwich. I am not downhearted yet. If I am to die for the cause, I shall die with a good heart, knowing that I die to save our hearths and homes.*

On the first anniversary of Percy's death his parents placed an 'In Memoriam' notice in the *Eastern Daily Press*. It included a popular verse, reflecting the anguish of the bereaved over the great distance between them and their loved one's resting place:

> *Far and oft our thoughts do wander*
> *To a grave far, far away.*
> *Where his comrades laid our loved one*
> *Who passed away, one year to-day.*
> *No one knows the parting*
> *Oh, what the parting cost!*
> *But God in His great mercy*
> *Has gained what we have lost.*

In addition, Percy's brother George and his wife Florrie and his sister Alice and her husband Harry Gascoyne placed a joint notice in the paper, noting that Percy had 'died of sickness at Dardanelles' along with the verse:

Some day we hope to meet him,
Some day we know not when,
We shall clasp his hand in a better land
Never to part again.

Percy Wiseman is buried at Portianos Military Cemetery, Lemnos, Greece, grave no. V.A.82, and commemorated also on the St Augustine's roll of honour. His photograph was donated to Norfolk Libraries Great War commemoration collection. He was awarded the 1915 Star and the British War and Victory medals. His older brother George would also die of disease, in 1919, while serving overseas.

Private 15565 Frederick James Lundy, 1st Battalion, Lincolnshire Regiment

Frederick James Lundy was born in Norwich in 1879, the eldest child of Frederick Lundy, a horsehair-sorter and gasworks labourer, and Harriet Lundy née Hayhoe, a silk-warper. In 1881 the family, including second child Nancy, was living in Hinde's Yard off St Augustine's Street. A third child, Albert James died in 1883, aged 1. By 1891 the family had grown with the addition of Harriet, Emma, a second Albert James and Herbert. By 1901, still in Hinde's Yard, the family had grown again with Nelly and Gladys. Frederick, 21, had moved a few doors along to lodge with Samuel and Hannah Pinfold, who seem to be described in the Census as either his grandparents or godparents (a relationship not recognised in the Census). At this time he was a welt-trimmer in the shoe trade. Later that year he married Emma Edith Steward. By 1911, still a welt-trimmer, Frederick lived at 6 Chequers Yard off Coslany Street with his wife and four children: Frederick, Arthur, Herbert and Ethel. The family later lived at 103 Norfolk Street in the Chapel Field area of Norwich.

Frederick enlisted in Norwich. His Army Service papers have not survived but his Medal Roll Index card notes he was first sent to France on 6 July 1915, which means he missed his sister Harriet's wedding to Sapper Charles Robert Marin at St Augustine's church on 22 July. Frederick's battalion, the 1st Lincolnshires, was engaged in the action at Hooge in July and August and in the second attack on Bellewaarde during the opening days of the Battle of Loos in

September. On 14 November the Battalion was transferred to the 62nd Brigade, 21st Division. That winter it was entrenched in Flanders, the war having stagnated to a cold, muddy stalemate. With no major battles the chief danger came from the everyday hazards of trench warfare. Private Frederick Lundy, 35, was killed in action on 23 December 1915. An In Memoriam notice in the *Eastern Daily Press* on the first anniversary of his death from his parents, sisters and one surviving brother, Herbert, notes, unusually, that he was killed by a sniper. Frederick is buried at Houplines Communal Cemetery Extension, Nord, France, grave no. I.A.31, and commemorated also on St Augustine's roll of honour as well as St Mary's Baptist church roll of honour, where he is mistakenly named 'F. Lindy'. *(See p.140.)* *Norfolk Roll of Honour* also lists him under both St Augustine and St Mary's Baptist church. He was awarded the 1915 Star and the British War and Victory medals. His brother Albert was killed in France in 1914. His sister Gladys's husband Ralph Gant, who is also commemorated on St Augustine's roll of honour, was killed in action in 1918.

Private 3/10811 Sydney Whittaker, 7th Battalion, Norfolk Regiment

Sydney (spelled Sidney in the birth register) Whittaker was born in the parish of St Augustine, Norwich, in 1890, the fourth child of William Whittaker, a shoe-finisher, and Susan Whittaker née Rout. His siblings were Susannah, William and Alice. In 1891 the family was at 17 Clarke Road in the parish of St Paul. It was still there in 1901, plus new addition, Leah, but minus William, who had married and left home in 1899. Susannah and Alice were now shoe-machinists. In 1911 Sydney, as he now called himself, married May Elizabeth Mason in Norwich. They later lived at 5 Howlett's Court off Botolph Street with their child, May Bessie. Sydney worked as a clicker (shoe-leather cutter) at this date. His parents meanwhile had moved to Waddington Street, Heigham, where they had begun their married life more than 30 years before and where they now kept a small shop.

Sydney enlisted in Norwich and was posted to the 7th Battalion, Norfolk Regiment, one of Lord Kitchener's new Service battalion formed in the frenetic weeks of August 1914 in order to supply the Army's increasing demand for recruits. The Battalion assembled for training at Shorncliffe, Kent, with barely any serviceable equipment and a shortage of experienced officers and NCOs. It was not until they moved to Aldershot in February 1915 that any serious training could be undertaken. Sydney's Army Service papers have not survived but his Medal Roll Index card notes he first went to France on 10 November 1915. The 7th Norfolks had been on the Western Front since May. By the time he joined them they were in their winter trenches near Béthune. Private Sydney Whittaker, 25, died of wounds here on 24 December 1915, Christmas Eve. He had survived the Front for little over six weeks. Three days earlier the Battalion had been caught in a gas attack while in trenches near Givenchy church. Protection against gas had improved chances of survival since the German's first use of gas at Ypres in the spring but was still rudimentary and unreliable. It is therefore possible Private Sydney Whittaker died of the effects of poison gas, probably chlorine, which caused the lungs to dissolve. On the first anniversary of his death his wife and parents placed an 'In Memoriam' notice in the *Eastern Daily Press*, including the popular patriotic verse:

He proudly answered his country's call,
He died a hero beloved by all.

Sydney Whittaker is buried at Calais Southern Cemetery, Pas de Calais, France, grave no. A.4.16, and commemorated also on the St Augustine's roll of honour (as 'Sidney Whittaker'). He was awarded the 1915 Star and the British War and Victory medals.

1916 – The Somme

Lance Corporal 15990 Albert William Mason, 8th Battalion, Norfolk Regiment

Albert William Mason was born in the parish of St Augustine, Norwich, in 1883, the second child of William Mason, a gas-fitter and whitesmith, and Sarah Ann Mason née Browes. In 1891, aged 7,

Albert was living at 13 Union Street, Heigham, with his father, older sister Rose and younger brother James. His mother was absent but not apparently deceased as his father is not listed as a widower. Also absent was Albert's youngest brother, William George, who may perhaps be the 3-year-old recorded in the Census in the care of a 65-year-old laundry worker, Louise Pettitt, in Cowling's Yard in the parish of St Swithin.

In 1901 the family was still at the same address in Heigham. Albert was a heel-builder in the shoe trade and James a shoe factory warehouseman. William had rejoined the family and was at school. Rose's occupation is undefined but in the continued absence of their mother she had probably taken over housekeeping duties. Their mother's absence from the 1891 Census may now be explained. The 1901 Census return for Norwich City Asylum, Hellesdon, lists an inmate named Sarah Mason, a 42-year-old married housewife described as a lunatic. Sarah also appears in the same institution's 1911 Census return. By this date the rest of the Mason family had gone their separate ways. Albert's father died in 1911, aged 51 and Albert had moved in with his sister Rose, now Mrs Hare, at 42 Leonards Street, St Augustine's. He was still a heel-maker. James was living in London, working as a porter in a drapery warehouse in Holborn Circus, while William George cannot be traced.

Albert enlisted in London, possibly as early as September 1914. He had perhaps followed James there to seek work. He was posted to the 8th Battalion, Norfolk Regiment, possibly after finding the London-based regiments over-subscribed. He first went to France on 2 November 1915. At this period the 8th Norfolks were in and out of the trenches near Albert in the Somme region, alternating with the 8th Suffolks. The regimental history notes that during December the Battalion was moved to Bussy-les-Daours to practice attacks on a full-scale model of a German trench system. Lance Corporal Mason, 33, died of wounds on 15 January 1916. (His death notice in the *Eastern Daily Press* placed by his sister, Mrs Rose Hare, says he died on 12 January, aged 32.) With stalemate along the Western Front that winter, his death was probably due to one of the everyday hazards of trench warfare, such as shelling or snipers. Albert is buried at the Corbie Communal Cemetery, the Somme, France, grave no. I.C.25, and is commemorated also on the St Augustine's roll of honour, where he is mistakenly listed as a private. He was awarded the 1915 Star and the British War and Victory medals. His brother James died in Flanders in 1917. *(See p. 135.)*

Sergeant 8975 Edward Henry Dennis, 2nd Battalion, West Yorkshire Regiment (The Prince of Wales's Own)

Edward Henry Dennis was born in Norwich in 1890, the second child of James Dennis, an auctioneer's porter, and Elvina Adelaide Dennis née Woods, a shoe-machinist. In 1891 the family, including Edward's brother James, was living at 4 Rosemary Lane in the parish of St Mary Coslany, so this may be where Edward was born. By 1901 the family had moved to 67 Barn Road in the parish of St Benedict. Edward now had two sisters, Christiana and Rosanne. By 1911 the family, including third daughter Elvina, had moved to 90 Magpie Road, just outside St Augustine's in the parish of St Paul. Edward's brother James and sisters Christiana and Rosanne (or Rose as she was known) were all employed in the shoe trade. Edward, however, was absent having enlisted in Norwich. The 1911 Census recorded him, aged 20, at Colchester Barracks, a private in the West Yorkshire Regiment. Although his Army Service papers have not survived, his regimental number indicates he joined up in 1908, aged 18. When Britain declared war against Germany on 4 August 1914 the 2nd West Yorkshire Regiment was garrisoned in Malta. A photograph of Edward presumably taken at this time shows him wearing KDs (the lighter, cotton, 'khaki drill' uniform issued in warm climates overseas) and holding his Wolseley pattern solar topi

59

bearing the Regiment's badge. He has corporal's stripes on his sleeves. The 2nd Battalion sailed for England on SS *Galicia* on 14 September, arriving in Southampton on the 25th. They were in France ten days later where they formed part of the 8th Division to the end of the war. The 8th was made up of pre-War Regular Army battalions that had been garrisoned overseas prior to August 1914. During the Battalion's first major action, on 18 December 1914 at Neuve Chapelle, it lost more than 120 men killed or wounded during a trench raid. During the Christmas Truce the Germans allowed its stretcher bearers to remove their dead from no man's land. In 1915 Edward married Maria Sarah Payne, who lived at 31 Rose Yard, St Augustine's.

Sergeant Edward Dennis, 25, was killed in action on the first day of the Battle of the Somme, 1 July 1916, the most calamitous date in the history of the British Army. What its planners had predicted would be literally a walk-over, confidently assuming the artillery barrage beforehand would have annihilated the German troops dug in opposite them, ended with 20,000 killed or missing and 40,000 wounded; and this on just the first day of a battle that was to stagger on for four and a half months and achieve little material gain. On 1 July the 8th Division's first objective was to capture German strongholds at Ovillers and La Boisselle opposite the centre of the British front line. Their first objective lay over a wide, exposed area of no man's land, which they had to cross in daylight. Huge numbers were machine-gunned here. Of the 723 officers and other ranks of the 2nd Battalion, West Yorkshire Regiment, who began the assault that morning just 217 were left alive at the end of the day. The bodies lay thickly entangled in the barbed wire or piled up in bomb craters for nearly three weeks before they could be recovered. It was noted that many of them had clearly died of their wounds after many hours or even days of suffering. Some, apparently, were found with open prayer books in their hands. This probably explains why Edward's family was unable to publish a death notice until 21 July. On 22 July the *Eastern Daily Press* printed a second, fuller family notice, including the verse:

Somewhere in France his body lies
Amid the battle's din;

But a spirit freed, death's power denies,
And leaves a world of sin.
Somewhere at home a tear is shed
And sorrow rends a breast;
But a trusting soul by pure faith fed,
Just whispers, 'God knows best'.

On the first anniversary of his death his parents, brother, sisters and widow placed an 'In Memoriam' notice in the *Eastern Daily Press*, including the verse:

Sleep on, dear one, and take thy rest,
They miss you most who loved you best.

Edward Dennis has no known grave. He is commemorated at the Thiepval Memorial, the Somme, France, and on the St Augustine's roll of honour where his rank is mistakenly given as private. In *Norfolk Roll of Honour* he is listed under two Norwich Anglican parishes, St Augustine's and St Paul's, as well as on the roll of honour of St Mary's Baptist church. *(See p.140.)*

Private 13354 Alfred Sidney Youngs, 'B' Company, 8th Battalion, Norfolk Regiment

Alfred Sidney Youngs was born in the parish of St Augustine, Norwich, on 4 April 1896, the eldest surviving child of Alfred Charles Youngs and Sarah Youngs née Custance, who were married in Norwich in 1895. At the time of his birth his parents were living in Leonards Street, St Augustine's. At this date Alfred's father worked in the local shoemaking industry, like his own parents, Walter and Elizabeth, who lived nearby in Cherry Lane. It was a trade Alfred would follow in his turn. His mother lived for much of her childhood in Rose Tavern, a two-room ale house in Oak Street where her father, Robert Custance, was the licensee. It was a milieu she would return to in later life with her husband. However, during Alfred's first few years of infancy she worked at home as a shoe-machinist, while her husband worked in a factory as a shoe-finisher. By 1901 the Youngs family, including baby Hilda, had moved to 6 Spencer Street in the parish of St James Pockthorpe. Alfred was a pupil at Angel Road Senior Boys School, which he left in 1910, aged 14. In 1911 the family, which now included Leonard, born 1903, and Stanley, 1906, was at 73 Waterloo Road, New Catton. In April 1914, Alfred's father gave up the shoe trade to become licensee of Victoria Tavern, a failing pub nearing the end of its days in Horace Street, Heigham. In November 1915 he was fined £1 for allowing beer to be sold to soldiers before noon and in 1916 the authorities refused to renew the license.

Alfred enlisted in Norwich on 1 September 1914, signing on for three years. He was posted to the newly established Service battalion, the 8th Norfolks. His attestation papers give his 'apparent age' as 19, he was in fact 18. A photograph taken around this time shows a fresh-faced youth who at only 5ft 3½ in height and weighing eight and a half stone was physically still barely more than a boy. On 9 September Alfred found himself in a vast, tented field known as St Martin's Plain at Shorncliffe Camp near Folkestone. The 8th Battalion was based here for the first month of its existence. Conditions were rudimentary and the camp's administration chaotic. They were short of everything from boots and tents to soap and cutlery. Uniforms and weapons were also in short supply and the men drilled in a motley collection of civilian clothes and khaki. The regimental history notes that bathing in the sea was compulsory every day at 5 a.m., whatever the weather. In the absence of experienced NCOs and officers, discipline was frequently handed out, unofficially and sometimes over harshly, by the men themselves. On 3 October the Battalion left Shorncliffe for Meeanee Barracks, Colchester, the men still clothed in a ragbag of civilian and military coats and trousers, and still without proper boots or rifles. In April 1915 they were moved again, to Codford Camp near Salisbury to undertake final battle training. By now they were almost fully equipped. During this period Alfred blotted his copy book on two occasions. At Colchester on 29 November 1914 he overstayed his pass by ten hours, for which he received six days' confined to barracks and loss of pay. He repeated the offence on 10 July 1915 at Codford, going AWOL for three days. For this more serious offence he was simply admonished and deducted three days' pay, the leniency of the punishment possibly due to the fact that the Battalion was expected to go overseas within days, though few, not even the officers, knew precisely when or where.

Finally, on 25 July 1915, after nearly 11 months of preparation, the 8th Norfolks embarked at Folkestone bound for Boulogne. For the remainder of the year they were almost constantly on the move around northern France, from trench to rest billet to trench, sustaining only slight casualties from the usual hazards of trench warfare, snipers and bombing. During this unsettled period news of their loved ones was very hard to come by for those left at home. In early October Alfred's father wrote to the Army Records Office, Warley, to enquire about his son's whereabouts, only to have to send a postcard later the same day to report that he was pleased to say he had just received news that he was safe and well. From January to July 1916 the Battalion prepared for the coming summer offensive on the Somme. On 1 July they were ready, in position in assembly trenches just north of the village of Carnoy waiting for the whistle that would signal them to go over the top. At some point in the ensuing battle Alfred received a gunshot wound to the abdomen, possibly during 'B' company's reinforcement of 'C' Company's costly assault on Pommiers trench south-west of Montauban. Such wounds, if not treated immediately, were invariably fatal due to shock, blood loss and the onset of septicaemia. On 3 July Alfred was carried to Casualty Clearing Station No. 5 at Corbie, where he died of his wounds on 4 July 1916, aged 19. (Army records say 20, perhaps because his age had been exaggerated by a year on enlistment.) In February 1917 the Army returned his personal effects to his family: a sad little bundle containing his identity disc, a tinder lighter, some letters, a devotional book, two rings, a purse, a three-penny piece, two farthings, some photos, a penny stamp and, oddly, some 'bullets', presumably empty shells collected as souvenirs.

On the first anniversary of his death his parents, brothers and sister placed an 'In Memoriam' notice in the *Eastern Daily Press* with the verse:

Far and oft our thoughts do wander
To a grave far, far away.
Where his comrades laid our dear one,
In a soldier's grave a year today.
We never knew the pain he bore
We never saw him die,
We only know he passed away
And never said 'Good-bye'.

At around the same date his father took over the license of the Club House Tavern, a pub in Post Office Court beside Norwich Provisions Market. He managed this pub until his death in 1933 after which his widow, Sarah, held the licence until 1938. Alfred is buried at Corbie Communal Cemetery Extension, the Somme, France, grave no. I.B.35. Although born in the parish his name does not appear on St Augustine's roll of honour, presumably because he had no close relatives living in the parish after the war. He is listed in *Norfolk Roll of Honour* in the parish of Holy Trinity in the Unthank Road area of Norwich. He was awarded the 1915 Star and the British War and Victory medals.

Lance Corporal 3/10136 Henry Meadows, 8th Battalion, Norfolk Regiment

Henry Meadows (known as Harry and also for some reason as 'Mike') was born in the parish of St Augustine, Norwich, in 1884, the second child of Harry Meadows, a tailor's cutter, and Priscilla Meadows née Boardman, who was originally from Colchester, Essex. In 1891 the family was living in Green Hills Road just to the north of St Augustine's. Harry, had an older brother Sidney, younger sisters Ethel, Mabel and Hilda, and a younger brother George. An uncle, Walter Meadows, also a tailor's cutter, lodged with them. By 1901 the family had moved to 129 Churchill Road in the parish of St James Pockthorpe. Sidney had now taken up the family trade of tailor's cutter, while Ethel was described in the Census as a tailoress. Mabel,

Hilda, George and new addition to the family, Charles, were all still at school. Harry, however, now 16, had begun work at Norwich Union as an insurance clerk. In 1907 he married Louisa Allen and by 1911 they were living at 44 Merton Road, a row of substantial terraced houses to the west of the city between Dereham Road and Bowthorpe Road. They had two children, Kathleen, born 1908, and Rosanna, 1910; a third, Donald, was born in 1911 after the Census was taken. The family later moved to Framingham Earl, village a few miles to the south of Norwich.

Harry Meadows enlisted in Norwich, possibly as early as September 1914 when the 8th Battalion, Norfolk Regiment, one of Lord Kitchener's New Army Service battalions, was established in Norwich. Many of its volunteer recruits were shop and clerical workers like Harry, with little or no military experience, hence the nickname of the 8th Norfolks, 'The Businessman's Battalion'. Harry and his fellow raw recruits were sent for training, first at Shorncliffe Camp in Kent, and then at Colchester throughout the autumn and winter of 1914, many probably still believing the war would be over by Christmas. In April 1915 the 8th Norfolks moved to Codford Camp on Salisbury Plain for further training and remained there until July. The 8th Norfolks, Harry with them, first crossed over to France on 25 July 1915, disembarking at Boulogne. For the remainder of the year and throughout the first half of 1916, they were in and out of the front line in the Somme region – at Bray, Albert, La Boisselle and Carnoy – without serious incident other than the usual hazards of trench warfare. A copy of a letter from Harry to his young son, Donald, now in the care of the Royal Norfolk Regimental Museum, is addressed 'from a hole in the ground in France'.

In the words of the regimental history, the 'comparatively uneventful history' of the 8th Battalion up to then came to an abrupt and bloody end on 1 July 1916, the first day of the Battle of the Somme. On this calamitous day, the 8th Norfolk's objective was the German front line south-west of Montauban. By the time it was relieved on 3 July, the Battalion had lost almost half its strength, killed, wounded or missing. Private Harry Meadows, 31, died of wounds on 8 July 1916 while at No.2 Stationery Hospital, Abbeville. Harry is buried at Abbeville Communal Cemetery, the Somme, France, grave no. V.8.4. Harry Meadows's name does not appear on the St Augustine's roll of honour. He is listed with three other men on the roll of honour in St Andrew's church, Framingham Earl, with the words 'Rest eternal grant, O Lord, these thy Servants & may Light perpetual Shine upon them'. He is also listed under the village of Framingham Earl in *Norfolk Roll of Honour* and commemorated on the Norwich Union Great War roll of honour in Surrey Street, Norwich. In 1920 *The Norwich Union Magazine* published a brief obituary:

Harry Meadows (familiarly known as 'Mike') was an enthusiastic angler, and would walk miles to try a piece of water that was supposed to contain fish. Long walks were a hobby, and he would think nothing of a 10 mile tramp after a long day at the Office.

He was awarded the 1915 Star and the British War and Victory medals.

Second Lieutenant Bertie William Benn, 8th Battalion, Norfolk Regiment, formerly Sergeant 3/10210, 9th Battalion, Norfolk Regiment

Bertie William Benn was born at Surrey Grove in the parish of All Saints, Norwich, on 7 February 1889, the eldest child of William Joseph Benn and Emily Benn née Huggins. Mr and Mrs Benn had nine children. Their names, in descending order of age, were Bertie, Walter, Arthur, Lilian Margaret (Maggie), Florence (Florrie), Hilda, Ethel, Cecil and William. Bertie's father had begun his married life in

1887 as a commercial traveller; his mother a farm labourer from Mulbarton, a village south of Norwich. By 1891 however, the Census describes his father as a journeyman butcher, meaning he had served an apprenticeship under a master butcher but was not yet fully qualified to set up his own slaughterhouse or butchery or train apprentices. For some reason he was unable to proceed any further in this line of business and was later employed as a porter, house painter and warehouseman. The latter had been his father's occupation. In 1891 the family, comprising at this date only Mr and Mrs Benn, Bertie and Walter, was living at 2 St Mark's Cottages off Hall Road, Lakenham; a southern suburb of Norwich a few minutes' walk from Surrey Grove where Bertie had been born. Bertie and Walter were pupils at St Mark's Boys School in Hall Road during the 1890s (Bertie was admitted on 7 January 1889, Walter on 12 November 1890), where they were contemporaries of Sidney Day, who was to win the Victoria Cross in 1917. By 1901 the family had moved to 20 Ebenezer Terrace off Sussex Street, St Augustine's. Here Bertie, 12, was working part-time as a baker's boy. Ten years later, the 1911 Census recorded him still with his parents in Ebenezer Terrace, working as a parks gardener.

Bertie Benn before the war

From 1910 until the outbreak of war in August 1914, in addition to his job as a gardener, Bertie also served part-time as a private in the 2nd East Anglian Field Ambulance, a Territorial unit of the Royal Army Medical Corps. On 7 September 1914, with the war only a month old, he volunteered for one year's full-time active service with the Army's Special Reserve. Passed medically fit, he was enrolled as a private in the 9th Battalion, Norfolk Regiment, which didn't officially come into existence until two days later. The 9th was one of Kitchener's New Army Service battalions, which were being hastily assembled all over the county to meet the increasing demands of the War Office for fresh troops as the small, pre-war Regular Army – the 'Old Contemptibles' – passed into history on the battlefields of northern France and Flanders. Composed mainly of civilian volunteers with little or no military experience, the 900-odd raw recruits that left Norwich that September were to spend the next 11 months roughing it, living under canvas in muddy fields at training camps at Shoreham in Sussex at first, then at Aldershot in Hampshire.

Bertie Benn (left) in the uniform of the East Anglian Field Ambulance

To begin with they hadn't rifles, uniforms or even proper boots but gradually organisation and conditions improved. Bertie's experience as a Territorial most probably counted, as he now advanced through the non-commissioned ranks comparatively quickly: to lance corporal (strictly speaking an appointment not a rank at this period) on 27 November 1914, to corporal on 8 April 1915 and then to lance sergeant (on unpaid promotion) on 21 July 1915. A letter written at this period to his brother Arthur, who had emigrated to Australia in 1913, survives in the Benn family's papers:

Shoreham Camp
14 March 1915

Dear Old Arthur,
I am sorry I have not written to you before, but I find out from home that you were getting on alright, so I did not worry. I reckon by the time you get this, I shall be in France sticking sausages, but will tell mother, to let you know how I get on. I

have just done 6 months in the Army, and have only got to go through a course of long range firing before I go away. I have had some rough times, in fact I often wonder how I have got through it all but I am in the best of health and shall not feel contented now, till the damned Germans are wiped right out. The money is the worst thing here, all we get is 6/- a week & it does not go far after we have paid for our washing, and got something to smoke. But I don't mind it is for a jolly good cause. I hope to have another stripe by the time this reaches you. I have only been home once since I joined, but I hope to go again before I go away. The war news seems to me to be very good & I think we shall get over the pond just in time to finish the beggars off. I should like you to have seen me in charge of the guard last Sunday, 15 men, on guard with fixed bayonets. I am going to have my photo taken before I go, & will send one to you as soon as I get them. I think this is all now hoping that you are quite well & hope the next time I write, the war will be over, Lce Cpl Benn receiving an Iron Cross for running away from the Germans.

From your Loving Brother Bert
If you write to me send letter home & mother will forward it on.

Corporal Bertie Benn

On 30 August 1915 Bertie went over to France with the 9th Norfolks for the first time, moving from Boulogne to bivouacs in Montcavrel where they received further training until 21 September. The Battalion was then marched over four gruelling days and 50 miles (83 km) to Béthune and into its first action, on 25 September 1915, at Lone Tree Hill during the Battle of Loos. The Battalion's first contingent had arrived in France less than a month earlier with 30 officers and 987 other ranks. By the time Bertie joined it, it had been reduced by casualties, illness and accident to just 16 officers and 555 other ranks. In such circumstances, promotion tended to be accelerated and on 1 October 1915 Bertie was made an acting sergeant, having, remarkably, risen from private to senior NCO in little more than a year. Even so, he still had one more promotion to go.

The winter and spring of 1915/16 were spent in and out of the trenches, with little going on other than a steady trickle of casualties from enemy shelling. Bertie's casualty form notes that in March 1916 he attended No. 16 Field Ambulance to have some dental work done. This was one of three Field Ambulance units (a kind of mobile field hospital rather than a vehicle) attached to the 6th Division, of which the 9th Norfolks was also now a part. Bertie was now drawing towards the end of his time with the 9th. Having impressed his superiors by the way he conducted himself as a sergeant he had been recommended by his CO for a commission and was sent to an Officer Cadet School (OCS). There were more than 20 OCS in the UK at this time. Unfortunately, Bertie's Service papers do not record which one he was sent to or when. On 25 June 1916 he was formerly discharged as a non-commissioned officer from the 9th Norfolks in order to receive a temporary commission as a 2nd lieutenant on probation. This was granted by the king on 27 June 1916. According to St Augustine's parish magazine he was the first man from the parish to be commissioned from the ranks. In fact he was the second. Herbert Pitcher (see section 'Four Survivors' Stories') had received a battlefield commission in March 1915. Two other St Augustine's men, Bertie's younger brother Walter Benn and Gordon Jode, were also commissioned from the ranks later. As seems often to have happened with soldiers when they became 'temporary gentleman', Bertie was posted to a different battalion, possibly to avoid the embarrassment of officers having to socialise with a fellow they had previously dealt with as a social inferior and to deter any of his barrack-room mates from taking advantage of their former association. In Bertie's case he was posted to the Norfolk Regiment's 8th Battalion.

Bertie had received his commission just as the British Army was about to experience the worst day in its history: 1 July 1916, the first day of the Battle of the Somme. On this day the 8th Norfolk's objective was to capture the German trenches outside the village of Montauban. In this they were partially successful but at a terrible cost with around 190 killed or missing, and more than 220 wounded. It isn't possible to say definitely whether or not Bertie took part in this battle, the Battalion's War Diary doesn't mention him and examination of his Service papers also draws a blank. However, in a letter to Bertie's brother, Arthur, their mother wrote: 'I think it was about the third battle since he got his commission that he was killed', which suggests he was present at the fighting from 1 to 3 July when the Battalion was relieved. However, a letter of condolence to his parents written by Captain Ashdown, Bertie's company commander, mentions that Bertie had been with them for 'a very short time … a few days', which suggests he only joined them after the catastrophe at Montauban. The 8th Norfolks spent the next two weeks rebuilding its strength in shelters and bivouacs around Carnoy and Albert. Between 9 and 13 July it received drafts of about 250 reinforcements, including 10 officers, from the Norfolk Regiment's 1st, 7th and 10th battalions, so perhaps Bertie joined the 8th Norfolks at this time.

Second Lieutenant Bertie Benn was killed in action on 19 July 1916, aged 27. In the early hours of the 19th, the 8th Norfolks received orders to return to Montauban to assist in the taking of the enemy-occupied Delville Wood to the north-east of the village. They were to begin their assault under cover of an artillery barrage at 6.15 a.m. Problems deploying to their designated jumping off position delayed the attack for an hour. A report written by the 8th Norfolks' CO, Lieutenant-Colonel Ferguson, described the moment in which Bertie was killed:

> *At 7.15 a.m. the two companies* [A & B] *advanced and met with a stubborn resistance, particularly on the left flank. The officers leading the first two waves of 'A' company were killed* [2nd Lieutenant Bertie Benn and Lieutenant Harry Mansfield MacNicol], *the men themselves suffering heavy casualties from machine gun fire and snipers concealed in trees. Several Germans surrendered as soon as we advanced but the men had become infuriated by the enemy's sniping methods and they were shot.*

The killing of surrendering enemy combatants, especially in the heat of battle, was unfortunately not uncommon as, for example, the massacre carried by a raiding party of 7th Norfolks near Monchy-le-Preux in the Arras sector in October 1917. During the Battalion's action at Montauban on 1 July officers going over the top had been allowed to wear ordinary battle tunics rather than the distinctive officer's coat so as not to present snipers with an obvious target. The ploy had been deemed a success with fewer than expected casualties among the officers but there is no mention of this tactic being employed again in the CO's 'lessons learned' report after the fighting at Delville Wood.

News of Bertie's death was delivered to his parents by telegram from the War Office on 3 August. Unusually, a copy is preserved in his Service papers. It is still a shock to see one of these official communications, which many thousands of families received during the war, the finality expressed so matter-of-factly:

> *Deeply regret to inform you 2 Lt B. W. Benn 8 Norfolk Regt was killed in action 19-20 July 1916 the army council express their sympathy.*

Bertie Benn had been an officer for just 23 days. Such was its brevity, notice of his commission wasn't published in the *London Gazette* until 18 August 1916, almost a month after his death. The October 1916 issue of St Augustine's parish magazine included a tribute by the rector, the Revd J. H. Griffiths, who wrote that he had known Bertie Benn 'for some years as a man of fine character'. The magazine included extracts from the letters of condolence received by his parents from Bertie's company and battalion COs. Captain Charles Frank Ashdown MC, officer commanding 'A' Company, 8th Battalion, Norfolk Regiment, wrote:

> *Dear Mr Benn,*
> *I feel that I would like to write a few lines to express to you and your family the deep sympathy I feel for you all in the death of your son, Second-Lieut. B. Benn, who was killed in action, on July 19th, whilst leading his platoon against the Germans, in certainly the hottest fight it has ever been my misfortune to be in. His platoon was in front and he was shot at the very*

commencement of the assault. I saw him shortly afterwards, and from what I could see and from what one or two of his men have told me, his death was instantaneous. He had only been with us a very short time, but in those few days, he proved his worth, and his death has been a real loss to me, as much from a personal point of view as a military one. He died doing his duty, in the forefront of battle, a very gallant gentlemen.

Lieutenant-Colonel Henry Gaspard de Lavalette Ferguson DSO, commanding officer, 8th Battalion, Norfolk Regiment, wrote:

Dear Mrs Benn,
One of my Company Officers has already written to you, but I feel I must write to you personally, to offer you my deepest sympathy in your great sorrow, at the loss of your son Lieut. Benn. He was killed in action on July 19th, whilst gallantly leading his men. Although your son had not been very long in my battalion, he made himself very popular with both his brother officers and men, and I myself mourn the loss of a very good officer. He had done well from the first day of joining us, and I had formed a good opinion of him. He was buried in the wood (together with two of his brother officers killed on the same day) he so gallantly helped to capture. [Lieutenant Harry Mansfield MacNicol and 2nd Lieutenant Walter Chapman Morgan.] *The graves are well looked after by those responsible for the work, and in due course your son's resting place will be marked with a cross. Any of his belongings that he left behind will, in due course, reach you. I would have written to you before this but I myself have only just left the fighting line, and had no opportunity of doing so. Again offering you my very deepest sympathy in your great sorrow and the loss to my battalion which your son's death has caused us all.*

Despite Colonel Ferguson's assurances, Bertie Benn's burial place, presumably in or near Delville Wood, was subsequently lost and he has no known grave.

Curiously, the death notice placed by his family in the *Eastern Daily Press* gave his date of death as 20 rather than 19 July. Perhaps because the War Office telegram gave his date of his death as 19–20

July, his family allowed him that officially sanctioned extra day of life. Something of the impact the news of the death of a loved one had on members of the close family may be gleaned from the distraught letter Bertie's mother, Mrs Emily Benn, wrote to her third son Arthur in Australia:

> *I have felt too much upset to write my dear boy its too terrible about our dear Bert I feel I shall never get over it we were so counting on seeing him home and now to feel I shall never see him again what shall I do … Dear boy he has not had much pleasure the last 19 months he has been out and in the fighting line since last August 1915.*

The Benn family were to have a long struggle with military bureaucracy to recover Bertie's effects and settle his estate. When his will was finally proved in 1919 his estate, left entirely to his mother, was £122 13s. 4d. Earlier, Mrs Benn had sought the help of the rector of St Augustine's church, the Revd J. H. Griffiths, to try to recover her son's possession, in particular and poignantly the sword she supposed all officers carried into battle. Internal Army correspondence among Bertie's Service papers reveal that there was some reluctance to tell her the truth, which is that it was extremely unlikely her son had ever purchased a sword (they were no longer general issue to infantry officers) and even if he had he would have been very unlikely to have worn it at the Front. Failing to get a sword she next tried to get his service revolver but this could not be traced; in fact the only personal effects recovered were his identity disc, some letters, a pocket notebook, a prayer book, some photos and his advanced pay book.

On the second anniversary of his death Bertie's parents placed an 'In Memoriam' notice in the *Eastern Daily Press*, including the verse:

> *What though in lonely grief we sigh*
> *For those beloved no longer nigh,*
> *Submissive would we still reply,*
> *Thy will be done.*

There is a separate family memorial to Bertie Benn in St Augustine's church, situated on the wall of the north nave aisle. It takes the form of an engraved marble plaque with the device of a crowned cross. At the base is a verse from the *Book of Revelations*: 'Be Thou faithful unto death and I will give thee a crown of life'.

The Benn Memorial

Bertie Benn is also commemorated at the Thiepval Memorial, Somme, France, and on the St Augustine's roll of honour. He was awarded the 1915 Star and the British War and Victory medals. Bertie's brother Walter was killed in action near Arras in 1917.

Private 17180 Frederic James Middleton, 7th Battalion, Norfolk Regiment, formerly Private, 8th Battalion, Norfolk Regiment

Frederic James Middleton was born in Duke Street in the parish of St Mary Coslany, Norwich, in 1887, the third child of Frederic Middleton, a printer's compositor, and Laura Middleton née Perowne, a surname of Huguenot descent. From at least 1891 the family was living at 2 Bantam's Yard in the parish of St Mary Coslany. In 1901 the children, in descending order of age, were Agnes, Ellen, Frederic, Alice, William, Kate, Winifred and Emily. The family was still living in Bantam's Yard in 1911, though now at No. 4. By this date it had suffered a number of tragedies. Alice had died towards the end of 1901, aged 12. Mr Middleton died in 1906, aged 48. William, 19, was an inmate at Norwich Incorporation Workhouse in Bowthorpe Road, where he was termed an 'imbecile'; and Winifred, 14, was a permanent resident at Dr Barnardo's Home for Incurable Children at Agra Mansions in Tunbridge Wells, Kent, where many of the children were crippled by rickets. Of those still living in the family home, Agnes was a shoe-fitter at Webster's factory in Calvert Street (later known as Batson & Webster in Fishergate), Ellen was a dressmaker, Kate was a book-binder at Jarrold's and Emily was still at school. Frederic, 23, was a baker for Wills Bakery.

Frederic enlisted in the Norfolk Regiment in Norwich, probably in 1915. His Service papers have not survived. On 4 September 1915 he married Eva White in St Augustine's church. He is described in the register as a private in the 8th Battalion, Norfolk Regiment, while Eva's father of 5 Pitt Street, St Augustine's, is described as a private in the National Reserves, 5th Battalion, Norfolk Regiment. After marriage Frederic and Eva lived at 4 Hooks Yard off St George's Plain.

Frederic first went to France on 10 December 1915, though whether with the 7th or 8th Battalion is not known. However, by the opening of the Somme offensive in July 1916 he was definitely in the 7th, which was held in reserve for much of the month, though subject to the normal hazards of trench warfare. Frederic, 28, died of wounds on 21 July 1916. Many of the wounded from the Somme were taken to the 5th Army's hospital at Étaples, and this is probably were Frederic died, given his place of burial. On 25 July the *Eastern Daily Press* published a family death notice, concluding with the words 'Though lost to sight to memory dear'. Frederic is buried at Étaples Military Cemetery, Pas de Calais, France, grave no. XIV.D.9, and commemorated also on the St Augustine's roll of honour. He is listed under the combined parishes of St Miles Coslany and St Martin at Oak in *Norfolk Roll of Honour*. He was awarded the 1915 Star and the British War and Victory medals.

Private 6731 Albert Want, 1st Battalion, Norfolk Regiment, formerly Private 4256 2nd and 3rd Battalions, Norfolk Regiment

Albert Want was born in the parish of St Martin at Oak, Norwich, in 1882, the fifth child of James Want and Emma Want née Coe. At this date the family lived at Hawke's Yard off Oak Street. Albert's father was a shoemaker, a trade Albert and his three brothers would follow in their turn. By 1891 the family had moved to 7 Esdelle Street, St Augustine's, a small two-up, two-down terraced house where Mr and Mrs Want raised eight children: John, Alice, Emma, James, Arthur, Albert, Ethel and Florence. They were still here in 1901, though without Emma, who had died in 1893 aged 19, eldest son John, and Albert, who had joined the Army.

On 1 August 1899 Albert enlisted in Norwich as a militiaman in the Norfolk Regiment's 3rd (Volunteer) Battalion. Aged 17 and a clicker (shoe-leather cutter) for a local shoemaker, Wyatts, he was already a part-time soldier in the 1st City of Norwich Rifle Volunteers. According to his Attestation papers, he had previously been rejected by the Army as 'under standard'. On this occasion the MO passed him fit for service. He was 5ft 2½ in height, weighed just 7 stone 2lbs (45.36 kg) and had dark brown hair, grey eyes and a scar on his forehead. (Four years later, on re-enlisting, he was half an inch taller and four pounds heavier.) Albert served as a full-time Regular for seven years between 1899 and 1906, first in the Norfolk Regiment's 3rd and then in the 2nd Battalion. While his Service papers are not explicit on where he served between 1899 and 1903, his medical record notes he received treatment for an unspecified ailment at Fermoy in County Cork, Ireland, in February 1900, and was hospitalised a year later during the 2nd Anglo-Boer War with 'debility' at Springfontein in the Orange Free State, the location of one of the infamous British concentration camps.

Judging by his Service papers, which are quite extensive, Albert seems to have been a real-life example of the stereotypical British soldier, Tommy Atkins. When he signed up for a further three years on 24 November 1903 his medical report describes a number of tattoos on both arms, including one with the words 'South Africa' above crossed flags on his right forearm along with a number of the stock-in-trade of the tattooist's art: hearts and daggers, clasped hands, flowers and pulchritudinous female forms. His conduct sheet is fairly sprinkled with outbreaks of minor misdemeanour, including using obscene language to an NCO, creating a disturbance in camp, returning to barracks drunk, being absent without leave, having a dirty rifle on parade, not complying with an order and being absent from parade. The majority of these offences occurred in 1904 when he was back in England after the Boer War with nothing much to do. Boredom was finally relieved in October 1905 when he began another tour of duty in South Africa, which lasted until November 1906 when he was transferred to the Army Reserve and returned to England. How he earned a living between 1906 and 1914 is not known. The 1911 Census records him as unemployed and living with his parents in Esdelle Street.

With war seeming to be inevitable in the summer of 1914 Albert was recalled to the colours on 5 August and posted to the 1st Battalion, Norfolk Regiment. Nine days later he was in France, arriving there two days before the main body of the Battalion, which was still sailing from Belfast where they had been garrisoned. The next fortnight was one of frantic activity. Now 32 and seven years out of training, Albert's feet did not survive the 1st Norfolks' first bit of serious marching, a two-day slog from the rail depot at Le Cateau to Dour in Belgium, a distance of about 27 miles (43km). On 22 August he was admitted to hospital with a sprained foot. By the time he was fit enough to rejoin the Battalion on 12 September, he had missed the Battle of Mons, II Corps' rearguard action at Le Cateau and the Battle of the Marne but was just in time to take part in the Anglo-French fight back at the Aisne and Ypres. Unsurprisingly, given what he had been through in the previous four months, Albert was taken ill on 13 December and had to be hospitalised with bronchitis and pleurisy, first in France and then in England, until 22 January 1915 when a sputum test found no evidence of T.B. and he was discharged and granted ten days' leave.

The following year and a half of Albert's life consisted of a bewildering series of postings. Returning from leave after his hospitalisation in February 1915, he was posted to the Regiment's Reserve Depot until July, then transferred briefly back to the 1st Battalion (without going to France) and then, on 3 September, was sent to France to join the 7th Battalion. On 22 October he was sent back to the Depot in England again, whereupon he sprained his back and had to be hospitalised. Out of hospital in November he was transferred again, this time to the Norfolk Regiment's 3rd Reserve Battalion, where he remained until the following spring. As in 1904/5, prolonged periods of idleness seem to have led to misconduct and in early April 1916 he forfeited six days' pay for being absent without leave for six days.

On 12 April 1916 Albert sailed for France for the third time, landing in Rouen on the 13th. It is not entirely clear which battalion he was attached to this time, possibly the 9th (there were few he hadn't been in at one time or another). Then on 25 May 1916 he finally re-joined the 1st Battalion, which he had last seen in France 16 month earlier. The 1st Norfolks were then entrenched near Arras and engaged in minor skirmishes. On 16 July it marched to Montauban in the Somme battle area. Between the 26 and 27 July it faced its sternest test of the war so far during the fighting in and around Longueval and Delville Wood, which the 5th Division had been tasked to recapture by Field Marshall Haig at all costs. In these two days of desperate fighting the 1st Norfolks lost 90 men killed in action and more than 150 wounded or gassed. At one point 'A' Company was reduced to the fighting strength of one platoon, the remainder having been buried by shelling. On the 31 July the 1st Norfolks were sent once more into the devastated village of Longueval, which was under almost constant heavy bombardment and in flames. Private Albert Want, 34, died here on 1 August 1916. The following day the Battalion, having lost a further 23 officers and men, was moved back to rest billets near Abbeville. Albert's body was never identified and he has no known grave. His father was notified of his death on 16 August. His mother was spared the agony of his loss, having died in 1915. Albert is commemorated at the Thiepval Memorial, Somme, France, and on the St Augustine's roll of honour. He was awarded the Queen's South Africa Medal with Cape Colony and South Africa 1901 Clasps for his service in the Boer War and the 1914 Star with Bar and the British War and Victory medals. Albert's brother Arthur also served as a private during the Great War, first in the Queens Royal (West Surrey) Regiment then in the Labour Corps.

Private 21099 Sidney James Scott, 'B' Company, 9th Battalion, Norfolk Regiment

Sidney James Scott was born in the parish of St Augustine, Norwich, in 1883, the second child of David Scott, a shoe-finisher (he is described on pre-1881 censuses as a cordwainer, an old term for a shoemaker) and Emma Priscilla Scott née Brighten, a silk-winder. His father, who was in his early fifties when Sidney was born, had been married before and widowed. As his older brother, David, died only a few months after he was born aged 3, Sidney (sometimes spelled Sydney) was in effect brought up an only child, a rare status in this era. The Scott family lived first in Howlett's Court off Botolph Street but by 1901 had moved to 51 Rose Yard off St Augustine's Street. By 1911 they had moved to 5 Old Yeast Yard off Muspole Street in the nearby parish of St George Colegate. Here Sidney was a shoemaker and the family's principal breadwinner now his father had retired from the shoe trade. In 1913 Sidney married Ethel Maud Victoria Staff. The couple lived at 15 King's Square off Globe Street in the Chapel Field area of the city. They had one child, Doris, born 1916.

Sidney's Army Service papers have not survived. The 9th Battalion, Norfolk Regiment, was established in Norwich in September 1914, one of the new Service battalions of Lord Kitchener's citizen army. It first saw action on the Western Front at the Battle of Loos in September 1915. However, given that Sidney was not awarded the 1915 Star, it is likely he only joined the Battalion after conscription in 1916, in which case his first experience of warfare would also have been his last. The 9th Norfolks entrained for the Somme battlefield on 2 August. On the 14th they went into front line trenches near the village of Mailly, some five or six miles north of Albert, where they were heavily shelled. Given that Sidney died in England on 21 August 1916, he must presumably have been brought home seriously wounded soon after the shell attack. His death was registered in West Derby, Lancashire, which included the First Western General military hospital in Fazakerley, Liverpool.

Sidney is buried in a Commonwealth War Grave Commission maintained grave at Norwich Cemetery, Bowthorpe Road, Norwich, grave no. 50/84. Although born in the parish of St Augustine his name does not appear on the parish's roll of honour. His father having died in 1913 and his mother the following year, there seems to have been no close relations left in the area to commemorate him. His name does, however, appear in *Norfolk Roll of Honour* under the Norwich parish of Holy Trinity. This was the parish church for the Globe Street area where presumably his widow and child lived. Sidney was awarded the British War and Victory medals.

Rifleman 4063 Sydney A. Palmer, 3rd Battalion, Rifle Brigade (The Prince Consort's Own)

Sydney Palmer was born in Norwich on 22 June 1884, the youngest of the seven children of Benjamin Palmer, a furniture broker (a dealer in used furniture), originally from Holt in north Norfolk, and Emma Palmer née Goodjohn from Polstead in Suffolk. Sydney's father died a few months after his birth, aged 41, and by 1891 the family had moved from the well-to-do Tombland area of the city to the rather poorer surroundings of 14 Esdelle Street in the parish of St Augustine. Sydney's older siblings at home at this date were Ernest, a plumber's apprentice; Kate and Alice, cigar makers; and Benjamin and Louise, like Sydney still at school. Their eldest sister, Emma, had married in 1888 and left home. Sydney attended St Augustine's Mixed Infants and Junior Boys School, and then, from 1 October 1895, Angel Road Boys School, which he left in July 1897 aged 13. The School's attendance register notes he was 'legally exempt' from staying on until 14, possibly because his widowed mother needed him to bring in a wage. By 1901, aged 16, he was a whitesmith (a maker of metal articles, usually from tin).

Sydney Palmer doesn't appear to be listed in the 1911 Census, at least not under the name he was born with. According to *Soldiers Died in the Great War* he enlisted in London, specifically at Hounslow, while resident in Hammersmith. While his Army Service papers have not survived one of his Medal Roll Index cards (unusually, he has two) records that he originally enlisted under the name 'Arthur Meachen', which was later crossed out and 'S. Palmer' substituted. His regimental service number on both cards, 4063, indicates that he enlisted in the Rifle Brigade sometime during 1910 or in early 1911. The 1911 Census records a Private Arthur Meachen, 23, born in

Norwich, at the Rifle Brigade's Winchester barracks. No one of this name, date and place of birth is recorded in the General Record Office's register of births, which is not surprising as the real Arthur Meachen of Norwich died in 1907, aged 27. The 1901 Census records this Arthur Meachen in Leonards Street, a street away from Esdelle Street where the 16-year-old Sydney was living at the time. Arthur Meachen's parents were Sydney's next-door-neighbours there, and their younger children presumably his playmates. *(See Alfred Meachen, p.96.)* It is unlikely the reason why Sydney enlisted under the name of a deceased neighbour will ever be discovered but the fact that he also took four years off his age (he was 27 in 1911 not 23) suggests he was trying hard to cover his tracks. Perhaps, he simply had personal problems he needed to escape from and, like countless young men before and after him, enlisted under an alias. Interestingly, someone named Sydney A. Palmer married an Alice Symonds in the City of London in 1910. No such couple appear in the 1911 Census, so perhaps it was from this relationship he was trying to escape.

It isn't clear when Sydney Palmer owned up about his real identity to the Army. One of his Medal Roll Index cards notes that his British War Medal and Victory medal were returned by his next-of-kin for amendment in 1921, suggesting that even at this date the Army was unsure about his true identity. His other Medal Roll Index card records that he first went to France on 20 December 1914. The bulk of the 3rd Rifle Brigade had landed in France as part of the 17th Brigade, 6th Division, on 12 September. By December it had already lost more than 100 men, so perhaps Sydney was sent with other reinforcements. Throughout 1915 until October, the 3rd Rifle Brigade was engaged in numerous actions in Flanders, in particular near Hooge where the German Army used *Flammenwerfer* (flamethrowers) for the first time. It then transferred to the 24th Division and shifted its area of operation to the Somme, where it spent most of the summer of 1916. On 17 August the 24th Division was set the task of capturing a strategically important position at Guillemont Railway Station, which it took and held until the 22nd, suffering heavy casualties. Private Sydney Palmer, 32, died of wounds on 22 August 1916, possibly, given his place of burial, while at Casualty Clearing Station No.5 at Corbie. Sydney is buried at Corbie

Communal Cemetery Extension, Somme, France, plot 2, row B, grave 106, and commemorated also on the St Augustine's roll of honour. He was awarded the 1915 Star and the British War and Victory medals.

Private 19816 Harry Purdy, 14th Battalion, Hampshire Regiment, formerly Private 17855, Bedfordshire Regiment

According to *Soldiers Died in the Great War* Harry Purdy was born in Woolwich, almost certainly a clerical error for Norwich. Woolwich District registers of birth for the 1880s and 1890s record no one of this name. Norwich District birth registers do, however, record a Harry Purdy born in Norwich in 1889. Harry Purdy was the son of Matilda Purdy, a laundry worker originally from Stiffkey in north Norfolk. She appears to have been unmarried and Harry's father's name is not known. In 1891 Harry was living at 246 Heigham Street, Norwich, with his mother, sisters Kate and Emily and younger brother William. By 1901 the family, which now included Alice, Eva and Hetty, had fallen into penury and were inmates of Norwich Incorporation Workhouse in Heigham. By 1911 the family was out of the workhouse and living at 110 Calvert Street in the parish of St George Colegate. Harry was absent, however, and may be the Norwich-born 'Henry' Purdy, 23, a kitchen porter in a London club noted in the Census living at St Giles's Christian Mission Boys Home, Holborn.

Harry Purdy's Army Service papers have not survived. *Soldiers Died in the Great War* says he was a Norwich resident when he enlisted in London. It also notes that before joining the Hampshire Regiment he had been in the Bedfordshire Regiment. His Medal Roll Index card indicates he was at Gallipoli in 1915, which logically places him in the Bedfordshire Regiment's 5th (Territorial) Battalion. The 5th Bedfordshires, part of the East Anglia Division, undertook Home defence duties from August 1914 to July 1915 when they sailed for the Dardanelles. Harry was posted to Gallipoli three months later, arriving on 3 October 1915, by which date the campaign had begun to disintegrate. By December the Anglo-French forces were being covertly withdrawn.

At some point Harry transferred to the 14th Battalion, Hampshire Regiment. Known as the 1st Portsmouth Battalion, it formed part of 116th Brigade, 39th Division, on the Western Front. The Battalion's first major action was during the Battle of the Somme near Hamel in the Ancre valley. In the early hours of 3 September 1916 the 116th Brigade attempted to capture German trenches below the heavily-defended Schwaben Redoubt, suffering many casualties as they tried to break though the barbed wire before being forced back to its jumping-off place. Private Harry Purdy, 28, was killed in action here. He has no known grave. Harry is commemorated at the Thiepval Memorial, Somme, France; on the Hampshire Regiment roll of honour in Winchester Cathedral and on the St Augustine's roll of honour. He was awarded the 1915 Star and the British War and Victory medals.

Lance Corporal 43119 Arthur Cannell, 1st Battalion, Norfolk Regiment, formerly Private 2223, 6th (Cyclist) Battalion, Norfolk Regiment

Arthur Cannell was born in New Catton, Norwich, on 7 January 1890, the eldest child of Arthur Cannell, a butcher, and Elizabeth Cannell née Hall. His father was the son of Abraham Cannell, who had run a family butcher's business in Bull Close Road in the 1880s. By the 1900s Arthur Cannell senior had his own butcher's shop at 67 Duke Street, which was also the family home at least up to the immediate post-War period. There were six children: Arthur was followed by Maud, then, after a considerable gap, by Louisa, Phyllis, Gladys and Frank. Between June 1896 and July 1901 Arthur was a pupil at Octagon Chapel Infants School then the Old Meeting House School, small, nonconformist schools in the parish of St George Colegate. Arthur next attended the Boys Model School in Princes Street. Founded in 1812 and maintained by charitable subscription, the Norwich Boys Model School provided a practical secondary education to the sons of those who could afford its small weekly fee. Four other men commemorated on St Augustine's roll of honour were pupils: Edward Halfacre, Clarence Neasham, Leonard Pert and Edward Sizer. All but Clarence, who emigrated to Australia before the war, also have individual memorials in the church. In 1911,

Arthur, 21, was working in the family's Duke Street shop, though as an accountant rather than an apprentice butcher.

Arthur enlisted in Norwich on 17 June 1915. His medical inspection found him fit for service and he was immediately embodied as a private in the 6th Battalion, Norfolk Regiment, a Territorial Force unit formed in 1908 more generally known as the Norfolk Cyclists. When war was declared in August 1914 it was decided the Cyclists were ideally suited to carrying out Home Defence duties around England's vulnerable east coast. Known colloquially as 'gas pipe cavalry', they pedalled along the country lanes from Wells to Gorleston on their sturdy BSA bicycles under the command of Lieutenant-Colonel B. H. Leathes Prior, who, despite his advancing years, gamely cycled at the head of the column through all weathers. Arthur seems to have impressed his superiors, for less than a month after enlisting, on 7 July 1915, he was appointed lance corporal on paid promotion. In 1915 all of the British Army's Cyclist battalions were grouped together as the Army Cyclist Corps. However, as it became more obvious that the campaign in France had become bogged down in the trenches, it was realised there was little use for a Cyclist Corps on the Western Front and gradually their personnel were posted to other units.

By the summer of 1916 the need for fit, well-trained men on the Western Front was acute and the majority of those remaining in the Norfolk Cyclists were now transferred to either the Norfolk Regiment's 1st or 8th Battalions. As Arthur went into the 1st Battalion it is likely he had been based at Bridlington on the Yorkshire coast with the 2/6th Norfolk Cyclists, a unit known as the 'Half Crown Holy Boys'. (In the pre-decimal era two shillings and sixpence or 'half a crown' was shown on price tickets as 2/6. The Norfolk Regiment's nickname, Holy Boys, is thought to derive from the figure of Britannia on its badge which Spanish peasants in the Peninsula War thought was the Virgin Mary.) On 26 July 1916 Arthur sailed from Folkestone to Boulogne. In common with the majority of Terriers during the national emergency, Arthur had signed the Imperial and General Service Obligation, which waived his right as a Territorial not to be sent overseas. On 30 July he was officially posted to the 1st Norfolks on the Somme, where they had very recently suffered terrible losses at High Wood, Longueval and

Delville Wood. Before joining them, the former Norfolk Cyclists spent about a week at the vast Army camp at Étaples near Boulogne as the various batches of reinforcements were consolidated. The new draft then met the battle-hardened surviving Old Contemptibles of the 1st Norfolks at their rest camp at Vauchelles–les-Quesnoy near Abbeville in early August for training 'in the conditions prevailing at the front', as the regimental history puts it.

Lance Corporal Arthur Cannell was killed in action a month later on 4 September 1916 in the fighting around Falfemont Farm, a strategically important position occupied by the Germans that overlooked the British front line near the village of Guillemont. This British feint was designed to cover a planned advance by French troops on the village of Combles to the east of the farm. The assault by the 1st Norfolks began at 3.10 p.m. The terrain was difficult, with steep ravines, and the Germans had the tactical advantage of the higher ground from where their machine guns wreaked havoc. By early evening the farm had been taken but the occupying troops from the 1st Norfolks' A, B and C companies were now subjected to an artillery bombardment from their own guns. Casualties were high, the 1st Norfolks losing 56 killed in action, another 94 missing believed dead and around 220 wounded. Three other St Augustine's men, Privates Loome, Plunkett and Scott, all 1st Norfolks, were killed at Falfemont Farm on the same day as Arthur, making this the highest number of casualties suffered by St Augustine men in a single day during the war. In addition to Arthur, seven other former Norfolk Cyclists were also killed here on this day: Privates E. Fox, C. S. Hicks, R. J. Lake, L. Sayer, W. R. Tubby, G. J. Woods and Harry Coxford, a brother of Walter Coxford. *(See p.150.)*

In October 1916 St Augustine's parish magazine published an obituary written by the rector, the Revd J. H. Griffiths:

> *Arthur Cannell was a parishioner and a regular attendant at our Church. He was one of those rare and loveable characters in which a kindly charity in judgement of others is blended with a firm attachment to those principles which mean everything to the true Christian. He was honest and upright, strong and true, in all relationships of life. … No one outside the immediate circle of his dear ones can tell what his departure has meant*

and will mean to them. Our hearts go out in deepest sympathy to his family and to her who worshipped with him and us at St Augustine's, and who one day had hoped to call his own in the most intimate of earthly relationships.

The person referred to in the last sentence was presumably Arthur's fiancée, who is only known as Lizzie from a death notice placed in the *Eastern Daily Press* on 20 September, which included the verse:

God in His tender care
Our loved one keepeth,
And whispers to our hearts
He is not dead, but sleepeth.

The parish magazine goes on to quote from one of Arthur's letters, in which he contemplates the very real possibility of his own death at the Front with apparent equanimity:

It may be that God will call me home, we cannot see into the future ourselves, if He does … bear it brightly, remember our Lord Jesus knows what is best in our lives … nothing is purposeless. Then what joy it will be when we shall all meet again, to be forever with Jesus, all our loved ones together, with no more partings. … Let us leave our future in our Master's keeping without any worry. Don't think I am writing this because I am low spirited because I really am not. I feel that now I am doing my duty and I never could feel that in England after we had our training.

Of one of the last letters Arthur had written home, the rector remarked: 'I can honestly say I have never read a more beautiful expression of calm Christian faith, courage and love, a courageous love, which made him forgetful of self and thoughtful in those last hours of awful danger of those at home.' In the April 1917 issue of the parish magazine the rector quoted approvingly from a letter written by an unnamed former Sunday School boy in France. It was almost certainly also from Arthur:

I am pleased to say that we've got a barn in our rest village where we hold a service on Sundays, so when I'm out I generally make a point of getting there if I can, as it makes one realise a little more that it is Sunday. We also hold a service there on Wednesdays, and last night I was able to get away to it, so it made quite a nice change. At the close of last evening's service we held a Communion Service, and nearly all the men stayed behind. It was glorious, and the old barn is so significant, just such a place as you might have imagined Christ in the days of his flesh to have used, and every one of the fellows is serious, there's no frivolity at these services, because you don't find fellows spending time there who are not really serious and in earnest. They all feel and know only too well how much Christ means to them when they are up in the 'line' and face to face with death! It doesn't require a beautiful building, nicely polished furniture, to come into touch with God. Oh, no, far from it. I can tell you, this experience has done me untold good, and I know there are many more like myself out here, so you can see this war is doing heaps of good in many ways, although perhaps it is difficult to realise just now.

After the war a large, engraved brass plaque to Arthur's memory was placed on the west wall of St Augustine's church to the right of the tower arch. It reads:

Semper Fidelis
To the glory of God and in loving memory of / Arthur Cannell /
6th Cyclist Norfolk Regiment
Killed in the battle of the Somme / Falfemont Farm /
September 4th 1916. Age 26.

This is followed by two Bible texts: 'Greater love hath no man than this; That he lay down his life for his friends', from St John's Gospel (15:13), and the words of St Paul: 'Not slothful in business / Thoroughly warm hearted / The Lord's own servant / Full of joyful hope, patient / Earnest, persistent in prayer', adapted from Weymouth's translation of Romans (12:11–12), which according the Revd J. H. Griffiths was a well-loved book of Arthur's and words 'specially applicable to the character of our dear friend'.

Arthur is buried at Delville Wood Cemetery, Longueval, Somme, France, grave no. XXV.K.5. He is also commemorated on the Boys

Model School Memorial in Norwich cathedral and St Augustine's roll of honour, where his rank is mistakenly given as private, as well as on the family memorial mentioned above, and on the Cannell family headstone in The Rosary (a non-denominational cemetery in Thorpe Hamlet, Norwich) in plot A4/12. Arthur Cannell was awarded the British War and Victory medals.

The Cannell family seem to have been closely connected with St Augustine's church. Arthur's sister Maud married Bombardier Arthur Holman of the Royal Artillery in the church on 4 July 1915. Five months after Arthur's death the Cannell family suffered a second bereavement when his father died. Though he had been in poor health for some time his death was sudden and unexpected. In March 1917 an anonymous contributor writing in the parish magazine described him as:

> a man much respected for his kindly unassuming manner, and for the uprightness of his business life. I have heard of him going into our poor yards and helping those who were in great poverty and distress. Additional pathos attaches to his death, coming as it does so soon after that of his much-loved son Arthur.

His funeral service was held in St Augustine's church and he was buried in the family plot in Rosary Cemetery. Arthur Cannell's cousin, Arthur Robert Allen (see p. 132), was killed in action with the Canadian Expeditionary Force in 1917.

Private 43262 Edward Henry Loome, 1st Battalion, Norfolk Regiment

Edward Henry Loome was born in the parish of St Mark, New Lakenham, a southern suburb of Norwich, in 1882, the second child of Edward Mark Loome, a Westminster-born carter and brewer's cooper, and Harriet Loome née Avis, originally from Barton Mills, Suffolk. By 1891 the family had moved from Pump Yard, New Lakenham, to Short Street in the parish of St Clement. There were now four children. Their places of birth, meticulously recorded in the 1891 Census, reveal some of the family's movements. Rosa, the eldest, a shoe fitter, was born in Chapel Field Road; Edward and his younger brother Sydney were born in New Lakenham, Ethel in New Catton and Maud in St Augustine's. In 1901 the family was still in St Augustine's, at 12 Esdelle Street. Rosa had married Herbert Jeffries, a coach builder, in 1900 and moved to Heigham. Edward, 19, was a journeyman baker, as was Sydney. Ethel was a 'tailoress', while Maud and the family's newest addition, Frederick, were still at school. In 1905 Edward married Ruth Susannah Mills. By 1911 Edward was a master baker and living at 34 Sussex Street, St Augustine's, with Ruth and their daughters Lily, May and Rosa. Edward's parents and three youngest siblings, Ethel, Maud and Frederick, were still in Esdelle Street; while Sydney was a private in the Army Service Corps at Bulford Camp, Salisbury, working as a baker.

Edward enlisted in Norwich. His Army Service papers have not survived. His lack of a 1915 Star medal suggests he was a 1916 conscript or possibly a late 1915 Derby Scheme volunteer. He would have been 33 or 34 at this date. He was posted to the 1st Battalion, Norfolk Regiment, which fought on the Somme in the summer of 1916. Private Edward Loome, 34, was killed in action on 4 September 1916, almost certainly at Falfemont Farm. He has no known grave. Two weeks after his death his family placed a death notice in the *Eastern Daily Press* with the verse:

His place is vacant, our hearts are sore,
Many may miss him, we miss him more.
His tender care, his loving face,
No one on earth can fill his place.

Edward is commemorated on the Thiepval Memorial, Somme, France, and on St Augustine's roll of honour, where his name is spelled 'Loombe'. He was awarded the British War and Victory medals.

Edward's father was a private in the Royal Defence Corps during the war. His brother Sydney continued to serve in the Army Service Corps, ending the war as an acting sergeant. His youngest brother Frederick was a gunner in the 3rd Norfolk Battery, East Anglian Brigade, throughout the war and was finally demobbed in 1920.

Private 43307 Ernest Edmund Plunkett, 1st Battalion, Norfolk Regiment, formerly Private 1965, 6th (Cyclists) Battalion, Norfolk Regiment

Ernest Edmund Plunkett was born in Norwich in November 1891, the fifth child of Walter Plunkett, a plasterer, and Eliza Plunkett née Joyce, a silk crepe factory hand. *(See the entry on his brother Walter Plunkett, p.106.)* In 1911 Ernest, 17, was living with his parents at 9 Rose Yard off St Augustine's Street and was employed, like his father and brothers, Walter and Edward, as a plasterer. By this date both of these brothers had married and set up their own homes. Their father, however, still included them in his household return, along with their deceased infant sister, Ethel, having, presumably, misunderstood the purpose of the Census. Ernest's other older brother, David, and older sister, Eliza, were also at home at this date and employed as confectioners. Also still at home were his four younger sisters: Emily, a 'tailoress', Alice and Ethel, both still at school, and Eva, born 1909, an infant. In 1912 eldest sister Eliza married George Self, listed as a lodger at the family home in 1911. After marriage they lived just down the yard, at No. 21. In 1915, second sister Emily married George Spauls, a shoemaker, and also moved down the yard, to No. 16. On 20 May 1916 David married Beatrice Skipper (Private George Skipper's sister) in St Augustine's church.

Ernest Plunkett enlisted Norwich on 14 March 1915 and was posted to the 6th Battalion, Norfolk Regiment, a Territorial unit known as the Norfolk Cyclists. Cyclist companies had first developed among Army Volunteers battalions in the 1880s. Between the Haldane Reforms of 1908 and 1914, fourteen Territorial cyclist battalions were formed in Great Britain, including the 6th Norfolks led by its stalwart, cycling C.O., Lieutenant Colonel B. H. Leathes Prior. In August 1914 the Norfolk Cyclists were set to work providing mobile defence around Norfolk's long and vulnerable coastline. A second battalion, designated the 2/6th Battalion, known colloquially as the 'Half Crown Holy Boys' was formed in October 1914 and posted to Bridlington, Yorkshire. *(See p.85.)* A short-lived third battalion, the 3/6th, was established in Norwich in May 1915 to act as a training reserve. Into this unit Ernest was initially posted. The newly formed collection of raw recruits, dressed in a motley collection of civilian clothes and khaki, was sent to Bear Rails camp in Windsor Great Park for basic training. By late November the 3/6th had begun to be broken up, with some officers and men transferring to the 2/6th in Bridlington, others to the 1/6th in North Walsham, Norfolk. On 21 December 1915 Ernest was appointed lance corporal and transferred to the 2/6th, still in Yorkshire.

By 1916 it had become clear to the War Office that the need to maintain coastal defence at home was outweighed by the need to supply the BEF on the Western Front with good quality soldiers. Most of the officers and men of the Norfolk Cyclists were now transferred to the Regiment's front line battalions, mainly to the 1st and 8th. Ernest's Army Service papers, however, have an undated rubber-stamped note saying he was posted to the 1/1st Hertfordshire Regiment, a Territorial unit attached to the 39th Division. On 17 February 1916, Ernest reverted to private, at his own request. This was common just before a unit went overseas as there were nearly always more NCOs than were needed. On 30 July 1916, he sailed from Folkestone to Boulogne, arriving at No. 17 Infantry Base Depot, part of the vast army camp at Étaples, on the 31st. From here he was transferred to the 1st Battalion, Norfolk Regiment, on 20 August 1916, receiving a new Army Service number.

Ernest's time with the 1st Norfolks was to last little more than a fortnight. He was reported missing in action on 4 September 1916. The date makes it very likely he was killed during the fighting at Falfemont Farm just south of Combles during the Battle of the Somme. Confirmation of Ernest death in action was reported by an officer of the 1/12th London Regiment (The Rangers) on 10 October. The Rangers had passed through the Falfemont Farm area on 14 September. Their official history notes that 'Of the farm itself no traces remained except a few scattered bricks'. According to his Army Service papers Ernest was buried 'in the vicinity of Leuze Wood' (nicknamed 'Lousy Wood' by the Tommies). The Rangers were entrenched in or close to the wood between 20 and 24 September, which is presumably when the burial took place. However, when the Imperial War Graves Commission disinterred the remains of soldiers buried in this area after the war it was unable to identify Ernest. A death notice was placed by his family in the *Eastern Daily Press* on 28 November 1916. It included the patriotic sentiment:

He proudly answered his country's call.
He lived as he died, beloved of all.

Ernest Plunkett is commemorated on the Thiepval Memorial, Somme, France, and on the St Augustine's roll of honour. Ernest was awarded the British War and Victory medals. The War Graves Commission mistakenly names him Ernest 'Edward' Plunkett.

Corporal 7185 George Robert Scott, 1st Battalion, Norfolk Regiment

George Robert Scott was born in Thorpe Hamlet, Norwich, in 1887, the youngest child of Thomas Scott, a wire-maker, and Eliza Scott née Wilson. In 1891 the family were living at 3 Blakeley's Yard off Pitt Street in the parish of St Mary Coslany. George's siblings at home at this date were Walter, James, Elizabeth, Maria, Edward and Emma. His eldest brother Thomas had left home and by 1901 all but George had also fled the nest. In 1911 George was still with his parents at the same address, employed, like his 67-year-old father, in making galvanised wire, probably at Barnard, Bishop & Barnard's iron foundry in Coslany Street, specialists in the production of wire-netting, which would later be deployed by the Army in the deserts of the Middle East during the war to provide temporary tracks over the sand.

George Scott enlisted in Norwich. Although his Army Service papers have not survived, his Service number indicates he enlisted as a Regular in the Norfolk Regiment sometime between September 1905 and June 1906. His Medal Roll Index card notes that he first entered a theatre of war (France and Flanders) on 16 August 1914. At some point he was promoted to corporal. As one of the original members of the BEF – one of the 'Old Contemptibles' – George was fortunate to have survived the back-foot fighting of 1914 trying to stem the German advance and the bitter trench warfare and gas attacks at Ypres in 1915, a 12-month period in which the 1st Norfolks lost more than 450 officers and men killed in action. Death finally caught up with him on the Somme in 1916. Corporal George Scott, 29, was killed in action there on 4 September 1916. The date of his death makes it likely he died in the fighting at Falfemont Farm during the Battle of the Somme. George is commemorated at the Thiepval Memorial, Somme, France, and on the St Augustine's roll of honour. He was awarded the 1914 Star with Bar and the British War and Victory medals.

Private 18231 Samuel Madgett, 9th Battalion, Prince of Wales's Own (West Yorkshire Regiment)

Samuel Madgett was born in the parish of St Benedict, Norwich, in 1892. His family background has proved somewhat difficult to unravel. His registered name at birth appears to have been Samuel Madgett Reeve. His mother, Rachel Mary Ann Elizabeth Madgett née Gready or Grady, was married at the time of his birth to Walter Reeve, a bricklayer's labourer. Rachel and Walter married in Norwich in 1876 and had at least seven children before the 1891 Census was taken: Charles, Hannah, Walter, Herbert, Minnie, Rachel and Agnes. During these years the family lived in the western Norwich suburb of Heigham, first at The Watering, a lane near the River Wensum close to the Gibraltar Gardens pub and later in Ely Street in the parish of St Benedict. Although Rachel was recorded as married in the 1891 Census, Walter was absent and not traceable elsewhere. Rachel, a brush-maker, was designated head of the household, suggesting she was now the family's main breadwinner. Living just around the corner in Heigham Street at this date was Samuel Madgett (also spelled Madget and Maggett in other records), an engine driver. Although he was also married, he appears to have been separated from his spouse of 14 years, Eliza, and sharing a home with his parents, sister and 12-year-old daughter Frances. Given that Samuel's birth was registered in 1892 under the name Samuel Madgett Reeve, it would seem safe to assume his father was Samuel Madgett and not his mother's absent husband, Walter Reeve.

By 1901, Rachel and her children had moved back to The Watering, Heigham. Living with them at this date was Samuel Madgett, the engine driver, designated a boarder while Rachel is now a widow. In 1910 Rachel Reeve and Samuel Madgett married, their estranged spouses having died in 1899 and 1906 respectively. By 1911 they were at 5 Flower Pot Yard off Oak Street. Samuel Madgett senior was now a furnace stoker for a sawyer and Rachel a charwoman (cleaner). Samuel, 19 (still listed as Samuel Reeve, stepson of Samuel Madgett) was a cord-winder for a rope-maker.

Samuel enlisted in Norwich, possibly in 1915. His Army Service papers have not survived, but other Army documents record him as Samuel Madgett rather than Samuel Reeve. This acknowledgement of his probable true paternity perhaps coincided with his 'stepfather' Samuel Madgett's death in 1914. The 9th Battalion, West Yorkshire Regiment, was raised in York in August 1914. It was a 'Kitchener' Service Battalion, part of the 32nd Brigade, 11th (Northern) Division. On 21 September 1915 Samuel landed at Gallipoli with other reinforcements to join the 9th West Yorks, which had been there since August but was now reducing operations prior to evacuation to Egypt. Transferred to the Western Front in 1916, the 9th Battalion's first major action was on the Somme in September during the Battle of Flers-Courcelette. Preparatory to this battle, the 9th West Yorks and the 8th Duke of Wellington's West Riding Regiment were ordered to take a German stronghold known as the *Wunderwerk* (Wonderwork), which defended the southern approaches to the village of Thiepval. An account of the assault on the Wonderwork was later given by Private Hepburn of the 9th West Yorks:

> *When our company went over the top and reached the German first trench it had been cleared of everyone, and our destination being a communication trench, leading from this we made there and had to dig for our lives, our artillery having battered the trench almost beyond recognition. Although open to heavy fire the nightlong and many of my comrades fell I was unhurt. Next night Fritz heavily bombarded our trenches and six men next to me but one were killed and huddled one on top another in the trench. How I escaped was marvellous.*
>
> *Yorkshire Evening Press*, 4 October 1916

While counted a success, the two Yorkshire battalions lost 128 men taking this position. Samuel was killed in action here on 14 September 1916. He has no known grave. Samuel Madgett is commemorated on the Thiepval Memorial, Somme, France, and on the St Augustine's roll of honour. He was awarded the 1915 Star and the British War and Victory medals.

Private 14878 Alfred Meachen, 9th Battalion, Norfolk Regiment

Alfred Meachen was born in the parish of St Augustine, Norwich, in August 1890, the sixth child of John Meachen, a shoemaker, and Emma Meachen née Jacobs. In 1891 the family was at 12 Esdelle Street, St Augustine's. Alfred's older siblings were Arthur, Maud, Robert, Florence and Walter. By 1901 the family had moved two doors down to No. 16 and now also included John, Ethel, Emma and Alice. Another daughter, Lily, was born later that year. Arthur, Maud and Robert worked in the shoemaking trade, like their father. Arthur had married just before the 1901 Census was taken, and moved around the corner to Leonards Street. He died in 1907, aged 28. *(See the entry for Sydney Palmer, p.81.)* Robert married in 1909 and moved to nearby Rose Yard. Of Alfred's other brothers, Walter married in 1910 and moved to Burrell's Yard in the neighbouring parish of St George Colegate. By 1911 the remainder of the Meachen family had moved to 25 Alma Terrace off Aylsham Road, just north of St Augustine's near St Augustine's School. By this date Alfred, 20, had joined the main family trade of shoemaking as a clicker (leather-cutter). His father, however, was now a vegetable hawker.

Alfred enlisted in Norwich, possibly as early as September 1914 when the 9th Battalion, one of Lord Kitchener's New Army Service battalions was established. The 9th Norfolks were sent to Shoreham in Kent to be trained and after a further period of advanced training near Aldershot, went over to France via Boulogne on 30 August 1915. The Battalion's baptism of fire came the following month in the Battle of Loos during the grim fighting in the quarries of Hulluch. For the remainder of the year and through the winter, spring and early summer of 1916, the 9th Norfolks served turns in and out of the trenches in the Ypres Salient in Flanders. In August it was moved to the Somme battlefield. Private Alfred Meachen, 26, was killed in action here on 15 September 1916 during the 9th Norfolks' assault on a German stronghold near the villages of Ginchy and Morval known as the Quadrilateral. A newly introduced secret weapon code named 'the tank', was supposed to have gone into the attack first but only one machine made it to the British front line, where the crew, mistaking men of the 9th Norfolks for Germans, opened fire, killing several. Following this incident of 'friendly fire' the depleted 9th advanced over no man's land and up a steep slope towards the Quadrilateral fort until stopped by a massive barrier of uncut barbed wire. Those who survived, crawled back to their trench under cover of night. The Battalion had lost more than 430 casualties, 160 killed in action, the others wounded or missing. Alfred is buried at the Guillemont Road Cemetery, Guillemont, Somme, France, grave no. VI.H.9. He is commemorated also on the St Luke's roll of honour. His name does not appear on St Augustine's roll of honour. He was awarded the 1915 Star and the British War and Victory medals.

Lance Corporal A/40113 Frederick Charles Clarke, 5th Battalion (Western Cavalry), (Saskatchewan Regiment), Canadian Expeditionary Force

Frederick Charles Clarke was born in Norwich on 17 March 1892, the sixth child of John William Clarke, a police court missioner, and Susannah Clarke née Hewitt, who came from Rockland St Mary in south Norfolk. Police Court Missionary Committees were first established in London in 1876 by the Church of England Temperance Society and are sometimes regarded as a forerunner to the national Probation Service established in 1907. There were more than 100 police court missioners spread over England's larger towns and cities working to help turn members of what society regarded as the criminal classes away from drink, crime and moral laxity. At first they simply stood bail for offenders who took the 'Pledge' and were deemed capable of reform, but gradually they took on such tasks as finding released prisoners accommodation, marital reconciliation, combating prostitution and helping 'difficult' children. As Norwich's police court missioner Frederick's father would have been a well-known local figure. In 1897 the *Eastern Daily Press* reported on his work in the parish of St James Pockthorpe, an area less than half a mile from St Augustine's that included what was generally regarded as the worst area of slum housing in Norwich. It was rife with what the newspaper politely termed the 'the single-room system': rooms rented by the night for the purposes of prostitution. William Clarke is described as a man of 'fiery energy and bubbling zeal':

He has to whip-up to duty the recalcitrant husband, he must exhort to matrimony those that are negligent about forms, and in many an affair d'amour it is his business, in the language of the people, 'to see the gal righted'.

In 1898 William Clarke was in the news again when he was called as a character witness in the trial of George Watt, a Norwich man on trial for murdering his estranged wife. Clarke had previously befriended him while trying to sort out his marital problems and later visited him in the condemned cell the day before he was hanged.

The 1901 Census records the Clarke family at 21 Sussex Street, St Augustine's. (The article quoted above says his office was in Sussex Street.) Here the Clarkes employed a domestic servant, Annie Chaney, who was no doubt kept busy by the family's eight children: Edith, Lily, Alice, John, Sidney, Frederick, Dorothy and Bertie. Two other children had died in infancy. While living here, Frederick was a pupil at Norwich's Old High Grade School. In 1911 Mr and Mrs Clarke were still at the same address with five of their children, including Edith, who was now an assistant police court missioner working alongside her father. In 1914 she was employed by the Chief Constable, though in what capacity is not known. In 1918 she was appointed as a uniformed employee of the detective staff, an appointment officially recognised by the Home Office in 1920, making her possibly the first policewoman in Norwich. Of the other children still at home in 1911, Alice was an elementary school teacher, John a law clerk, and Dorothy and Bertie still at school. Three children had flown the nest. Lily had married the rector of St Giles, Norwich, the Revd Archibald Jones, in 1909. Sidney and Frederick had emigrated to Canada.

Assisted-passage schemes allowed young men and women to seek a new life and better employment prospects in Britain's Dominions and Colonies. The Government of Canada at this time was vigorously promoting immigration with guaranteed employment in farming and domestic service. Sidney went first, in March 1907 aged 16. Frederick followed in 1909 when he reached 16, sailing from Liverpool on the *Empress of India* on 13 August. On arrival in Quebec on 19 August, he stated that his final destination was Humboldt, Saskatchewan where he was going to join his brother and become a farmer. Their youngest brother Bertie would follow them in March 1914.

Neither Sidney nor Frederick can be found in the 1911 Census of Canada and the next documentary record for Frederick is when he enlisted, attesting to his willingness to serve in the Canadian Overseas Expeditionary Force (CEF) at Humboldt, Saskatchewan on 20 December 1914, aged 22. His medical record notes that he was 5ft 6 in height, the average height of an English man of that era, with fair hair and brown eyes. He had a birth mark above his left knee. His religion was Church of England and his civilian trade farmer and gasoline engineer. He had no previous military experience. His father, now of Willow Bank, Heathfield, Salhouse, Norfolk, was named next-of-kin.

The 5th Canadian Infantry Battalion was put together at Camp Valcartier, Quebec, in 1914 from a number of small cavalry militia units based in the western provinces, hence it was sometimes known as the Western Cavalry although it was only ever an infantry unit. Another name for them was the 'Red Saskatchewans', probably after its distinctive red insignia patch. The 5th Battalion embarked on SS *Lapland* from Quebec on 26 September 1914, arriving in England on 17 October. After four months training it went over to France to join the 2nd Brigade, 1st Division, CEF, on 13 February 1915, fighting in the 2nd Battle of Ypres in April and the Battle of Festubert in May, and suffering heavy casualties. In June 1916 the CEF was severely tested by a German feint in the Ypres Salient, designed to draw British forces away from the build-up of manpower and *matériel* on the Somme. A counter attack on a point of high ground known as Mount Sorrel by the 1st and 2nd Canadian Divisions regained no territory but lost many men as they advanced over open ground in full view of the enemy's machine guns; a dress rehearsal for the carnage on the Somme later that summer. The Mount was finally taken on 13 June, with the 5th Battalion being held in reserve. Frederick was wounded in June, probably during this battle, but not seriously and was soon able to return to his Battalion.

Lance Corporal Frederick Clarke, 24, was reported missing presumed killed in action during the Battle of the Somme on 27 September 1916. He has no known grave. At this date the 5th Canadians were in Hessian Trench on the Albert Front. The day was spent consolidating the positions it had captured the previous day while a furious duel was fought over their heads by the opposing artillery batteries. The Battalion's War Diary records that its casualties this day were 56 killed with more than 300 wounded and 122 missing. Just over six weeks later, an obituary appeared in the *Eastern Daily Press*:

> *Mr J. W. Clarke, the Norwich Police-Court Missionary, has received news of the death at the front of his third son .... His captain writes that he was wounded whilst assisting in taking a trench, and when making his way to a dressing station was again hit, this time fatally.*

St Augustine's Parish Magazine that December included a reflection on Mr and Mrs Clarke's grief by the Revd J. H. Griffiths, their suffering accentuated by the news that two of their other sons on active service were lying critically wounded in hospital. One was 2nd Lieutenant John William Clarke, 9th Battalion, Norfolk Regiment, who was wounded on the Somme on 19 October 1916. He had been in France less than three months. The other was Private Bert Clarke, who had enlisted in the CEF in Humboldt, Saskatchewan, in July 1915. Both recovered and survived the war. The rector observed:

> *In face of sorrow such as that which has fallen on Mr and Mrs Clarke, we long to speak and yet feel tongue-tied. We realise only too poignantly, that 'the heart knoweth its own bitterness,' and that it is very, very difficult for others to sympathise so effectively as to give any ease of heart and soul. We are reminded of the lines:*
>
> > *Console if you will – we can bear it.*
> > *'Tis a kindly wasting of breath;*
> > *But not all the talking since Adam*
> > *Can make death to be other than death.*

The verse is a slightly misquoted stanza from 'After The Burial' by American poet James Russell Lowell, its blunt realism in sharp contrast to the sentiments usually found in local death notices. Frederick is commemorated at the Vimy Memorial, Pas de Calais,

France. His name does not appear on St Augustine's roll of honour. He is commemorated (as Fred Clarke) on the war memorial in Salhouse churchyard and is listed under Salhouse in *Norfolk Roll of Honour*. Frederick is also commemorated on the Saskatchewan War Memorial in the Wascana Centre, Regina. The online Saskatchewan Virtual War Memorial gives his home address in Canada as Golden Acre, a settlement south-west of Humboldt. He was awarded the 1915 Star and the British War and Victory medals.

Private 5610 George Bailey, 1/6th Battalion, Durham Light Infantry, formerly Private 5559, Norfolk Regiment

George Bailey was born in Norwich in April 1891, the fourth child of the curiously named Saddleton Lily Bailey, a butcher, and Elizabeth Bailey née Warnes. The Bailey family lived in Magpie Road in the parish of St Paul. George had three older siblings: Saddleton, Philip and Elizabeth, and three younger: Ethel, Hilda and Willie. Three others had died in infancy. George was a pupil at Bull Close Boys School from 21 August 1900 to 11 May 1905, leaving just after his 14th birthday. The 1911 Census reveals that four of the older children, including George, worked in the local shoemaking industry, George as a 'maker', probably in the making room where soles and heels (uppers and bottoms) were assembled. All the Bailey children were still living in the parental home in Magpie Road in 1911 except Philip, who now lived in New Catton, a suburb to the north of St Augustine's. Philip had been in the Army, first as a Territorial in the 4th Battalion, Norfolk Regiment, and for about three months as a Regular in the Lincolnshire Regiment, before buying his discharge in 1907. In 1910 he enlisted again, first in the Royal Horse Artillery and then in the Royal Field Artillery, serving in South Africa and India before finally being discharged as physically unfit for further active service in July 1914.

George Bailey enlisted, probably as a 1916 conscript, in Norwich and served first as a private in the Norfolk Regiment before transferring to the 1/6th Durham Light Infantry (DLI), a Territorial battalion. On 5 November 1916, during the final days of the Battle of the Somme, the 1/6th DLI, together with two other DLI Territorial battalions, were ordered to capture a prominent topographical feature of the battlefield known as the Butte de Warlencourt, an ancient, man-made mound of chalk that rose from the surrounding flat landscape like a bleached skull. Entangled with barbed wire and riddled with tunnels, this enemy-occupied position dominated the battlefield opposite the British front line at Le Sars. It had been repeatedly attacked since October but never taken and was regarded as virtually unassailable. When the three Durham Territorial battalions turn came they suffered heavy casualties while bogged down in no man's land below the Butte, eventually forcing their way to the top only to have to withdraw a few hours later when German reinforcements came up. Reported missing in action, it would be ten months before George's death was confirmed, possibly after identifiable relics were recovered from the battlefield. His father by then was dead, having died in October 1916. With confirmation, George's mother and siblings could finally place a notice in the *Eastern Daily Press,* including the verse:

We miss you and mourn you in silence unseen
And dwell on the memories of days that have been.

George Bailey is buried at Warlencourt British Cemetery, Pas de Calais, France, grave no. VII. 22, and is commemorated also on the St Augustine's roll of honour. He was awarded the British War and Victory medals.

Private 42144 Edward Clarke, 5th Company, Machine Gun Corps, formerly Private 2272, 6th (Cyclist) Battalion, Norfolk Regiment

Edward Clarke was born in Norwich on 5 June 1894, the fifth surviving child of Benjamin Edward Clarke, a shoemaker, and Mary Ann Clarke née Hoy, a shoe-machinist. The family were recorded in the 1901 Census at 3 Magpie Road, where they had been since at least 1891. Their children, in descending order of age, were Thomas, Maria, Joseph, Arthur, Edward, Ernest, Elsie, Lily and Benjamin. In 1905 Thomas joined the Royal Navy on a 12-year-term (he eventually retired having served 22). By 1911 the family had moved to Howard Court at the back of 77 Pitt Street, St Augustine's. Three of Edward's brothers, including 14-year-old Ernest, were employed, like their parents, in shoemaking. Edward, 16, was working in the printing trade, though later he too joined the family's shoemakers as a clicker (leather-cutter).

Edward enlisted in Norwich on 12 July 1915 and was posted initially to the Norfolk Regiment's 6th (Cyclist) Battalion, a Territorial unit mainly engaged in Home Defence duties around England's vulnerable east coastline. At 5ft 6 he was two inches below the minimum height requirement for a Territorial Cyclist, but exceptions were made for men of good physique and character. On enlisting he signed a declaration that he was willing to serve overseas. Pre-war Terriers had enlisted on the understanding they would only be mobilised for Home Defence duties. He was initially placed in the newly formed third formation of the Norfolk Cyclists, the 3/6th, and sent for training at Bears Rail Camp in Windsor Great Park. He later transferred to the 2/6th Norfolk Cyclists, known colloquially as the 'Half Crown Holy Boys'. *(See p.85.)* The 2/6th Norfolk Cyclists were garrisoned in Bridlington on the Yorkshire coast until the spring of 1916. Gradually, as the demand for trained men grew, members of the 6th Cyclists were drafted to other units, mainly to the Norfolk Regiment's 1st, 8th and 9th battalions. Edward, however, was formally discharged on 25 May 1916 and on the following day enlisted in the Machine Gun Corps (MGC) in Grantham, Lincolnshire, the home of the Army's Machine Gun Training Centre. He went over to France via Folkestone and Boulogne on 17 July 1916 and joined the MGC's Base Depot at Camiers on 18th. On 6 August 1916 Edward was posted to the 5th Company, Machine Gun Corps, attached to the 5th Brigade, 2nd Division, on the Western Front. He was killed in action, aged 22, on 13 November 1916, the first day of the Battle of the Ancre. A month later his family placed a death notice in the *Eastern Daily Press*, including the verse:

> *Sleep on, dear one, and take thy rest,*
> *We miss you most, who loved you best.*

On the first anniversary of his death his brother Arthur, sister-in-law Alice, parents and other siblings placed two 'In Memoriam' notices in the paper. A third, from someone called only 'Bosie', possibly his fiancée, included the verse:

> *In the bloom of life death claimed him,*
> *In the pride of his manhood days.*
> *None knew him but to love him,*
> *None mentioned his name but with praise.*
> *None knew how sad his parting was,*
> *Or what the farewell cost;*
> *But God and His holy angels*
> *Have gained what I have lost.*

Edward Clarke is buried at Waggon Road Cemetery, Beaumont-Hamel, Somme, France, grave no. E.3, and commemorated also on the St Augustine's roll of honour. He was awarded the British War and Victory medals.

Edward's eldest brother Thomas served in the Royal Navy throughout the war, rising from leading seaman to petty officer in 1918. Younger brother, Private Ernest Clarke, 1/5th Battalion, Norfolk Regiment, was killed in action in Palestine in 1918. *(See p.166.)*

Private 7400 Ernest Bearman, 2nd Battalion, Norfolk Regiment

Tracing Ernest Bearman's family background has proved difficult. *Soldiers Died in the Great War* gives his place of birth as St Augustine's, Norwich, while the 1911 Census records an Ernest Bearman, also born in St Augustine's, as a private in the Norfolk Regiment in the 'Overseas Military'; presumably with the 2nd Battalion, which was garrisoned at Belgaum in India at this date. His age, 24 in 1911, means he was born in 1886 or 1887; however, the birth of no one of this name was recorded by the General Register Office in Norfolk in these years or indeed at any time in the 19th century. By contrast the surname was fairly common in Essex at this period and it seems likely Ernest was in fact born there, probably in Braintree in 1887. Growing up in Norwich from an early age, he may simply have assumed he was born there too when he came to enlist.

Ernest's mother's seems to have been Sarah Ann Chinery, an Essex silk-weaver who married Samuel Bearman in 1873. She had at least two children with him, Sarah and Lillie, before he died in 1884. By 1891 she was married again, to James Thompson, a Norwich-born shoe-riveter. In the Census that year she was recorded living with him in Braintree with two children described as her husband's step-children, Lillie and Ernest. Her other daughter, Sarah, seems to have disappeared. Despite the fact that Samuel Bearman died two years before Ernest was born, he was registered at birth with his surname. Whether his mother's second husband, James Thompson, was his biological father or merely his stepfather is not known. Sometime between 1891 and 1901, the Thomson/Bearman family moved to Norwich and in the 1901 Census were recorded living in Heath Road, St Paul, a parish adjacent to St Augustine's north-eastern boundary. By 1911 Ernest's mother, who was still working as a silk-weaver, was widowed again and living on her own in Swan Yard in the parish of St Martin at Oak, another parish adjacent to St Augustine's. Ernest himself, as previously noted, was now in the Army and garrisoned in India.

Although Ernest Bearman's Army Service papers have not survived, his regimental number suggests he enlisted in 1907 when he was 19 or 20. Following Britain's declaration of war against Germany on 4 August 1914, the 2nd Norfolks moved from India to the Middle East, embarking at Bombay on SS *Elephanta* on 6 November and disembarking in the Persian Gulf nine days later. Here they formed part of the 18th Indian Brigade, 6th Indian Division, which fought running battles with the Turkish Army and Arab insurgents up and down the River Tigris until it was finally trapped and besieged at Kut in December 1915. Four months later starvation forced the garrison there, under the command of Major General Sir Charles Townshend, to surrender. The British and Indian troops at Kut had suffered terrible hardships during the siege and following surrender around 70 per cent of the British troops, made prisoners of war, died of malnutrition, disease and exposure on the forced march to Turkish camps in Anatolia. Townshend and most of the senior officers were segregated from the other ranks and imprisoned in comparative comfort. Private Ernest Bearman died in Mesopotamia while a POW on 23 December 1916. He has no known grave.

Ernest Bearman is commemorated at the Haidar Pasha Cemetery, Turkey. His name does not appear on the St Augustine's roll of honour. He is, however, listed under the parish of St Barnabas, Heigham, Norwich, in *Norfolk Roll of Honour,* and commemorated also on that church's Great War memorial board. He was awarded the 1915 Star and the British War and Victory medals.

1917 – Palestine, Arras, Messines, Passchendaele

Lance Corporal 84690 Walter Edward Plunkett, 207th Field Company, Corps of Royal Engineers

Walter Edward Plunkett was born in Norwich in 1883, the first child of Walter Plunkett, a plasterer, and Eliza Plunkett née Joyce, a crape (silk) factory hand. In 1891 Walter, his parents and siblings Edward, Eliza and David, were at 10 Osborne's Yard in the parish of St Martin at Oak. That November, fifth child Ernest was born. By 1901 the family had moved to 4 Church Alley in the same parish. There were now four more children: Emily, Alice, Elizabeth and Ethel. Another Ethel had died of acute bronchitis in 1897, aged 19 months. Walter, 17, was a bricklayer's labourer. Edward, 16, was absent, however, a private in the Militia at Colchester Garrison. While the Census doesn't say which regiment he was in, it may have been the Norfolk Regiment's 4th Battalion, formerly known as the East Norfolk Militia. Later in 1901 the family moved to 2 Cartwright's Court in the neighbouring parish of St Mary Coslany. Walter's grandparents and uncle Herbert, a shoemaker, lived there too, at No. 5. In November Elizabeth, aged 2, died of the measles. A year later Gladys died of pneumonia, aged 17 months. Infant mortality in England at this period was very high, estimated at around 15 deaths per 100 of population, the result of insanitary conditions in over-crowded urban areas and the lack of affordable or effective healthcare.

In 1905 Walter married Martha Susannah Self, described as a 'factory sweeper' in the 1901 Census. Their first child, Ivy, was born in February 1906 while they were living at 2 Kerrison's Yard in the parish of St George Tombland. Their second, Alice, was born in July 1907, by when they had moved to 4 Campling's Yard in the parish of

St Saviour. Next came Emily, born August 1908; then Walter, born October 1910. By 1911 Walter, Martha and the children had moved to 5 Chequers Yard in the parish of St Miles Coslany. Here they had two more children: Henry Arthur, born February 1913, who died of 'epidemic diarrhoea' 7 months later, and Henry David, born May 1914. According to the 1911 Census, Walter, like his father and brothers Edward and Edmund, was a plasterer. This was the first census in which people were able to complete their own household return forms. This sometimes led to interesting mistakes. Walter's father, who was now at 9 Rose Yard off St Augustine's Street, clearly misunderstood the purpose of the Census, erroneously including his sons Walter and Edward, both of whom had married and left home, in his household return. Walter and Edward are also recorded in their own homes, so it wasn't simply a matter of them being under his roof on Census night. In addition, he included his deceased daughter Ethel, though not, curiously, his other dead children. At some point during the war Walter and Martha moved to 14 Fellmonger's Yard off St Martin-at-Oak Wall Lane in St Augustine's, where Walter for the first time became a registered voter.

Walter enlisted in Norwich. His Army Service papers have not survived. He was posted to the Corps of Royal Engineers. Presumably, his 15-odd years in the building trade fitted him for this branch of the Army. The fact that his Medal Roll Index card (which mistakenly records his forename as William) shows no entitlement to the 1915 Star might indicate he was conscripted in 1916, however, the history of his unit, the 207th Field Company, suggests he probably enlisted when it was established in Norwich in February 1915. The 207th Field Company was a wartime establishment, raised to provide engineering support for Kitchener's 5th New Army. Known as the Norfolk Company it was attached to the 38th Division (later re-designated the 34th Division) along with the 208th and 209th. The 207th spent the summer, autumn and early winter of 1915 at camps near Ripon, Yorkshire, and on Salisbury Plain, Wiltshire. It embarked for France on 8 January 1916 where, despite being an engineering unit, it took part in a number of combat actions during the Battle of the Somme between July and September 1916, notably at the Battle of Albert, 1–3 July, when it helped capture the Scots and Sausage Redoubts.

Lance Corporal Walter Plunkett, 33, was killed in action on 14 January 1917. The 34th Division was not engaged in any particular action on this day so it is likely he was a victim of one of the commonest hazards of trench warfare, shelling. Sapper Arthur Norman Lake, also of the 207th Field Company, was killed five days later by shell fire. On 8 February 1917 the *Eastern Daily Press* published a notice of Walter's death from his widow Martha with the verse:

> *A bitter grief, a shock severe*
> *To part with him we loved so dear,*
> *Our loss is great, we will not complain,*
> *But hope in Heaven to meet again.*

In March 1917 St Augustine's parish magazine printed a brief obituary. After noting that another of Mr and Mrs Plunkett's sons had fallen in action, it quoted from a letter from Walter's CO:

> *It has always been a pleasure to be with him. He was very willing and full of pluck, and was always cheerful. He was a great favourite of mine and very popular with the whole Company.*

Walter Plunkett is buried at Brewery Orchard Cemetery, Nord, France, grave no. IV.F.12. and commemorated also on the Royal Engineers (34th Division) memorial in Norwich cathedral cloisters and St Augustine's roll of honour, which mistakenly lists him in as a private. He was awarded the British War and Victory medals.

Each of Walter's three brothers served in the Army during the war. Private Edward William Plunkett, who had been in the Militia in 1901, served with the Norfolk Regiment. (This was probably the 9th Battalion, as he went to France on the same day as that Battalion, 30 August 1915). He was later in the Labour Corps. Gunner David Plunkett served in the Royal Garrison Artillery, enlisting in Norwich on 9 December 1915 and serving with the heavy guns until discharged in November 1919, suffering from a common occupational hazard of artilleryman, deafness. Walter's youngest brother, Ernest Plunkett, was killed in action on the Somme in 1916. (See p. 91.)

Sapper (Instructor Mechanic) 85613 Arthur Norman Lake MM, 207th Field Company, Corps of Royal Engineers

Arthur Norman Lake was born in the parish of St George Colegate, Norwich, in 1883, the second surviving child of Frederick William Lake, an upholsterer and paper-hanger, and Sarah Lake née Harper, an umbrella-maker machinist working from home. In 1881 Arthur's parents and their first child, Fred, were at 36 Pitt Street. The southern end of Pitt Street, now part of Duke Street, was then in the parish of St George Colegate; so this is presumably where Arthur was born. The family were still there in 1891 and now included Emily. Interestingly, all the children had the middle name Norman,

 including Emily, the probable explanation being that their parents believed they would thereby have a claim to a legacy endowed by Alderman John Norman in the 18th century. In 1901 the family was still in Pitt Street, though minus Fred, who had married in 1898 and moved to Gorleston. Arthur, 18, was now an apprentice book-binder. In 1907 he married Eliza Alice Francis and by 1911

they were at 12 Eade Road, New Catton, a suburb just north of St Augustine's. Their only child, Elsie Norman, was born in 1909. They later lived at 7 Rosebery Road, New Catton. Arthur was now a binder of accounts ledgers at Jarrold & Sons.

Arthur enlisted in Norwich. The 207th Field Company, Royal Engineers, along with the 208th and 209th companies, was known as the Norfolk Company. It recruited in Norwich in February 1915 as part of the newly established 34th Division but did not go to France until January 1916. During the summer it took a part in the Somme offensive, at the Battle of Albert and at Bazentin Ridge and Pozières Ridge. On 21 October 1916 Arthur's award of the Military Medal (MM) for bravery in the field was gazetted in the *London Gazette*. Sapper Arthur Norman Lake, 34, was killed in action on 19 January 1917. Lance Corporal Walter Plunkett, who was also in the 207th Field Company, had been killed in action five days earlier. *(See p.106.)* On the first anniversary of Arthur's death the *Eastern Daily Press* published 'In Memoriam' notices from his widow, his parents and his siblings. The latter contains additional information about the circumstances of his death. Describing him as an 'Instructor Mechanic', it mentions he was 'killed in France by an enemy shell while engaged on work for the benefit of the troops', and concludes with the words: 'Gone from sight, but his life work lives'. Arthur is buried at the Brewery Orchard Cemetery, Nord, France, grave no. IV.F.13. *Norfolk Roll of Honour* lists him under St Mary's Baptist church, Norwich. He is commemorated on the St Mary's Baptist church roll of honour, on Jarrold's Great War memorial tablet and on the 34th Norfolk Division, Royal Engineers memorial in Norwich cathedral cloisters. A photograph of him wearing the MM ribbon on his tunic was placed in Norwich Library's roll of honour collection after the war. He was awarded the British War and Victory medals and the Military Medal.

Private G/20150 Archibald Claude Marshall, 2nd Battalion, The Queen's (Royal West Surrey) Regiment, formerly Private 2965, Suffolk Regiment

Archibald (known as Archie) Claude Marshall was born in the parish of St Augustine, Norwich, in 1897, the fifth child of William Marshall, a shoe-riveter, and Keziah Marshall née Hawkins. At the beginning of their married life his parents lived at 3 Cattermoul's Yard off Pitt Street, St Augustine's. By 1901 they had moved to 20 Gildencroft, St Augustine's. Archie's older siblings were William (known as Percy), Frederick, Maud and Edith; his younger, Arthur (who died in 1902, aged 2), Beatrice, Walter, Donald and John. By 1911 the family had moved to 128 Cowgate in the parish of St Paul. Although not recorded as a widow, Archie's mother is listed as the head of the household in the census that year, which has then been crossed out. Archie's father is absent.

Archie enlisted in Norwich and served with the Suffolk Regiment before being transferred to the 2nd Battalion, The Queen's (Royal West Surrey) Regiment. The Queen's 2nd Battalion suffered heavy casualties in the opening days of the Battle of the Somme. However, having survived the slaughter here, Archie was killed in action in

Flanders on 14 March 1917 during one of the costly and largely fruitless assaults on the Hindenburg Line to which the German Army had recently made a strategic withdrawal. On 13 March the 2nd Battalion received orders to capture the enemy's trenches at Bucquoy, which reconnaissance had established were formidably defended by machine-gun posts and thick rows of barbed wire. The Battalion's War Diary notes:

> *1.00am, zero hour, enemy artillery put an intensive barrage in front of their trenches and swept ground with machine gun fire. Owing to light rain and heavy state of ground, men had great difficulty in keeping their feet and when they fell their rifles clogged with mud. Eventually small parties got to the other side of the hostile wire but could not get through the third line of it owing to its thickness. At 3.00 am, orders issued to withdraw. Carried out by 4.50 am. Relieved and returned to Bolton Camp. A wet and cold night.*

The Battalion lost around 20 men in this failed assault, including two officers, 2nd lieutenants Furze and Limbrick, both 19, like Archie. Archie is buried at The Queens Cemetery, Bucquoy, Pas de Calais, France, grave no. II.A.8. He is not listed on the St Augustine's roll of honour. He was awarded the British War and Victory medals.

Private 18486 and 201807 Ernest George Jolly, 1/5th Battalion, King's Own Scottish Borderers

Ernest George Jolly was born in the parish of St Martin at Oak, Norwich, on 25 February 1896, the second child of Rosetta Jolly. His father's name is not known. His mother was the daughter of a blacksmith and was herself a 'shoe fitter', presumably of horses. In 1901 Edward was at 5 Globe Yard, Heigham, a western suburb of Norwich, with his mother and brother Percy in the household of Charles Harper, a house painter. Ernest and Percy are described in the Census as Mr Harper's stepsons, though there is no record of their mother having married him. A third child, Alice, is described as Mr Harper's daughter, though it isn't clear whether Rosetta was her mother. Ernest was a pupil at Quay Side School in Norwich from 7

January 1908 to 1910 when he left, aged 14. According to the School's attendance register his home address was 20 Old Yeast Yard off Muspole Street. Charles Harper is described as his guardian. By 1911 the family had moved to 27 Stone Masons Square off St George's Street. Ernest, 15, was now a machine feeder in the shoe trade and is described as Mr Harper's son and recorded as 'Ernest G. Harper'. Household returns in this year were for the first time completed by the head of the household, who here was Charles Harper. Ernest's older brother Percy had by this date left home and was a hotel porter in St Leonard Hythe, Kent. Ernest's sister or possibly half sister, Alice, now had two sisters, Maud and Lily Harper. During the war period Ernest's mother, his named next of kin, was at 5 Catherine Wheel Opening off St Augustine's Street.

Ernest enlisted in Norwich, signing on under his mother's maiden name. How a Norwich shoemaker ended up in the 1/5th King's Own Scottish Borderers, a Territorial battalion known colloquially known as the 'Kosbies', is a conundrum. His Army Service papers have not survived but the fact that he was not entitled to a 1915 Star medal suggests he was conscripted in 1916. Certainly, he was with them before 1917 when all other ranks serving in Territorial battalions were assigned a new six-figure regimental number. Perhaps the Scottish regiment needed men who could repair boots. The 1/5th Kosbies was then rebuilding its strength in Egypt after the disastrous Gallipoli campaign. Ernest was killed in action in Palestine on 19 April 1917 during the Second Battle of Gaza in which the 1/5th Kosbies lost more than 80 men. Two other St Augustine's men, Albert Fox and William Mason, were also killed or died of wounds received in this battle. Ernest is commemorated at the Jerusalem Memorial, Israel, and on St Augustine's and St Mary's Baptist church rolls of honour (he is mistakenly named 'F. Jolly' on the latter). In *Norfolk Roll of Honour* he is also listed under both St Augustine's (his surname spelled 'Jolley') and St Mary's Baptist church. He was awarded the British War and Victory medals.

Ernest's brother Percy Jolly was a private in the 1/4th Battalion, Norfolk Regiment during the war, serving at Gallipoli until invalided out in October 1915, transferring back in England to the Norfolk Regiment's 11th (Reserve) Battalion before finally moving to the Labour Corps' Agricultural Company No.667.

Private 1602 and 200086 William Henry Mason, 1/4th Battalion, Norfolk Regiment

William Henry Mason was born in the parish of St Edmund, Norwich, in 1895, the second child of Henry Mason, a dyer and finisher of crape (silk), and Mary Ann Mason née Playford. Registered at birth as Henry William Mason, his forenames seem to have been swapped about at regular intervals throughout his brief life; William Henry, however, was how the Army recorded him. His mother was his father's second wife. His first wife, Susannah, had died in 1888, aged 31, and he had married Mary Ann Playford a few months later. William's mother, besides bearing eight children, four of whom died in childhood, was a professional foster mother. In 1901, when the family was at 11 Thompson's Yard off Fishergate in the parish of St Edmund, William's siblings included older sisters Mary and Alice and younger Ethel. The household also included a foster child, Ernest, aged 1. By 1911, the family had moved a few hundred yards away to 5 Loose's Yard off Magdalen Street. William's mother had two foster children in her care at this date, Edward and Ethel. William, 15, was now a shoe-finisher.

William Mason enlisted in Norwich and served in the 1/4th Battalion, Norfolk Regiment. While his Army Service papers have not survived, his Medal Roll index card notes he arrived in the Dardanelles on 6 August 1915. The 1/4th and 1/5th Battalions, Norfolk Regiment, had sailed from Liverpool on RMS *Aquitania*, a fast, sleek Cunard liner that had been launched in 1913 and had only completed three voyages before being commandeered for war work. Her sister ship, the *Lusitania*, had been torpedoed and sunk that May, with the loss of more than 1,100 lives. After the disastrous campaign at Gallipoli, where the Norfolk Regiment lost more men to disease and exposure than enemy action, 1/4th Norfolks were transferred to Egypt where they spent the whole of 1916 defending the Suez Canal sector from Turkish attacks. This mainly comprised digging miles of trenches in the sand and building a chain of forts in the desert alongside the Canal. After a fairly uneventful year, the 1/4th Norfolks were sent into action again in early 1917, marching across the Sinai desert to In Seirat, where an attack on Turkish-occupied Gaza was in preparation. On 19 April, the 163rd Brigade, including the 1/4th and 1/5th Norfolks, advanced in line and in daylight across open country, like soldiers of the Napoleonic era, against the Turkish Army's well-prepared and heavily armed defences outside Gaza, suffering extremely heavy casualties. Such were their losses during the 2nd Battle of Gaza that both battalions virtually ceased to exist as effective fighting units from this day Private William Mason was killed in action here on 19 April 1917, aged 22. William is commemorated at the Jerusalem Memorial, Israel, and on the St Augustine's roll of honour, where he is listed as 'H. W. Mason'. He is also commemorated on St Saviour's roll of honour in Magdalen Street. He is listed as Henry W. Mason under St Augustine's in *Norfolk Roll of Honour*. His parents lived at 24 Rose Yard, St Augustine's, after the war, hence presumably William's inclusion on the parish's roll of honour even though he does not appear to have lived there himself. He was awarded the 1915 Star and the British War and Victory medals.

Private 22258 Robert Fuller, 12th (Bristol) Service Battalion, Gloucestershire Regiment, formerly Trooper 19928, Hussars of the Line

Robert Fuller was born in the parish of St Augustine, Norwich, in 1896, the third child of Samuel Fuller, a shoe finisher, and Mary Ann Fuller née French. In 1901 the Fuller family was at 5 Hinde's Yard off St Augustine's Street. Robert had two older siblings, Arthur and Elizabeth, and three younger, Nellie, Charles and Eva. In 1911 Robert was still here with his widowed mother and siblings. Arthur had moved to Bristol, where he was an assistant master at a boarding school. Robert, 14, had left school and was a blacksmith's assistant.

Robert Fuller enlisted in Norwich. His Army Service papers have not survived but his entry in *Soldiers Died in the Great War* notes he was formerly a trooper in the Hussars of the Line. In 1914 there were 12 Hussar regiments of the line (units of Regular Army cavalry). Recruits were initially placed in the Corps of Hussars and after training posted to one of the 12 regiments. It is not known which one Robert went to but presumably his experience as a blacksmith would have fitted him for the role of farrier. His Medal Roll Index card notes that he first served in an overseas theatre of war in the Balkans, which he entered on 16 August 1915. At this date 'Balkans' was Army code for Gallipoli. The Anglo-French expeditionary force did not reach the other main Balkan's Front, Salonika, until October. As no British cavalry regiments served at Gallipoli, it seems probable Robert went there as a private in an infantry battalion, perhaps the Gloucestershire Regiment's 7th Battalion, the only one of its battalions to go there. At some point Robert transferred to the 12th Gloucestershires, which at the close of 1915 was attached to the 5th Division on the Western Front. Robert, 21, was killed in action on 20 April 1917 during the Battle of Arras. A death notice appeared in the *Eastern Daily Press* on 5 May 1917. Shortly after the second anniversary of his death the paper printed an In Memoriam notice: 'To memory sacred – From his sorrowing Mother, Brothers, and Sisters'.

Robert Fuller is buried at Sucrerie Cemetery, Ablain-St Nazaire, Pas de Calais, France, grave no. 1.A.12, and is commemorated also on St Augustine's and St Luke's rolls of honour. He was awarded the 1915 Star and the British War and Victory medals.

Private 40244 William Sydney Anthony William Mutton, 1st Battalion, Royal Dublin Fusiliers, formerly Private 5418 and 29392, 5th Battalion, Norfolk Regiment

William Sydney Anthony Mutton was born in the parish of St Augustine, Norwich on 15 May 1896, the second or possibly third child of William Frederick Mutton, a shoemaker, and Maude Ellen (known as Nellie) Mutton née Browne. His father, who was usually known as Frederick, came from a family of Norfolk marshmen on Halvergate marshes. William, or Willie as he was known, was baptised in St Augustine's church on 13 January 1902, aged 5. He was a pupil at Angel Road Boys School until he was 14. The 1901 Census records Willie and his parents at 52 Magpie Road, St Augustine, with his widowed grandmother, Mary Browne; his uncle, Herbert Browne and his older sister May Blanche, who died in 1908, aged 16. The 1911 Census records that his mother had had three children. Now only Willie remained. The name of the third child is not known. By this date Willie had left school and was a French-polisher. Grandmother Browne was still living with the family in Magpie Road, though uncle Herbert seems to have gone.

Willie was conscripted in Norwich on 27 March 1916. His Army Service papers have not survived; however, according to supplementary information held by the Commonwealth War Graves Commission he was a member of the 5th Battalion, Norfolk Regiment, prior to transferring to the Royal Dublin Fusiliers, known colloquially as the Blue Caps. The Norfolk Regiment's 5th Battalion was based in Egypt in the spring of 1916 but as there is no indication on his Medal Roll Index card that he ever went there it is likely he was held in one of the Battalion's second-line Reserve units, the 2/5th or 3/5th, in England, before trans-ferring to the Irish regiment. Whether Willie joined the 1st Battalion, Royal Dublin Fusiliers, in time to take part in the Battle of the Somme is not known. On 1 July 1916 the Blue Caps lost more than 300 men, mainly to German machine-gun fire, in a failed attempt to take Beaumont Hamel. Private William Sydney Mutton, 20, was killed in action near Monchy-le-Preux during the Battle of Arras on 20 April 1917. He has no known grave. His parents and fiancée Ada placed a death notice in the *Eastern Daily Press* two and a half weeks later. It included the verse:

We little thought when we said goodbye
(We were parted for a time) that you so soon should die.
The foreign grave was the bitterest blow,
None but aching hearts can know.

On the first anniversary of his death his parents placed an 'In Memoriam' notice in the *Eastern Daily Press* with the words: 'No nobler cause had he than to lay down his life for the freedom of others'. His photograph was subsequently placed in Norfolk Library's Great War memorial collection. Willie is commemorated at the Arras Memorial, Pas de Calais, France, and also on St Augustine's roll of honour. He was awarded the British War and Victory medals. Due to his regimental affiliation he is also commemorated in *Ireland's Memorial Records 1914-1918,* published by the Irish National War Memorial Committee in 1923.

Private 205949 Albert Fox, 'A' Company, 1/4th Battalion, Norfolk Regiment, formerly Private 4559 Norfolk Regiment

Albert Fox was born in the parish of St Mary Coslany, Norwich, on 13 October 1897, the sixth surviving child of Frederick George Fox, a shoemaker, and Ellen Jane Fox née Perrement. *(For more on Albert's background see Frederick Fo, p.176.)* In August 1904 Albert, 6, was enrolled as pupil of the Old Meeting House School, a nonconformist establishment in the parish of St George Colegate. At this date he was at 5 Dog Yard, Oak Street. By 1911 the family had moved to 18 Leonards Street, St Augustine's. Albert, 13, was now a 'newsboy'. In 1915 he married Mabel Eastoe, a dressmaker. They lived at 6 Beehive Yard. Later that year their only child, Doris, was born.

Albert enlisted in Norwich on 25 May 1915, joining the 1/4th Battalion, Norfolk Regiment. Interestingly, Albert and his brothers Frederick and Ernest have consecutive regimental numbers (4559, 4558, 4557 respectively), suggesting that they joined up on the same day. Aged 18, Albert declared he was 19; a crucial difference as officially soldiers could not go overseas until they were 19. It wasn't to matter as it would be nearly nine months before he left England. On 15 February 1916, he embarked at Devonport on the transport ship HT *Saturnia*, arriving in Alexandria 11 days later. From here the Battalion moved to Mena Camp at the foot of the Great Pyramid at Cairo. The 1/4th Norfolks formed part of the 163rd Brigade, 54th Division, which after the rigours of Gallipoli was now stationed in Egypt to defend the strategically vital Suez Canal along a string of fortified posts in the desert. Water and rations were brought up daily by camel from the nearest railhead. For a young man from Norwich whose only previous experience of sand had probably been the beach at Great Yarmouth, this must have been an extraordinary experience.

In February 1917 the 163rd Brigade was ordered to march across the Sinai desert into Palestine, where British operations to drive out the Ottoman Turks had finally begun. On 27 March the Brigade was held in reserve on a ridge above Gaza while British and Anzac forces attempted to capture the city. Having seriously underestimated the Turkish Army's strength and tenacity, they were forced to retire to In Seirat, where they remained for three weeks while a second assault on Gaza was planned. Albert was wounded on 19 April during the Second Battle of Gaza, an even more disastrously misjudged action than the First, in which British and Anzac forces again suffered heavy casualties, many dying while advancing in line in broad daylight like soldiers of the Napoleonic era, across open desert and scrubland towards well-defended Turkish positions. It is thought casualties on the British side alone amounted to over 6,500 killed, wounded or missing, half of these from the 54th Division. Such were the losses of the 1/4th and 1/5th Norfolks, they virtually ceased to exist as operational battalions after this battle. Two other St Augustine men, Privates E. G. Jolly and W. H. Mason also died in this battle. Albert died of wounds received at the Second Battle of Gaza at the 53rd (Welsh) Casualty Clearing Station at Deir el Belah, Palestine, on 21 April 1917. According to the casualty form among his Army Service papers he had been shot in the mouth. Albert is buried at Deir el Belah War Cemetery, Gaza Strip, Palestine grave no. A.117, and commemorated also on the St Augustine's roll of honour. He was awarded the British War and Victory medals.

Albert's family placed a death notice in the *Eastern Daily Press* on 3 May 1917, including the popular memorial verse:

> *He sleeps beside his comrades*
> *In hallowed graves unknown;*
> *But his name is written in letters of love*
> *In the hearts he left at home.*

On 17 September 1917, the paper published a letter from Lieutenant Roland Charles Larking of the 1/4th Battalion, Norfolk Regiment:

Dear Sir,

I am now home on leave from Palestine, and on my return journey took photos of the graves of the following Norfolk men, who died from wounds received at Gaza on April 19th: – Ptes Hill, G. Balaam, A. Fox and A. Lister. I do not know the addresses of their relatives. I thought you would not mind putting a notice in your paper to the effect that the relatives of these men can have photographs on application to me.

The following day the paper published an editorial expanding on Lieutenant Larking's offer:

We have seen the photographs which Lt. Roland C. Larking has brought home from Palestine on his present leave. Near Gaza, in an old Bedouin garden surrounded by a cactus fence, a well-kept cemetery has been made. A careful record of internments has been organised with the view possibly to a more permanent memorial scheme. Mr Larking has been among the graves with his camera, and found several bearing the names of Norfolk men. Some of these photographs he has already distributed among grateful relatives, but four remain upon his hands. He has at present no clue to the whereabouts of the relatives of these cases.

Whether Albert's family ever saw the photographs is not known. Albert's widow Mabel later lived at 39 Philadelphia Lane off Aylsham Road in north Norwich and remarried, becoming Mrs Longbone. In October 1917 she wrote to the War Office regarding the return of her late husband's personal possessions at the time of his death: '2 discs, Ingersoll watch & chain, 1 pipe, 1 letter, 1 card, 4 shoulder titles [brass badges identifying his regiment], 1 cap badge'. This list is fairly typical of a First World War private soldier's meagre effects. Those whose relatives died on the battlefield rather than in hospital rarely even had this much returned.

Albert's brother Frederick Fox, a sergeant-major in the East Yorkshire Regiment, died of wounds in March 1918. His other brother, Ernest, served in the Norfolk Regiment and survived the war. Their father, Frederick, was actually the first member of the family to join up, enlisting as a volunteer private in the Norfolk

National Reserve, an early form of Home Guard, in January 1915 aged 48. In December 1917 he was posted to the newly formed Royal Defence Corps, whose duties included guarding docks and railways. He was demobbed in May 1919.

Lance Corporal 43165 Alfred McPherson Cossey, 1st Battalion, Norfolk Regiment

Alfred McPherson Cossey was born in Brighouse in the West Riding of Yorkshire in 1895, the second child of John Cossey, a Norwich-born pharmacist, and Mary Dorcas Cossey née Elliott, who was born in Dunboyne, County Meath, Ireland. His parents were married in Dublin in 1890 and his older brother Sydney was born in Dunshaughlin, County Meath, in 1893. By 1895 the family had moved to Brighouse. They were still there in 1901. By 1906 they had returned to Norwich, where Alfred's sister, Alice, was born. His grandfather, John Cossey, had run a 'druggist' shop in St Augustine's Street, Norwich, in the 1860s. In 1911 the family were living at 46 Aylsham Road but by 1914 they had moved to 16 Pitt Street, St Augustine's. At this date Sydney was assisting his father in the family pharmacy business.

Alfred enlisted in Norwich. His Army Service papers have not survived but he appears to have been a 1916 conscript. He was killed in action near Arras on 23 April 1917, aged 22, and has no known grave. On this day the 1st Battalion, Norfolk Regiment, was engaged in the Battle of La Coulotte near Lens during the latter phases of the Arras offensive. An assault against the German front line in front of the village of La Coulotte by British and Canadian troops met uncut wire and machine guns, and had to withdraw under a heavy barrage, an all-too-common and all-too-fatal scenario. The 1st Norfolks suffered heavy casualties here with 37 killed, more than 130 wounded and 24 missing in action. Another St Augustine's man in the 1st Norfolks, Henry Clarke, was fatally wounded in this action. *(See p.124.)* Alfred is commemorated at the Arras Memorial, Pas de Calais, France, and also on the St Augustine's roll of honour. He was awarded the British War and Victory medals. His brother, Sydney, served as a private in the Royal Army Medical Corps and survived the war.

Private 43297 Percy William Swann, 1st Battalion, Norfolk Regiment; formerly Private 1868, 6th Battalion (Cyclists), Norfolk Regiment

Private William Swann's name appears with two others out of alphabetical order on the last panel on the right of St Augustine's roll of honour chancel screen. This suggests his name was a late addition, possibly added after the screen was installed in January 1920. While *Norfolk Roll of Honour* also lists a William Swann among the casualties from St Augustine's parish, no one of this name is listed in *Norwich Roll of Honour*, which unlike *Norfolk Roll of Honour* doesn't associate casualties with Anglican parishes or nonconformist congregations. Furthermore, no one of this name appears in any of the decennial censuses as a resident of the St Augustine's area between 1881 and 1911. The Commonwealth War Graves Commission's (CWGC) Debt of Honour Register has eight First World War privates named either William or W. Swann. None appears to have had any obvious connection with Norwich or Norfolk, or to have served in the Norfolk Regiment. Curiously, however, the General Register Office's register of Army Deaths does list a Private William Swann of the Norfolk Regiment who died in 1917. Cross referencing this soldier to the CWGC database reveals that he was also known as Private Percy William Swann. Fortunately, this soldier's Army Service papers have survived and these provide a family connection with St Augustine's that may explain his inclusion on the parish's roll of honour.

Percy William Swann was born in the village of Knapton in north Norfolk in 1890, the only son of George Swann, a shoemaker, and Ann Swann, described as a washerwoman, of The Cottages (later known as The Council Houses), Knapton. Percy had five older sisters, Gertrude, Elizabeth, Florence, Laura and Alice. Interestingly, in the 1891 Census, aged 10 months, he is named William rather than Percy William, suggesting he was familiarly known by his second forename.

Percy William enlisted in Norwich on 12 January 1915 and was initially posted to the Norfolk Regiment's 6th (Cyclist) Battalion, a Territorial unit. During 1915 and the first half of 1916 the Norfolk Cyclists were employed in Home Defence duties round the vulnerable east coast. In July 1916, however, the Battalion was broken up and its officers and men distributed to various fighting battalions overseas. On 30 July Private Swann was posted to the 1/1st Battalion, Hertfordshire Regiment, and embarked with them at Folkestone for Boulogne, from where he was sent to No. 17 Infantry Base Depot, part of the vast army camp at Étaples. On 10 August 1916 he was posted to the 1st Battalion, Norfolk Regiment, which was then in rest billets at Vauchelles-les-Quesnoy near Abbeville. Here he was given a new number 43297. The 1st Battalion had just taken part in fierce fighting on the Somme around Longueval and Deville Wood. A fortnight later it was engaged in another desperate battle, this time at Falfemont Farm on 3 September, where it lost more than 150 officers and men, including four men from St Augustine's. Three weeks later it was in the thick of it again, at Morval. On 29 September the Battalion boarded a train at Dernancourt for Longpré in order to join the 1st Army on the Bethune Front. During the journey Private Swann for some reason left the train without permission and on being challenged by an NCO made an 'improper reply'. Conditions on troop trains on the Western Front, especially for other ranks, were scandalously squalid and uncomfortable. The trains were notoriously slow and the carriages resembled cattle trucks rather than passenger compartments, with little or no sanitation and limited access to fresh water, food or even benches. For this act of insubordination 'in the field', for which technically he could have been court-martialled and, if found guilty, shot, William received 28 days Field Punishment No.1 (the maximum sentence a commanding officer could impose without a court martial), which consisted of being cuffed and fettered to the wheel of a gun carriage or stake for up to two hours each day out in the open, as well as hard labour, extra drill and loss of pay. Percy seems to have been forgiven by 21 November, when he was sent on a trench mortar course, which lasted until 4 December when he rejoined the Battalion and spent winter in the trenches.

Private Percy William Swann was killed in action on 23 April 1917 during the final phase of the Battle of Arras. During an action near La Coulotte 'A' Company was placed in the first line of the assault, putting four enemy machine guns out of action before being stopped by uncut barbed wire and more withering machine-gun fire. At the end of the day the survivors withdrew under cover of darkness to their starting point, where they continued to be shelled. The Battalion had lost around 40 men in this botched action with many more wounded or missing. Percy was among those reported missing in action. His father was notified by telegram on 19 May and on 21 June he wrote to the Army Records Office seeking any information on his son's whereabouts. None was forthcoming. In fact it would not be until 1 February 1918 that the Army officially regarded Percy as having died on active service. A declaration form completed by his father in May 1919 listed the names and addresses of Percy William Swann's closest blood relations: his parents and his five sisters. Interestingly, one unmarried sister, Florence Swann, lived in Eade Road in Norwich, just to the north of St Augustine's parish; another, Laura Louisa Swann, who had married her first cousin Archibald Swann, lived at 12 Leonards Street, St Augustine's. It may therefore have been one or both sisters who saw to it that their only brother's name was added to the St Augustine's roll of honour. As to whether he ever lived in the area, no evidence has been discovered. Percy William is commemorated on the Arras Memorial, Pas de Calais, France; on the Knapton roll of honour (where his full name and regiment are given) and in *Norfolk Roll of Honour* under Knapton where he is called William Swann; and also possibly on the St Augustine's roll of honour, if the William Swann listed there is indeed the same man. He was awarded the British War and Victory medals.

Corporal 6221 William Woodcock, 1st Battalion, Norfolk Regiment

William Woodcock was born in the parish of St Augustine, Norwich, in 1886, the fifth child of Charles Woodcock, a baker, and Eliza Woodcock. His parents had 14 children, only eight of whom survived into adulthood: Charles, Harriet, Flora, Herbert, William, Albert, Eliza and Nellie. In 1891 the whole family was squeezed into a small terraced house at 50 Esdelle Street. William's father died in 1903 and his widowed mother later lived in Whiting Court off Magdalen Street with three of her unmarried children: Herbert, Eliza and Nellie. In 1906 William married Maria Elizabeth Barber, a shoe-machinist, and by 1911 they were at 20 Cross Street off Sussex Street with their first child, Maria, aged 3. At this date William was working as a shoe and boot-finisher. A second child, William, was born in 1913. They were still here in 1914 when William was listed on the Norwich Electoral Register.

William Woodcock enlisted in Norwich before the war. His Army Service papers have not survived. Curiously, he enlisted under the surname Eastoe, for what reason it is unclear. It may have been his mother's maiden name; there is no record that his parents ever married. His Medal Roll Index Card notes that he declared his real name to be Woodcock on 17 August 1914, perhaps after realising that his wife, whom he had married as William Woodcock, might not receive her separation allowance as his legitimate spouse.

William joined the BEF in France on 15 September 1914. His first experience of action would probably have been in the fighting along the La Bassée Canal on the Festubert Front in October. Given that the 1st Norfolks were in trenches in the Wulverghem sector that Christmas, it is quite possible he witnessed or even took part in one of the famous impromptu football games between British and German troops here during the unofficial Christmas Truce. William survived the Battle of the Somme in 1916 and at some point was promoted to corporal. Corporal William Woodcock, 31, was killed in action on 23 April 1917 during a costly and unsuccessful assault on Vimy Ridge during the Battle of Arras. On 10 May 1917 his 'sorrowing wife and children' published a death notice the *Eastern Daily Press* with the words 'He answered his country's call'. William is commemorated on the Arras Memorial, Pas de Calais, France, and on St Augustine's roll of honour. He was awarded the 1914 Star with Bar and the British War and Victory medals.

Private 3/4854 Harry Henry (or Herbert) Clarke, 1st Battalion, Norfolk Regiment

According to *Soldiers Died in the Great War*, Harry Henry Clarke was born in the parish of St Augustine, Norwich. The name is fairly common and it is difficult to pinpoint his family background with any certainty. The most likely candidate is a Harry Clarke, listed in the 1891 Census at 3 Winter's Yard off Pitt Street, St Augustine. This Harry was the youngest child of Isaac Clarke, a labourer and shoemaker, and Emma Clarke née Burroughs, a silk-warper. If Harry

Clarke in *Soldiers Died in the Great War* is this Harry Clarke, then his name was actually Harry Herbert Clarke, born in Norwich in 1882. The household of Isaac and Emma Clarke in 1891 included five children, Lydia, George, William, Caroline and Harry; their eldest children, John and Eliza, having left home by this date. By 1901 the family had moved to 13 Old Yeast Yard off Muspole Street in the nearby parish of St George Colegate. Harry was now the only child still at home and was working as a general labourer. By 1911 Harry's father, 75, was a widower, at 15 Fullers Hall beside the River Wensum to the west of St Augustine's, now working as a painter and decorator. Harry does not appear to be living in Norwich at this date and it is possible he is the Harry Clarke of Norwich in lodgings in Lewisham, London, working as a meat salesman. However, the 1913/14 Norwich Electoral Roll includes a Harry Clarke, possibly the same man, listed as a resident at 4 St Martins-at-Oak Wall Lane, St Augustine's, which suggests he had moved back to Norwich by this date.

Harry Clarke enlisted in Norwich. His Army Service papers have not survived, though the prefix 3 to his regimental number suggests he was in the Norfolk Regiment's 3rd (Reserve) Battalion prior to being posted to the 1st Battalion, a common route into this Regular Army battalion by post-August 1914 recruits. His Medal Roll Index card notes he first went to France on 9 March 1915. At this period the 1st Norfolks were occupying trenches near St Eloi in the Ypres Salient. During April and May the 1st Norfolk Regiment, part of 15th Brigade, 5th Division, was engaged in repeated attempts to seize and hold a series of topographical vantage points beside the Ypres–Comines railway line. After a relatively quiet winter and spring the 1st Norfolks were thrown into the meat-grinder that was the Battle of the Somme in July 1916. On 25 July 1916 Harry was admitted at Le Treport Hospital on the French coast with a gunshot wound to the left foot. He had presumably received this during an abortive preliminary assault on strongly defended German positions at High Wood near Longueval on 23 July, in which the 1st Norfolks had lost one killed in action and 15 wounded. It is not known when he returned to the Front.

Private Harry Clarke died of wounds on 28 April 1917, possibly, given his burial place, while at Casualty Clearing Station No. 22 in

Bruay. He had almost certainly received his fatal injury five days earlier at the Battle of La Coulotte during the Arras offensive, a disastrous but all-too-common encounter between human flesh and uncut barbed wire and machine-gun fire, in which the 1st Norfolks lost 37 killed in action, more than 130 wounded and 24 missing. Another St Augustine's man in the same battalion, Alfred Cossey was among those killed in this action. *(See p.120.)* Harry is buried at Bruay Communal Cemetery Extension, Pas de Calais, France, grave no. F32. His name does not appear on St Augustine's roll of honour. He was awarded the 1915 Star and the British War and Victory medals.

Rifleman S/8439 Ernest Henry Barber, 'D' Company, 8th Battalion, The Rifle Brigade (The Prince Consort's Own)

Ernest Henry Barber was born in Norwich in 1889, the fourth surviving child of Charles Barber, a foundry worker like his father before him, and Mary Agnes Barber née Fitt. By 1891 the family had moved to Colchester: to 30 Artillery Street South near the Garrison, where Ernest's father was employed as an iron-moulder. Ernest had four siblings at this date: William, Charles, Nellie and younger brother James. By 1901 the family was back in Norwich, at Starling's Yard in the parish of St Saviour. Mrs Barber was now a widow and the family's main breadwinner as a horsehair-weaver. Eldest son William had left home; Charles, 15, was an errand boy; Nellie, Ernest and James were still at school, and newest addition, Harry, was still an infant. By 1911 Mrs Barber had moved to 94 Calvert Street in the parish of St George Colegate. Ernest and Charles, both shoe-finishers, were now the only children still at home. Nellie, also employed in the shoe trade as a machinist, was living with her brother William and sister-in-law Flora, who ran a shoe-repair business in King Street, Norwich. James cannot be traced and Harry was with his maternal grandfather and step-grandmother in Cat and Fiddle Yard off Botolph Street.

Ernest enlisted in Norwich and went over to France to join the BEF on 6 July 1915. The 8th Battalion, Rifle Brigade, was a light infantry Service battalion, formed in Winchester in August 1914. It had been on the Western Front since May 1915, as part of the 41st Brigade, 14th (Light) Division. Over the span of Ernest's service with the 8th Rifles it was engaged in numerous actions, most notably at Hooge and Bellewaarde in 1915, Delville Wood and Switch Trench on the Somme in 1916 and the 1st Battle of the Scarpe in April 1917. Rifleman Ernest Barber, 28, was killed in action on 3 May 1917, in a costly attack on the German front line near Chérisy during the closing days of the Battle of Arras, an action known as the 3rd Battle of the Scarpe.

'D' Company, in which Ernest was then serving, was ordered to form part of the 8th Rifles' first-wave, assaulting companies. It was held in position on the right of the British front line until 2.45 a.m. when it went over the top. In the dark the men had only the noise and flashes of the creeping barrage in front of them as their guide as they inched forward over no man's land. At 4.30 a.m. 'D' Company reached the village of Chérisy and by-passed it. A patrol sent into the village found only dead German soldiers there. 'D' Company then consolidated its position on the main road leading out of the village near a landmark known as *la statue de Saint-Michel* – the battered remains of a large statue of the Archangel Michael in the act of spearing Satan under his feet. Here it came under heavy machine-gun fire and shelling, which prevented any further advance for three to four hours. Eventually, what was left of the 8th Rifles was ordered to withdraw to their original jumping off point in order to escape being cut off by German reinforcements then coming up in strength. Ernest was initially listed among those reported missing.

Another St Augustine's man in the 8th Rifles, Leonard Pert, was also killed here on this day with around 50 other riflemen. *(See p.128.)* Ernest is commemorated at the Arras Memorial, Pas de Calais, France, and on St Augustine's roll of honour. He was awarded the 1915 Star and the British War and Victory medals. Ernest's brother Charles enlisted in Norwich on 30 March 1915 and was posted to the Royal Field Artillery. He served in France and Palestine, ending his military career in Egypt in 1920 with the rank of bombardier.

Rifleman S/17986 Leonard Harry Pert, Signal Section, 'C' Company, 8th Battalion, Rifle Brigade (The Prince Consort's Own)

Leonard Harry Pert was born in Norwich in 1891, the first child of Harry Pert, a shoe manufacturer, and Alice Pert née Griffiths. His parents were married in St Augustine's church by the Rev W. A.

Elder in 1890 and began their married life at 48 Pitt Street, St Augustine's, the home of Leonard's grandfather, James Pert, who ran his own boot and shoemaking business and shop there. In 1895 his grandfather died and Leonard's father inherited the business. By 1901 the family, which now included Stanley, born 1893, had relocated to 31 Pitt Street across the road. The family was still there in 1911. Leonard was now an assistant teacher, employed by Norwich Town Council, while Stanley was a clerk in a local brush factory. According to his obituary in the *Eastern Daily Press*, on 17 May 1917, Leonard:

> *received his early training under Mr J. D. Wright at the Presbyterian School, which he attended eight years without a miss. His name was always on the list at the annual prize distribution. He obtained a pupil teacher's scholarship in July 1906 and attended the Municipal Secondary School* [in Duke Street] *two years* [Leonard was also a student at the Boys Model School in Princes Street]. *On leaving college he obtained an appointment under the L.C.C* [London County Council] *and at the outbreak of the war was serving as head assistant at the Nynehead Street Boys' Council School, Deptford.*

Leonard Pert enlisted (or, given the date, was conscripted) in Deptford, London, on 5 February 1916. At this date he lived at 15 Cranfield Road, Brockley. According to his Attestation papers he had been a member of the 10th Battalion (Duke of Cambridge's Own),

Middlesex Regiment, a Territorial battalion, for a year and a half until 2 November 1913, when his contracted time expired and he was discharged. After being conscripted he was held in the Army Reserve until posted to the Rifle Brigade on 29 April 1916. Between May and August Leonard trained with the Brigade's 14th Battalion; a New Army Reserve battalion then camped at Belhurst Park. On 4 May he was appointed temporary lance corporal, reverting to rifleman at his own request on 5 August. Such requests were common before embarking for active service overseas as there were always fewer positions for NCOs in an expeditionary force than in an establishment in Britain. On 24 August he landed in France and was posted to the Rifle Brigade's 8th Battalion, which he joined in the field on 9 September. Ten days later he received his baptism of fire during the 8th Rifles' costly assault and capture of a German defensive position between High Wood and Deville Wood known as Switch Trench. Leonard may very well have seen British tanks in action here for the first time, strange lumbering machines prone to break down and an unfortunate reputation for firing on their own side. The Rifle Brigade here lost more than 100 men killed and 320 wounded.

Rifleman Leonard Pert, 25, was killed in action during the Battle of Arras on 3 May 1917. This was the first day of an action known as the 3rd Battle of the Scarpe, designed to push back the Germans onto their rear defences. 'C' Company, in which Leonard was then serving, was ordered to support 'B' and 'D' companies on the left and right of the front line near the village of Chérisy. They went over the top at 3.45 a.m. and by 7.00 a.m. had by-passed Chérisy and crossed the River Sensée, digging in under shelling and heavy machine-gun fire near a landmark known as *la statue de Saint-Michel* – a large statue of the Archangel Michael spearing Satan under his feet. In the early afternoon, as enemy reinforcements came up threatening to cut them off, the Rifle Brigade fell back to their original positions having suffered heavy casualties. The planned combined assault of artillery barrage, tanks and infantry failed to mesh and the attack was called off on the 4th. Despite the extraordinary gallantry and skill of the riflemen the attack had been an utter and costly failure. Leonard's obituary, using words presumably extracted from his commanding officer's letter of condolence to his parents, described how:

He went out under a heavy bombardment to repair the
telephone wire which had been cut, and while doing this he was
struck by a shell, his death being instantaneous.

It goes on to say that he did good work and how much his death was regretted by the officers and men of his battalion, and how much it will be regretted among his large circle of friends in his native city. His parents placed a death notice in the *Eastern Daily Press* on 17 May 1917 (repeated the following day) with lines from a hymn by George Matheson described as Leonard's favourite verse:

O love that wilt not let me go
I rest my weary soul in Thee;
I give Thee back the life I owe,
That in Thine ocean depths its flow
May richer, fuller be.

Leonard is commemorated at the Arras Memorial, Pas de Calais, France; on the Boys Model School Memorial in Norwich cathedral; and on the rolls of honour of St George Colegate and St Augustine. He is also listed under both St Augustine's and St George's parishes in *Norfolk Roll of Honour*. Leonard has an individual memorial in St Augustine's church in the form of a stained-glass window in the south nave aisle depicting an angel at Christ's empty tomb below a dove descending, witnessed by Mary Mother of Christ and Mary Martha. The memorial is based on a design by Art Nouveau-inspired Norwich architect George Skipper and made by William Morris & Co. of Ruskin House, Rochester Row, Westminster. It has a Biblical inscription (Matthew 28:6) and memorial text:

He is not here, He is risen as He said
To the glory of God and in loving memory of
Leonard Harry Pert who was killed in battle in
France May 3rd 1917 aged 25
This window erected by his parents

As shop owners and manufacturers, Leonard's parents were presumably somewhat better off than the majority of families in the St Augustine's area. Even so, the cost of their son's memorial window

must have placed a considerable burden on their finances. Such installations within Anglican churches required a Faculty from the Archdeacon, who relied on a report on its appropriateness drawn up by the Diocesan Consistory Court. The Faculty papers, held at Norfolk Record Office, note that the design of the window was approved at a Vestry meeting in St Augustine's parish on 9 April 1918, that is, during the war and less than a year after Leonard's death. Permission for the parish to erect a memorial stained glass window was granted by the bishop of Norwich on 27 July 1918. A photograph *(above)* of Leonard in civilian clothes was donated to Norwich Library's Great War roll of honour photographic archive by his family. He is one of three teachers who lost their lives in the war commemorated in St Augustine's church. *(See Edward Halfacre, p. 236, and Edward Sizer, p. 220.)*

Private G/11304 John Daniel Shorten, 7th Battalion, Royal Sussex Regiment

John Daniel Shorten was born in 1897 in parish of St Mary Coslany, Norwich, the fourth child of George Shorten, a boot and shoe-finisher working at home, and Kate Shorten née Middleton, who was originally from Sheffield. A first child, Robert, had died in 1892, aged 1, while they were living in Newbegin's Yard off St Mary's Plain. By 1901 the family was at 3 Sun Yard off Oak Street in the neighbouring parish of St Miles Coslany. At home at this date, in addition to John, were his older siblings Florence and George and younger sisters Martha and Kate. Two more children, Sidney and Gladys, born in

1903 and 1905 respectively, completed the family. Mrs Shorten died in 1909, aged 37 and by 1911 the family had moved to 5 Dial Yard off Barrack Street in the parish of St James Pockthorpe. John was a pupil at the Old Meeting House School and later at the Quay Side School, which he left at 14 in 1912.

While John's Army Service papers have not survived, his regimental number suggests he was conscripted between April and May 1916. The 7th Battalion, Royal Sussex Regiment, was one of the first 'Kitchener' Service battalions, established in Chichester just eight days after Britain's declaration of war against Germany on 4 August 1914. It formed part of the 36th Brigade, 12th (Eastern) Division, which fought on the Western Front throughout the war. Following a short period of training in England it is possible John was pitched straight into action on the Somme in the summer of 1916. The 7th Royal Sussex fought in the battles of Albert, Pozières and Le Transloy during the Somme offensive, losing more than 250 officers and men killed in action and more than twice that number wounded or missing. The Battalion's next major engagement was during the Battle of Arras the following spring. Having survived the 1st Battle of the Scarpe and the Battle of Arleux in April, Private John Shorten, 19, was killed in action on 3 May 1917 in the last major engagement of the Battle of Arras, the 3rd Battle of the Scarpe. Two other St Augustine's men, Riflemen Barber and Pert of the 8th Rifle Brigade, also died in this disastrous action. *(See p.126 and p.128.)* A notice of John's death appeared in *Eastern Daily Press* just over a month later. His father remarried in 1917, and he and his new wife, Georgina, were living at 155 Cowgate off Magdalen Street at this time. John is commemorated at the Arras Memorial, Pas de Calais, France, and on the Royal Sussex Regiment Great War roll of honour in St George's Chapel, Chichester cathedral. He was awarded the British War and Victory medals.

Private 675635 Arthur Robert Allen, 2nd Infantry Battalion (Eastern Ontario Regiment), Canadian Expeditionary Force

Arthur Robert Allen was born in Norwich on 23 April 1898, the third child of Arthur Vincent Allen, a butcher, and Louisa Allen née

Cannell. He had two older sisters, Louisa and Rosa, and two younger, Ada and Florence. In 1901 the family was living at 16 St Leonard's Road, Thorpe Hamlet, where Arthur's father ran a small family butcher's business. Arthur's mother was a daughter of Abraham Cannell, whose family owned several butcher's shops in Norwich. Arthur Cannell was a cousin. *(See p.84.)* Arthur Allen's mother died in 1905, aged 38, and by 1911 the family had moved to 49 Botolph Street, St Augustine's, then a busy street of small shops, factories and modest dwellings that connected St Augustine's Street with Magdalen Street, the two main retail streets in north Norwich. Here Arthur's father ran another butcher's shop, assisted now by his eldest daughter Louisa. The business does not seem to have prospered, for in 1913 Mr Allen emigrated to Canada, taking with him his three youngest children: Arthur (15), Ada (11) and Florence (9). Assisted-passage schemes, some funded by the Canadian Government itself, some by prominent businessmen and phil-anthropists such as Russell James Colman of Colman's Mustard fame, provided subsidised tickets for the Atlantic crossing for the unemployed and under-employed. Thousands of men and women left Britain's shores for the first time in this way, only for many of the men to return a few years later and die on the Western Front.

On 27 May 1913 the Allen family sailed from Liverpool on SS *Franconia*, arriving in Portland, Maine, USA, on 4 June. Their final destination was the town of Ingersoll in Ontario, Canada. While still aboard ship in harbour they were visited by a Canadian Government Employment Agent. These agents received a commission from the Canadian Government for every immigrant they placed with employers seeking labourers or domestic servants. While Mr Allen senior obtained work as a labourer, the teenaged Arthur was assigned to domestic work. Ada and Florence were too young yet to be employed.

The next known event in the Allen family story occurred on 21 February 1916 when Arthur visited the recruiting office in Kintore, Ontario, where he was living at the time, to attest his willingness to serve His Majesty King George V in the Canadian (Overseas) Expeditionary Force (CEF). According to his Attestation papers he was at this date working as a labourer and had no previous military experience. An obituary published in a south-west Ontario newspaper, *St Mary's Journal Argus*, notes that Arthur had been employed on a farm in the township of East Nissouri prior to enlisting. Although his actual date of birth is noted in his papers, his 'apparent age' was given as 18. He was in fact 17 and legally too young to be sent overseas on active service for which the recruit needed to be aged at least 19. All too often during this time of crisis such regulations were ignored. The following day, having been passed fit by a medical board in the nearby town of Ingersoll, Arthur was formally enlisted in the CEF. His medical record notes he was 5ft 5 in height, had a fair complexion, blue eyes and light brown hair. His religious denomination was Methodist. His father, whose address was recorded 'R. R. No. 2, Ingersoll, Ontario', was named as next-of-kin. 'R. R.' probably stands for railroad, so it seems likely he was employed on the railway there. Interestingly, Ingersoll is only 15 miles from the Ontarian town of Norwich. Perhaps it was this familiar name that had drawn the family to this part of Canada.

Initially, Arthur was placed in the 168th Infantry Battalion, also known as the Oxford County Regiment, a local reserve unit of enlisted men awaiting posting overseas. He was then transferred to the 2nd Battalion (Eastern Ontario Regiment), the bulk of which had been in France since February 1915. It is not known when he joined the CEF on the Western Front but according to his obituary in *St Mary's Journal Argus* he saw action during the Arras Offensive of April 1917 when the Canadians, at very heavy cost, captured Vimy Ridge. Private Arthur Robert Allen died of wounds on 5 May 1917, aged 19. The probable date of his wounding is 3 May during the capture of Fresnoy in the Third Battle of the Scarpe when the 2nd Battalion CEF was sent across no man's land near Willerval north-east of Arras at a cost of more than 350 casualties. His obituary provides a vivid description of the circumstances:

> *During a night attack on the fortified village of Fresnoy-en-Gohelle the troops were shelled and machine gunned mercilessly by the Germans. The lead company from the 2nd Battalion was able to force its way through the wire and capture the western edge of the village. Two companies of the 2nd came forward and mopped up the village, killing or capturing all Germans found in the dugouts and ruined houses. Private*

Allen was hit by small arms fire, was evacuated, and later died.

A death notice appeared in the *Eastern Daily Press* in Norwich, England, six weeks later, presumably placed by his older sisters, Louisa and Rosa, who had remained in England. It included the popular memorial verse:

He sleeps beside his comrades,
In hallowed graves unknown,
But his name is written in letters of love,
In the hearts he left at home.

In fact, his grave is not unknown. Arthur Allen is buried at Aubigny Communal Cemetery Extension, Pas de Calais, France, grave no. II.F.82. His place of burial suggests that he died at the 1st Canadian Casualty Clearing Station, which was based at Aubigny-en-Artois at this date. Although he still had close relatives living in St Augustine's, Arthur's name does not appear on the St Augustine's roll of honour, excluded perhaps by relatives who shared his Methodist faith and might have objected to his commemoration in an Anglican church. He was one of five St Augustine's men to die whilst serving with the Canadian Expeditionary Force.

Private G/8127 James Edward Mason, 11th Battalion, Queen's (Royal West Surrey Regiment)

James Edward Mason was born in Norwich in 1885, the third child of William Mason, a gas-fitter and whitesmith, and Sarah Mason née Browes. *(For James's background see p.57.)* In 1911, James, 26, was living at his place of work, 7 Holborn Circus, London – the warehouse and emporium of Thomas Wallis & Co. Ltd, General Drapers & Complete Household Furnishers – where he was a warehouse porter, one of 148 men and 53 women employees living on the premises.

James enlisted in Piccadilly, London. The 11th Battalion, Queen's (Royal West Surrey) Regiment was a 'Kitchener' Service battalion formed in Lambeth on 16 June 1915. After nearly a year in training the 11th went over to France in May 1916 where it formed part of the 123rd Brigade, 41st Division. James's Army Service papers have not survived but it is likely he would have fought at the Battle of Flers on the Somme during September. In June 1917 the 11th Battalion took part in the Battle of Messines in Flanders. Private James Mason was wounded here, probably on 7 June. From the battlefield he would probably have been taken to one of two casualty clearing stations, CCS 10 or 17, at Remy Siding, where he died of his wounds on 11 June 1917. His sister, Mrs Rose Hare, placed a death notice in the *Eastern Daily Press* ten days later. James is buried at Lijssenthoek Military Cemetery, Poperinghe, Belgium, grave XV.G.15. He is also commemorated on St Augustine's roll of honour and in the Book of Remembrance in the Council Chamber of Lambeth Town Hall, London. He was awarded the British War and Victory medals. James's older brother Albert was killed in action in France in 1916.

Private 242484 Samuel Ernest Laccohee Baker, 1/5th Battalion, Norfolk Regiment, formerly Private 22109, Norfolk Regiment

Samuel Ernest Laccohee Baker was born in Norwich in 1872, the eldest child of Samuel Laccohee Baker, a cabinet-maker, and Charlotte Gertrude Baker née Harrison, a shoe-trimmer. Samuel's grandfather, also called Samuel, was a cordwainer, an old term for a shoemaker. He would have made shoes entirely by hand, using traditional methods, probably at home. Samuel's parents were married in Norwich in 1872, only a few months before he was born. His mother was a domestic servant at the Three Pigeons public house in St Benedict's Street, so he may well have been born there. *Soldiers Died in the Great War* records his place of birth as 'St Bernard's', probably a transcription error for St Benedict's as there is no such parish in Norfolk. Laccohee is a Norwich 'Stranger' surname, thought to derive from a family of Walloon or Flemish weavers, La Cohie, who settled in Norwich in the late 16th century. Each member of the Samuel Baker's family had this as a middle name, as did several other Walloon-descended Norwich families. A trust set up in the 1830s to help educate those who could claim descent from a

Norwich Huguenot family probably accounts for this custom. In 1881 the family was at Freeman's Court in the parish of St Giles. The Baker household included Samuel's siblings, Arthur, Ellen and Henry, as well as his widowed grandfather in his seventies and still working, though now as a porter and messenger. In 1883 Arthur died, aged 9. In 1886 Grandfather Samuel died, aged 79. By 1891 the family had moved to Wilde's Court in the parish of St Stephen. Samuel now had three more siblings: Rose, William and John. Samuel, 18, was now a clicker (leather-cutter) in the shoe trade. In 1896 he married Ellen Elizabeth Bartram and by 1901 they were living at 113 Millers Lane, New Catton, with their daughter Hilda. By 1911 they had moved to 70 Grapes Hill. Samuel was still in the shoe trade but now as a pressman and Hilda had been joined by Nellie, Bessie and Samuel.

Samuel Baker enlisted in Norwich. His Army Service papers have not survived though his regimental numbers indicate he was a Territorial before they were given new six-digit numbers in January 1917. His age is problematic. Whether a volunteer or a conscript, he was too old. He would have been 41 or 42 at the start of the war, when the upper age limit for recruits was 30 (it was raised to 35 shortly afterwards). The upper age limit for conscripts under the Military Service Act of 1916 was 41 by which date he was 43 or 44, so, presumably, he lied about his age. His Medal Roll Index card gives no date for first entry into an overseas theatre of war, so it is possible he did not join the 1/5th Norfolks in Palestine until June or even July 1917 when it was rebuilding its strength after the heavy losses it had suffered at the 1st and 2nd battles of Gaza in March and April.

Private Samuel Baker, 45, was killed in action in Palestine on 13 July 1917. Not much was happening at this date and the Battalion's only casualties (three) were from Turkish shelling of their trenches outside Gaza. Official confirmation of his death reached Norwich quickly. His widow placed a death notice in the *Eastern Daily Press* only six days later. It included the words 'In the midst of life we are in death'. His photograph, showing him in uniform holding a small dog was placed in the Norfolk Library's Great War memorial collection by his family. He has no known grave. Samuel is commemorated at the Gaza War Cemetery, Gaza Strip, Palestine, and on the St Augustine's roll of honour. He was awarded the British War and Victory medals.

Private 25242 Arthur Cropp, 2nd Battalion, Norfolk Regiment

Arthur Cropp was born in the parish of St Augustine, Norwich, on 13 June 1895, the fourth surviving child of Harry Hunt Cropp, a shoemaker, grocer and general dealer, and Elizabeth Cropp née Gowing. Arthur's paternal grandparents, Philip Hunt and Maria Hunt née Cropp, had married in Norwich in 1868, four years after his father was born. It was presumably for this reason Arthur's father bore his mother's maiden surname, marrying under the surname Cropp in 1882 and being registered as Cropp in the 1891 and 1911 censuses, though not, curiously, in the 1901 Census when the whole family was recorded as [Forename] C. Hunt.

In 1891 the family, including Arthur's older siblings, Harry, George and Ernest, was at 29 Muspole Street in the parish of St Mary Coslany. In 1897 a younger sibling, Walter, died in infancy; another, Elizabeth, had died aged less than a year old just before the 1901 Census was taken in April, then Ernest died later that year, aged 2. By 1901 the family, including new additions Ethel and Arthur, had moved to 53 Bull Close Road in the parish of St James Pockthorpe, where Arthur's mother ran a grocery shop assisted by her eldest son, while their father worked at home fitting up (rough-cutting leather) for the shoe trade. By 1911 the family had moved again, to 5 Silver Road, Sprowston, a northern suburb of Norwich. Only four of the Cropp children survived into adulthood: George,

Ethel and Arthur, who were all still home assisting in the family's grocery business, and Harry, the eldest, who had married in 1904 and was living in Wodehouse Street off Silver Road, where he was running his own grocer's shop. On 11 February 1915 Arthur married Kate Robina Carey. They lived at 33 Spencer Street near Silver Road. A son, Donald, was born later that year.

Arthur enlisted in Norwich and served in the 2nd Battalion, Norfolk Regiment. His Army Service papers have not survived, but he appears to have been a 1916 conscript. He seems to have joined the 2nd Norfolks in Mesopotamia (part of present-day Iraq) as it was being comprehensively rebuilt. The bulk of the old, pre-war Regular Army battalion had been decimated by battle, disease and hunger before, during and after the siege of Kut and the bulk of its surviving remnants had gone into brutal captivity following the Kut garrison's surrender to the Turkish Army on 29 April 1916. A new, provisional 2nd Battalion was assembled in Basra, partly from stragglers from the old 2nd Norfolks who had been lucky enough not to have been among the besieged of Kut, but mainly from raw, inadequately prepared recruits straight from Britain, Arthur among them. The chief dangers they faced in Basra during 1916 were from heat-stroke and disease, in particular diphtheria and cholera. In February the 37th Brigade (14th Indian Division), of which the new, provisional 2nd Norfolks now formed a part, moved up from Basra to cross the Tigris and support the 1st Indian Army Corps' attempt to retake Kut. On 25 February 1917, as the Turkish Army was withdrawing from Kut, the 2nd Norfolks began to pursue them along the road to Baghdad. It was here Arthur was shot in his right leg and was taken for treatment at the 3rd Brigade General Hospital in Kut. Following the capture of Baghdad in March 1917, the 2nd Norfolks found themselves garrisoned at Baqubah about 50 km north-east of Baghdad for six months. At the height of summer conditions were excessively hot, dry and dusty, and in their insanitary, overcrowded encampment there was a serious outbreak of diphtheria. According to the regimental casualty list Arthur died of heat-stroke on 17 July 1917 at No. 3 Echelon, Basra, the location of the Mesopotamia Expeditionary Force's General HQ. However, given that he was buried in Baghdad, this seems unlikely. Arthur is buried at Baghdad (North Gate) War Cemetery, Iraq, grave no. IV.K.7. He was awarded the

British War and Victory medals. Although born in the parish, Arthur's name does not appear on St Augustine's roll of honour. He does, however, appear on St Mary's Baptist church roll of honour and on St Miles Coslany's roll of honour. To add to the confusion, *Norfolk Roll of Honour* lists him under the parish of St James Pockthorpe, where his wife and parents now resided.

Arthur's father was a Baptist Sunday school teacher and a leading member of the Norwich Baptist congregation that worshiped at St Mary's Baptist church in the parish of St Mary Coslany. On 11 December 1921 a memorial service was held in St Mary's for 24 members of the Baptist Men's Adult School 'who gave their lives for others'. The January 1922 issue of *Norwich Church*, a local Baptist magazine, notes that during the ceremony a war memorial was unveiled by Arthur's father: 'Brother H. Hunt Cropp, a teacher, who had lost a son in the war, and has been with the School since its commencement'. The war memorial in St Mary's Baptist church today *(below)* is a post-Second World War replacement for the original, which was destroyed by enemy bombing in 1942.

Private 6887 and 328195 Walter Ralph, 'A' Company, 1/1st Battalion, Cambridgeshire Regiment, formerly Private 6047, Norfolk Regiment

Walter Ralph was born in Norwich in 1892, the tenth surviving child of Henry John Ralph, a whitesmith and iron-foundry fitter, and Sarah Ann Ralph née Thurston. The family lived at 27 Leonards Street, a two-up, two-down terraced house in St Augustine. It must have been rather crowded. The 1911 Census records that Mrs Ralph had had 14 children; 11 were still living: Henry, Alfred, May, Maud, Herbert, Joseph, Ernest, George, Ethel, Walter and Arthur. Four of Walter's elder brothers were foundry workers like their father, as was Walter.

Walter's Army Service papers have not survived. *Soldiers Died in the Great War* records that he was in the Norfolk Regiment (possibly the 1st Battalion) before transferring to the Cambridgeshire Regiment. He was probably a 1916 conscript. The Cambridgeshire Regiment was one of only three British regiments composed entirely of Territorial battalions. Formed from the 3rd Volunteer Battalion, Suffolk Regiment in 1908, it comprised one front line battalion, the 1/1st, and three Reserve or Depot battalions. A part of the 118th Brigade, 34th Division, the 1/1st Cambridgeshires served with distinction on the Somme in 1916, particularly at the Schwaben Redoubt. Private Walter Ralph, 24, was killed in action on 31 July 1917. This was the first day of the 3rd Battle of Ypres (later known as Passchendaele), during an action known as the Battle of Pilckem Ridge in which the 1/1st Cambridgeshires lost more than 60 officers and men killed in action. He has no known grave. Ralph is commemorated at the Ypres (Menin Gate) Memorial, Ieper, Belgium, and on St Augustine's roll of honour. He was awarded the British War and Victory medals.

Ralph's younger brother, Private Arthur Ralph, served in a number of Reserve or Depot units with the Norfolk, Suffolk and Northamptonshire regiments before being transferred to the Labour Corps with which he finally went to France in August 1918 as part of an Area Employment Company.

Private 9694 John Henry Abigail, 'B' Company, 8th Battalion, Norfolk Regiment

Shot at dawn, Flanders, 12 September 1917. *(For Private Abigail's story see 'The 'necessary entracte' – the life of Private John Henry Abigail' on p.263.)*

Second Lieutenant Walter Horace Benn, 7th Battalion, Norfolk Regiment, formerly Corporal 52018, 28th Battalion, Middlesex Regiment (The Duke of Cambridge's Own)

Walter Horace Benn was born in Norwich, probably in the southern suburb of Lakenham, on 11 October 1890, the second child of William Joseph Benn and Emily Benn née Huggins. *(For more on Walter's family background see p.66.)* By 1901 the family had moved from Lakenham to 20 Ebenezer Terrace off Sussex Street, St Augustine's. Walter was a pupil at Norwich Municipal Secondary School, a Higher Grade school in nearby Duke Street. The 1911 Census records him still living with his parents in Ebenezer Terrace, aged 20, and employed as a correspondence clerk. On 3 August 1914, the day before the declaration of war against Germany, he married Ada Bertha Bunn in St Augustine's church. His trade, as stated in the marriage register, was now shoe-trimmer, though for which firm is not known. According to the Census, Ada was also a shoe-trimmer, specialising in fancy needlework. Like Walter she came

from a large family and also had eight siblings. After marriage Walter and Ada lived at East Bungalow in Brundall, a village a few miles east of Norwich near the Norfolk Broads. Prior to enlisting Walter was promoted to manager of the shoe-preparing department. His relatively rapid promotion perhaps reflected the drainage of skilled manpower from industry into the armed services.

Walter attested his willingness to serve in His Majesty's Armed Forces on 7 December 1915, four days before the end of the Derby Scheme of voluntary enlistment in which men committed to active service at a later date, if required. The scheme was particularly popular with older and married men as it demonstrated they weren't shirkers or cowards but postponed their actual call-up indefinitely. It was generally understood that the youngest and those unmarried would be mobilised first. Walter was now placed in the Army Reserve pending mobilisation, which for him occurred on 10 April 1916. He was now posted to the 28th Battalion, Middlesex Regiment, a Reserve unit kept in England for training purposes. He clearly made a good impression, for on 12 June, only two months after mobilisation, he was appointed lance corporal. On 1 September 1916 most of the regimental Reserve battalions were amalgamated into a series of training cadres. Walter was now transferred to the 102nd Battalion, a Training Reserve unit based at Corunna Barracks, Aldershot. Here on 16 December he was promoted again, to acting corporal. Not long after this he was recommended by his CO for a commission without even having attained the rank of full corporal. The slaughter on the Western Front fell disproportionately on junior officers and the Army had a desperate need for suitably qualified replacements. It was decided, reluctantly by many, to seek officer material outside the usual pool of the public school-educated gentry in order to find 'temporary gentlemen' from among the 'other ranks'. Walter's brother Bertie had himself been promoted from the ranks in June 1916, only to be killed on the Somme three weeks later. On 3 January 1917 Walter was posted to the 18th Officer Cadet School at Prior Park, Bath. On 15 February he wrote from there to the War Office on behalf of his parents, who were seeking information regarding back pay and unpaid allowances due to them as next of kin of his late brother Bertie. On 24 April he received a temporary commission as a 2nd lieutenant on probation. He had expressed a preference for the Norfolk Regiment and he was duly posted to the 7th Battalion, then entrenched near Arras, part of the 35th Brigade, 12th (Eastern) Division. He arrived in France on 19 June 1917.

Second Lieutenant Walter Benn, 26, was killed in action six weeks after arriving on the Western Front. Having fought each other to a standstill at Arras in the spring, British and German divisions glared at each other across no man's land throughout May, June and July until around 9 p.m. on 2 August when the sound of a horn was heard coming from the German lines. The 7th Norfolks at this moment were defending the Front in a series of evocatively named trenches: Pick Cave, Pick Avenue, Saddle Support Trench, Hook Trench and Tool Trench. German reconnaissance aircraft had buzzed back and forth over the Front all day, directing their artillery to rain down mortar shells and gas. Then at 9 p.m. the Germans launched a major trench raid. At this moment, Walter was on duty with 'D' Company in the centre of the line. This was the first trench to be overrun, forcing the rapid evacuation of its survivors. On their left, the officer in command of 'C' Company, 2nd Lieutenant Merwyn Allen, realising they were in danger of being similarly overrun, led his men out of their trench and drove off the enemy with bayonets until he was shot through the head and killed. Another officer from 'C' Company went over to see if he could make contact with the remnants of Walter's 'D' company but never returned and was presumed killed or taken prisoner. The 7th Norfolks suffered about 90 casualties, killed, wounded or missing in this raid. Their CO, Lieutenant Colonel F. E. Walton, writing up the incident later, made what seems to be the first and last mention of Walter in the Battalion's War Diary:

> 'D' Company was in charge of Sec Lieut F. A. HAYLOCK with Sec Lieut BENNS [sic]. The latter was killed early in the evening by a rifle bullet. Sec Lieut HAYLOCK, assisted by Sergt J. S. JOHNSON constructed a bombing block in TOOL TRENCH and personally reconnoitred the position. The enemy barrage ceased at about 10 p.m.

The phrase 'early in the evening' suggests Walter died before the trench raid began, perhaps shot by a sniper during the earlier barrage, which had started at around six. Second Lieutenant Frank Arthur Haylock, a Norfolk man who survived the war and became the rector of Booton church, was, like Walter, promoted from the ranks, having enlisted as a private in the 28th Battalion, Canadian Expeditionary Force. Sergeant James Samuel Johnson DCM MM and Bar, was killed in action on 14 October 1917 in what seems to have been the away leg of this raid, a notorious occasion in which discipline appears to have broken down and the British raiding party, having captured a German trench, killed at least 200 German soldiers who had already surrendered. Walter's Army Service papers note repeatedly that he was attached to the Machine Gun Corps after being commissioned, presumably the 35th Brigade's Machine Gun Company; however, neither the 7th Norfolk's nor the 35th MGC's war diaries for this period appear to have any mention of him.

Ada received the dreadful telegram informing her of her husband's death on 9 August. Papers held among Walter's Service papers record the distressing struggle she had with military bureaucracy to obtain a death certificate and a copy of his will, as well as to recover his meagre personal effects: a wrist watch, a pocket book, some photos, a leather purse, a collar stud, two tie pins and a photo case with photo and a lock of hair – Ada's? The lack of the necessary documents left her in straitened financial circumstances, as without them she could not obtain the pay and allowances lying in Walter's Army bank account or claim the insurance money due to her on her husband dying on active service. The intervention of the rector of St Augustine's, the Revd J. H. Griffiths, eventually helped move matters along. After several letters and much red tape it was finally established that Walter had either not left a will or it had been lost. Ada had therefore to go to Probate to establish her right to her late husband's estate, which when it was proved in 1919 amounted to a little over £126.

There is a separate family memorial to Walter and his older brother Bertie situated in the church's north nave aisle: an engraved marble plaque with a crowned cross. At the base is a verse from the Book of Revelations: 'Be Thou faithful unto death and I will give thee a crown of life'. *(See p. 75)*. The part that relates to Walter reads:

Also of Lieut W. H. Benn / (of the 7th Norfolk) /
Brother of the above / Who died in action in France /
August 2nd 1917 Aged 26 years.

A photograph of Walter in officer's uniform was placed in the Norfolk Libraries' Great War memorial collection. Another photograph in the Royal Norfolk Regimental Museum shows him arm-in-arm with a young woman, presumably Ada. Walter is buried at Monchy British Cemetery, Monchy-le-Preux, Pas de Calais, France, grave no. I.F.33, and is commemorated also on St Augustine's roll of honour and on a brass plaque in St Laurence church, Brundall. He was awarded the British War and Victory medals.

Private 41960 William Sidney Willsea, 1st Battalion, Essex Regiment, formerly Private 27011, 3rd (Reserve) Battalion, Norfolk Regiment

William Sidney Willsea was born in the parish of St Augustine, Norwich, on 18 March 1891, the fourth child of Albert Joshua Willsea and Phoebe Willsea née Armes, who had married in Norwich in 1868. His father was an iron-worker and later a shellfish dealer. His mother was a brush-maker. William had three older siblings: Joshua, James and Ethel, and a younger sister, Edith. In 1901 the

family was at 15 Cross Street off Sussex Street, St Augustine's. William was a pupil at St Augustine's Junior Boys School. His mother died in 1903 and in 1910 his father remarried, to a widow, Mrs Lucy Clara Nichols. By 1911 William, 20, had moved with his father, step-mother, younger sister Edith and step-sister Phyllis Nichols to 23 Oak Street, and was working as an assistant in his father's shellfish business. In 1913 William married Clara Blyth. They lived at 45 Sussex Street and had a daughter, Mabel, born 1914.

William enlisted in Norwich on 1 November 1916 and was posted first to the Norfolk Regiment's Reserve, the 3rd Battalion, then to the 1st Battalion, Essex Regiment. His Army Service papers have not survived but given the date of his death, 16 August 1917, he was almost certainly killed in action, aged 26, at the Battle of Langemarck during the 3rd Battle of Ypres. His death notice did not appear in the *Eastern Daily Press* until almost a month later, suggesting he was initially reported missing. The *Eastern Daily Press* published one each from his widow, sisters, brothers and sisters-in-law, and from his father and stepmother. His widow's included the verse:

O, why was he taken so young and fair,
One of the best, we all loved so dear.
Hard was the blow that compelled me to part
With one so long and dear to my heart.
Wife and little girl

William is commemorated at the Tyne Cot Memorial, Zonnebeke, Belgium, and on St Augustine's roll of honour. He was awarded the British War and Victory medals.

William's eldest brother Joshua was a private in the Cheshire Regiment and then the Labour Corps. His elder brother James was a private in the Royal Army Medical Corps. Both survived the war.

Gunner 875892 (formerly 2269) Percy Hewitt, 95th Brigade, Royal Horse Artillery and Royal Field Artillery (Territorial Force)

Percy Hewitt was born in the parish of St Augustine, Norwich, in 1892, the eighth child of Robert William Hewitt, a bricklayer's labourer, and Martha Hewitt née Clarke. Percy's older siblings were Charles, Alice, George, William, Ada, Edith and Ernest. He also had a younger brother, Herbert. In the 1891 Census the family was in Heigham but had presumably moved to St Augustine's by 1892. By 1901 the family had moved to 142 Aylsham Road, though without Charles and Alice who had left home. By 1911 the family had moved again, to 34 Berners Street, Mile Cross, a north-western suburb. Now only Ada, Edith, Percy and Herbert were still at home. The 1911 Census records that Percy, 19, was a porter at a blind asylum, possibly the Norwich Asylum and School for the Indigent Blind on Magdalen Street.

Percy enlisted in Norwich, probably as a 1916 conscript. His Army Service papers have not survived but *Soldiers Died in the Great War* records that he served in Territorial Force brigades of both the Royal Horse Artillery (RHA) and the Royal Field Artillery (RFA). Gunner Percy Hewitt, 25, died of wounds on 26 September 1917. The Commonwealth War Graves Commission notes that he was serving in the 95th Brigade RFA at the time of his death, which was attached to the 21st Division at this date. It is possible, therefore, that

Percy died of wounds received on the first day of the Battle of Polygon Wood during the 3rd Battle of Ypres. Percy is buried at the Westouter Churchyard Cemetery, Heuvelland, Belgium, grave no. II.E.4. He is not commemorated on the St Augustine's roll of honour. He was awarded the British War and Victory medals.

Private 30755 William Robert Bovill,
1st Battalion, Devonshire Regiment,
formerly Private 19415, Wiltshire Regiment

Unravelling William Robert Bovill's ancestry has proved problematic. He may have been born in Norwich in 1896 or 1897, the son or possibly adopted son of Walter James Bovill, an Army pensioner who was then a timekeeper at a silk crepe factory, and Mary Bovill. His earliest appearance in national records under the name William Robert Bovill does not occur until the 1911 Census, when he was recorded, aged 13, living with his parents and three younger siblings, Annie, Walter and Flossie, at 7 Bertie Road off Vicarage Road, New Catton, a northern suburb of Norwich. The births of none of these children (who are all recorded in the Census, like their mother, as born in Norwich), were registered under the surname Bovill by the General Register Office, suggesting they were registered under their mother's maiden name, which is not known. William's parents, Walter and Mary, were not in fact married, for the very good reason that Walter was married already and had a second family in another part of Norwich.

Born in Portsmouth in 1859, the son of a timber merchant, William's father, Walter James Bovill had married Ellen Blanch Williams of North Camp, Farnborough, in the bride's parish church on 11 March 1886. According to the marriage register he was a 'Drum Major in the Regiment' and garrisoned in St Helier, Jersey. Ellen was the daughter of a prison warder. By 1901 a Mrs Ellen Bovill, presumably the same person, was a laundress living in Mousehold Street in the parish of St James Pockthorpe, Norwich, with her children Ellen, Medora, Geletty and James. The children's places of birth – the Channel Islands, Ireland and Norwich – suggest the peripatetic life of a soldier's wife. Her widowed father, James Williams, the former gaoler, was also a member of the Mousehold

Street household. In the same Census Walter Bovill is recorded on his own in Royal Oak Yard off Oak Street and employed as a gaslighter at a silk mill, possibly St Mary's Mill, also in Oak Street. Whether they had permanently separated is not known. By 1911 Ellen Bovill had moved to Longs Yard, Fishergate, with her daughters Medora and Geletty, and new additions Aileen and Edna. Ellen and James are absent. Ellen Bovill is described in the Census unusually as both married and head of the household, suggesting she and Walter were now living completely separate lives but were not able or willing to divorce. Bizarrely, the 1911 Census return self-completed by Walter Bovill states he had been married for 24 years, though clearly not to the woman he was currently sharing a home with.

William enlisted in Norwich. His Army Service papers have not survived but his Medal Roll Index card records that he first went overseas on 5 November 1915 to join the 1/4th Battalion, Wiltshire Regiment, then garrisoned in India, first in the Meerut Divisional area and later in Poona, before being transferred to the 75th Division in Palestine in September 1917. At some point, William was posted to the 1st Battalion, Devonshire Regiment in Flanders, part of 95th Brigade, 5th Division. He was killed in action during the 3rd Battle of Ypres (later known as Passchendaele) on 4 October 1917, aged 20. On this day, 13 British and ANZAC Divisions of General Plumer's 2nd Army advanced along an eight-mile front to the north-east of Ypres, churned by incessant rain and shelling into a murderous swamp. The bitter fighting here became known as the Battle of Broodseinde, one of the so-called 'bite and hold' battles of the 3rd Ypres. Judged an Allied victory and a turning point in the war, the ground gained was just 700 yards at a cost of 26,000 casualties, killed, wounded or missing, on the British and ANZAC side alone. The 1st Devons lost 56 men killed in action with more than 200 wounded or missing. William appears to have been counted among the missing presumed dead as his Medal Roll Index card has a note 'Death Regarded 4.10.17'. He has no known grave.

William's connection with St Augustine's parish is probably explained by the fact that his father, Walter, is recorded in the 1916 Electoral Roll as owning or leasing property at 6 Leonards Street, St Augustine's, a property right which entitled him to vote in local and general elections before universal male suffrage was introduced in 1918. In the 1918 'Absent Voters' Electoral Roll for Norwich, William was also registered as a voter, though in fact posthumously, at 6 Leonards Street. A Mrs M. A. Aldous of 13 Napier Street, Norwich, is listed as his sister by the Commonwealth War Graves Commission. A Mary Ann Bovill married a Frederick Aldous in Norwich in 1923. She is presumably the same person, though no sibling relationship has been discovered with William. William is commemorated at the Tyne Cot Memorial, Zonnebeke, Belgium, and also on St Augustine's roll of honour. He was awarded the 1915 Star and the British War and Victory medals.

Private 31793 Walter George Coxford, 11th Battalion, Northumberland Fusiliers, formerly Private 218157, 1/1st Battalion, London Regiment (Royal Fusiliers)

Walter George Coxford was born in Norwich in 1894, the fourth child of George Coxford, a shoemaker, and Elizabeth Coxford née Newman. In 1901 the family was at 18 Rosebery Road, New Catton, a suburb north of St Augustine's. At this date there were seven brothers: William, 18, a packer in the shoe trade, Leonard, Sydney, Walter, Harry, George and John. The family was still here in 1911 and now included Ada, Donald, Nellie and May. Walter's two eldest brothers had left home: William was a salesman in Beverley, Yorkshire, while Leonard was only a few streets away from Rosebery Road in lodgings occupied by ten members of the Brown family. This was an era when such large families were almost the norm. The 1911 Census records that Walter's mother had 13 children including three who had died in infancy. Four days after the Census was taken Leonard married his landlord's daughter, Harriet Brown in St Augustine's church.

Walter Coxford enlisted in Norwich, probably as a 1916 conscript. While his Army Service papers have not survived, his entry in *Soldiers Died in the Great War* notes that before joining the Northumberland Fusiliers he had served in the Royal Fusiliers, the London-based regiment. Moreover, his six-figure Service number indicates he was a member of one of the Royal Fusilier's affiliated Territorial battalions, the 1/1st Battalion, London Regiment, in early 1917 when all serving

Terriers were renumbered. Walter seems to have gone over to France for the first time with this unit. A letter written in France at the end of August by his younger brother Harry to their mother mentions that Walter had recently been seen in a rest camp by a friend. The 1/1st Battalion, London Regiment, fought on the Somme in the Abbeville sector as part of the 56th (London) Division from 1 July through to the end of October, suffering around 350 casualties.

It isn't known when Walter was transferred to the Northumberland Fusiliers but it was certainly before 22 September 1917 when he married Gladys Nellie Wilson in St Augustine's church. The couple's stated address in the register was 36 Leonards Street, St Augustine's, the bride's parents' home. Their married life was all too short. Three weeks after the ceremony Walter was dead, killed in action during the 3rd Battle of Ypres on 14 October 1917. The 11th Northumberland Fusilier's War Diary records that between 11 and 16 October the Battalion was entrenched at Joist Farm near Dickebusch where the front line consisted of no more than a very muddy trench strung between a series of rain-filled shell craters. Here they endured constant shelling, losing over the five days they were on duty here 22 killed, 67 wounded and nine missing. On the morning of the 14th, the War Diary records that 'C' Company was very heavily shelled, losing around ten men including two of its platoon commanders. Interestingly, another of the Battalion's casualties this day was also a Norwich man, Private Henry Dickerson.

Walter's bride of three weeks, now his widow, placed a death notice in the *Eastern Daily Press* on 6 November 1917 with the verse:

I shall not forget him, I loved him deeply,
For his memory to fade from my mind like a dream,
The lips need not speak, when the heart mourns sincerely,
And thoughts often dwell where they seldom are seen.

Walter parents', brothers' and sisters' notice, published on the same day as his widow's, remembered both Walter and Harry, who had died on the Somme in 1916. It included a verse and two lines of prose that are openly critical of war and British jingoism:

Dear sons and brothers, we mourn you
Victims of war's cruel reign,

Cut off in your early manhood
Through man's lust for power and gain.

Another loved one sacrificed, a lifelong sorrow.
This is the price we pay for England's boasted greatness.

Considering how rigidly controlled the press was during the war, it is extraordinary that this very rare example of public dissent got past the censor. War-weariness and disillusionment among both the troops and civilians was mounting in 1917. Although hardly reported at home, there had been widespread mutinies in the armies of Britain's principal allies, France, Italy and Russia. British and Anzac soldiers had rioted at Étaples in September. This was also the year in which decorated war poet 2nd lieutenant Siegfried Sassoon wrote his famous letter to *The Times*, critical of the government's conduct of the war. Little if any of these events are likely to have been known to the Coxford family but their outburst in the local newspaper's deaths column is indicative of a nationwide sense that it had already sacrificed too much – and would it ever end? Walter has no known grave and is commemorated at the Tyne Cot Memorial, Zonnebeke, Belgium, and also on the roll of honour in Christ Church, New Catton. He is not commemorated on St Augustine's roll of honour. He was awarded the British War and Victory medals.

Four of Walter's brothers were members of the armed services during the war. Leonard was a rigger in the Royal Flying Corps and Royal Air Force until 1919. Sydney was a private, first in the Norfolk Regiment and then in the 1/7th Battalion, Royal Warwickshire Regiment, in France in 1917. George was a private in the 2nd (City of London) Regiment and the Royal Fusiliers. Harry was a private in the Norfolk Regiment's 2/6th (Cyclist) Battalion, and 1st Battalion, and was killed in action on the Somme on 4 September 1916 during the fierce fighting at Falfemont Farm where four St Augustine's men died: Arthur Cannell, Ernest Loome, Ernest Plunkett and George Scott. In 2007 Ronald Coxford published *A Half Crown Holy Boy* based on letters his uncle Harry Coxford wrote to his mother and other family members while serving with the Norfolk Regiment. These frequently mention Walter. Harry appears to have been the first of the brothers to enlist. As rumour spread in the latter half of 1915 that some sort of compulsory enlistment might be introduced,

Harry sought to reassure his worried mother that Sid and Walter were unlikely to be called up, recommending that they 'fit a yarn up & say they're on war work or something like that'. Inevitably, both were called up. On 28 August 1916, Harry mentioned in a letter to his mother that he had just written to Walter, then in a rest camp. 'I dare say he could do with it after being up the line. I hope I shall see him before long, so long as we can keep safe and well it don't matter about roughing it.' They would never see each other again.

Private 3/7471 Thomas Elsegood, 7th (Service) Battalion, Norfolk Regiment, formerly Private, 3rd (Reserve) Battalion and 1st Battalion, Norfolk Regiment

Thomas Elsegood was born in the parish of St Mary Coslany, Norwich, in 1893, the second child of Thomas Elsegood, a weaver, and Amelia Elsegood née Bulldeath. He had three sisters: Emily, who died in 1896 aged 10; Rose, who died in infancy in 1901; and Alice, the only one to outlive him. Born in 1899 she died in 1978 aged 78. The 1901 Census records the family at 3 Cartwrights Yard in the parish of St Mary Coslany. At this date Thomas's parents were silk-weavers; his father had previously been a horsehair-weaver and would be so again. The family was still at Cartwright Yard in 1911, by which date Thomas, 17, was a shoemaker.

Thomas enlisted in Norwich on 31 December 1912 and was posted to the 3rd (Reserve) Battalion, Norfolk Regiment. His surviving Army Service papers include a reference obtained by the Regiment's recruiting officer from Albert Parnell, foreman at Sexton & Sons, one of largest shoe manufacturers in Norwich with a factory in St Mary's Plain. Prior to leaving the firm on 19 December 1912 due to 'slackness of trade', Thomas had worked there for five or six years, having presumably started straight from school, aged 13 or 14. At 5ft 4 Thomas was two inches below the average height for the period but was otherwise considered suitable Army material despite having flat feet. Other than drill and musketry practice, he seems not to have been required to do much soldiering until 8 August 1914, four days after Britain's declaration of war against Germany, when he was mobilised in Norwich and transferred to the Norfolk Regiment's 1st Battalion, the bulk of which was busy preparing to sail from Belfast to join the British Expeditionary Force in France. By the time Thomas joined them in France at the beginning of September the 1st Norfolks had already fought at Mons and was now fighting a rearguard action to within sight of Paris.

Nothing more is known of Thomas's movements until March 1915. The 1st Norfolks were then entrenched close to St Eloi near Ypres in Flanders. It was a relatively quiet period in this sector but the daily hazards of trench warfare went on regardless. Here on the 7th Thomas received a shrapnel wound to the head and neck, necessitating hospitalisation, first at Poperinghe and then at Rouen for 10 days. He rejoined his unit on 29 March. During April the 1st Norfolks fought in the 2nd Battle of Ypres where they were principally engaged in trying to capture a commanding mound of earth known as Hill 60. The 2nd Battle of Ypres went on until 25 May and is chiefly remembered for the first recorded use of chlorine gas as a battlefield weapon. On 5 May the 1st Norfolks had 75 casualties from gas while at St Eloi. During June the Battalion was entrenched at Verbranden Molen. Here on 11 June, Thomas was wounded again, shot in the leg, fracturing the tibia (lower leg bone), which required hospital treatment in Rouen. This time his wound was judged a 'Blighty one', one of the highly prized wounds that without being life-threatening, got you shipped home. Thomas embarked for England on 16 June where he remained for nine months. On arrival he was immediately transferred, at least on paper, from the strength of the Norfolk Regiment's 1st Battalion to its Depot at Britannia Barracks in Norwich while hospitalised. On 10 September, having presumably recovered sufficiently to return to non-combatant duties, he was posted to his pre-war unit, the 3rd (Reserve) Battalion and sent for training at Halton Park Camp near Wendover in Buckinghamshire. This estate, owned by Baron Alfred de Rothschild, had been made available to the War Office in 1914 and would later become a Royal Flying Corps aerodrome. At this period, however, estate land had been dug up to replicate a Western Front trench system for training troops in trench warfare. Here on Monday 4 October 1915 Thomas was arrested for having overstayed his pass by 44 hours and 20 minutes. There may have been extenuating circumstances as he was given a relatively light punishment of three days confined to barracks with apparently no deduction of pay. On 23 March 1916, Thomas returned to France and served there throughout the Somme campaign. It isn't clear from his papers whether he now rejoined the 1st Norfolks; indeed there's a suggestion he may have transferred, at least on paper, to the Regiment's 7th Battalion, part of the 35th Infantry Brigade, 12th (Eastern) Division. According to his Active Service form, on 29 July he was temporarily attached to the 70th Field Company, Royal Engineers, which, like the 7th Norfolks, was part of the 12th Division. Then on 8 August he was posted to the 7th Norfolks.

On 6 April 1917, Thomas was attached to No. 143 Siege Battery, Royal Garrison Artillery, a heavy howitzer unit. It was presumably while attached to this battery that he fell foul of military discipline for a second time and much more seriously. On 13 April, he was tried by Field General Court Martial, charged with what basically amounted to looting, an offence for which, if found guilty while on active service in a foreign land, the maximum punishment allowed under the Army Act then in force was death. No British soldier was executed during the First World War for this offence and it seems that in Private Elsegood's case the charge against him were deliberately modified to exclude mention of looting or plunder. It was alleged that on 9 April 1917, the first day of the Battle of Arras and three day after joining No. 143 Siege Battery, he had entered an unoccupied, furnished room in Arras, the property of a Madame Langlart, a French citizen, and stolen a table knife, a looking glass, an ivory whistle and a brooch. On the main charge, that of 'conduct while on active service in prejudice of good order and military discipline' the court found him not guilty. On an alternative charge of 'committing an offence against the property of a citizen of the country in which he was serving' he was found guilty and sentenced to nine months 'IHL' (imprisonment with hard labour). Three months of this were immediately remitted by Brigadier General Berkeley Vincent, commander of the 35th Brigade at Arras, who had only recently narrowly escaped death when a shell buried him alive and killed most of his staff. The sentence was promulgated, that is, read out to the soldier in front of as many of his comrades as could be mustered, on 2 May.

It isn't clear where Thomas served his sentence but it seems to have been in France rather than Britain, perhaps at one of the railheads or ports where men were needed to do hard, physical labour all day every day. He was released on 2 September, two months early, and returned to the 7th Norfolks; meaning he had only had to serve four out of the original nine month sentence. Early release would prove to be a death sentence as 39 days later on 14 October 1917 Private Thomas Elsegood, 24, was killed during a British trench raid near Monchy-le-Preux south-east of the town of Arras. He has no known grave. The 7th Norfolks' War Diary notes of this bloody encounter: 'Our men could not be prevented from killing those that surrendered and it is estimated that at least 200 Germans were killed by the raiders'. Only 30 prisoners were taken. The regimental history published after the war omitted all mention of the fact that German soldiers who had already surrendered had been killed, implying instead that matters had simply got out of hand in the heat of battle: 'The men appear to have been particularly exasperated by a long series of trench bombardments at this time, for little quarter was given'. The British losses amounted on the day to 23 killed or died of wounds, including five platoon commanders, 11 missing and 38 wounded. Thomas is commemorated at the Arras Memorial, Pas de Calais, France. He is not listed on the St Augustine's roll of honour. He was awarded the 1914 Star with Bar and the British War and Victory medals.

Thomas's father served as a private in the Royal Defence Corps between 3 February 1915 and 24 May 1918, when he was discharged aged 58 due to sickness. He was then awarded the Silver War Badge.

Private T/290094 Arthur William Copland, 42nd Divisional Train, Army Service Corps

Arthur William Copland was born in the parish of St Mary Coslany in 1880, the second child of Henry Samuel Copland, an upholsterer, and Harriet Copland née Hannah. In 1881 the family, including Arthur and his sister Kate, was at 2 St Mary's Plain. They later moved to Heigham, an industrial suburb west of St Mary Coslany; first to Northumberland Street and then, by 1901, to Heigham Street. The family now included Leonard and Henry. By this period,

Arthur, 20, was a currier (leather worker). In 1908 he married Edith Yallop, a tailor's presser, and by 1911 they were living at 165 Heigham Street. They had three daughters: Bessie, Edith and Hilda.

Arthur enlisted in Norwich and was posted to the Army Service Corps (ASC), the British Army's logistics experts. His Army Service papers have not survived and the next known fact is that he was killed in action in Belgium on 17 October 1917. At the time of his death he was in the ASC's 42nd Divisional Train, the supply column of the 42nd (East Lancashire) Division. Between late September and early November, the 42nd Division was defending the western-most extent of the trench system that ran from the Belgian coast to Switzerland. Their sector near Nieuport (Nieuwpoort) was comparatively quiet at this period; however, the usual hazards of trench warfare were ever-present even in the quietest sector of the Front. The War Diary of another 42nd Division unit, the 1/8th Battalion, Manchester Regiment, notes that on the day Arthur died enemy shells fell on Coxyde (Koksijde), which was several kilometres behind the front line, the shells fired perhaps by one of the German's super heavy howitzers nicknamed 'Big Berthas'. Two other ASC personnel, Corporal George Hushen and Lance Corporal W. G. Young died on the same day and are buried in the same cemetery as Arthur, which suggests they were all killed in the same incident. Arthur is buried at Coxyde Military Cemetery, Koksijde, Belgium, and commemorated also on St Barnabas roll of honour, Heigham. *Norfolk Roll of Honour* lists him under St Barnabas's parish but with the wrong first initial, 'H' rather than 'A'. He was awarded the British War and Victory medals.

Lance Corporal 2050 Clarence Frederick Neasham, 2nd Infantry Battalion (New South Wales), Australian Imperial Force

Clarence Frederick Neasham was born in Bournemouth, Hampshire, on 12 November 1895, the first child of Frederick Neasham, a soldier and, later, tram driver, originally from Whorlton, County Durham, and Ellen Jane Neasham née Dix of Norwich. His parents were married in Norwich in 1894 while his father, a trooper in the King's Dragoon Guards, was stationed there. By the time of Clarence's birth his parents had moved to Hampshire, following the Regiment's move to Aldershot. In 1897 a second son, Leonard Victor, was born in Bournemouth. A third, Ronald Leslie, was born in Aldershot in 1899.

By March 1901 the Neasham family was back in Norwich, at 114 Beaconsfield Road, a street of substantial, late-Victorian terraced houses off Magdalen Road in the parish of St James Pockthorpe. Over the following decade the family moved house regularly, though within a very narrow compass, around this part of Norwich. Clarence's father had retired from the cavalry by this date and was now a tramcar driver on the city's newly laid electric tram system. Clarence attended Bull Close Junior Boys School from 11 April 1904 to 12 March 1906, when the attendance register notes he left the neighbourhood. Interestingly, he was registered under his second forename, Fred. His home address now was 121 Knowsley Road, one road north of Beaconsfield Road. Five weeks after leaving Bull Close

Juniors he was admitted at Bull Close Senior Boys School, where he remained until 21 November 1909, leaving soon after his 14th birthday. He then received a further 10 months' secondary education at the Boys Model School in Princes Street in the commercial heart of the city. His home address was now 21 Stacey Road on the west side of Magdalen Road. On leaving the Model School on 3 November 1910, the attendance register notes that Clarence took a job in a shop selling diary produce. By 1911 the Neashams had moved again, one road north of Stacey Road to 42 Guernsey Road. The family had by now grown with the addition of two daughters, Audrey, born in 1904, and

Dorothy in 1908. Clarence, 15, was now employed by the General Post Office as a telegraph messenger. In March the following year he was appointed an assistant postman.

On 27 June 1913 Clarence, aged 17 years and 7 months, enlisted for four years' service in the 1st East Anglian Brigade, a Territorial unit of the Royal Field Artillery. Clarence's trade, as stated on his Attestation papers, was now a blacksmith's striker for the Norwich Tramway Company. Presumably, he had taken up the chance to work in the engineering workshop of his father's employer. Men who signed up for part-time soldiering with the Territorials agreed to attend a fixed number of weekend drills, hence their nickname, 'Saturday Night Soldiers', as well as an annual fortnight-long camp out, usually in August. The Territorials' role in Britain's armed services was purely defensive; its members had no obligation to serve overseas unlike Regular servicemen. Territorials were able to retain their full-time employment and live at home, while the allowance they received was a useful supplement in poor households. Becoming a Terrier also provided many young men with the sort of camaraderie and opportunity for adventure that 50 weeks a year in a factory or office could probably never provide.

On 6 February 1914, having completed less than a year of his agreed four years' service, Clarence was honourably discharged at his own request under the provisions of paragraph 156(3) of the Territorial Force Regulations. There had to be a very good reason to be granted a discharge and Clarence certainly had one, for by this date he had been living in Australia for at least two months. His absence from drill between October 1913 and February 1914 was, for some reason, not noted in his record. Despite having emigrated less than four months after joining up, his Service papers state he had completed 248 days' service, which was clearly impossible. The conclusion that discreet veils were drawn and blind eyes turned in the case of a young man of good character, the son of an old trooper, cannot be discounted.

Clarence embarked on SS *Indrapura* at Tilbury on 14 October 1913, bound for Melbourne. Little is known about his first years in Australia. A few clues may be gleaned from his obituary and from the soldier's will he wrote in October 1915 while in a military hospital in the Mediterranean in which he left £10 to a Mrs Jane Appleby of

Brilliant Street, Bathurst, New South Wales. According to Clarence's obituary, published in *The Bathurst Times* on 13 December 1917, Mrs Appleby was Clarence's aunt. A brief notice of her death appeared in the *Sydney Morning Herald* in 1925: 'Mrs Jane Appleby, a resident of south Bathurst, for many years a prominent worker in the Anglican Church, died in Sydney.' Clarence's obituary mentions that he had been employed by the railway engineering workshop in Bathurst for 18 months prior to enlisting. In Sydney on 13 January 1915 Clarence attested his willingness to serve in the Australian Army, claiming to be 21 when he was 19, which is curious as the minimum legal age for enlistment in the Australian Imperial Force (AIF) was 18. Competition for places in the Australian expeditionary force was intense and Clarence may have calculated he stood a better chance of getting in if he appeared to be slightly more mature. However, this wasn't his only exaggeration. His father, named as next of kin, was described as a sergeant-major in the King's Dragoon Guards, whereas he appears never to have risen above the rank of corporal. He also claimed to have served six months in the Royal Field Artillery when he had barely served three – falsehoods designed, presumably, like adding two years to his age, to better his chances of his being immediately accepted for military service overseas. In fact, he probably needn't have worried. His medical report gives his height as 5ft 9, about 3 inches above the average adult male of this period. His work as a blacksmith's striker had presumably helped develop his physique as he was half an inch taller than when he joined the Territorials in Norwich 19 months earlier. Passed fit for service, he took the oath which formally enlisted him in the AIF the following day at Liverpool, New South Wales.

Curiously, the Australian Nominal Roll for the Great War lists Clarence as a lance corporal in the 1st Light Horse Regiment; however, nothing in his surviving Army Service papers corroborates this. His first posting was on 12 March 1915, when he was placed in the 1st Australian Army Division's 5th Reinforcements Battalion, which was then training raw recruits preparatory to them joining the 2nd Australian Infantry Battalion (New South Wales Regiment) at Gallipoli. In a little over two months Clarence would be there too. On 13 April 1915 he embarked from Sydney on HMAT *Kyarra*, an elegantly appointed, Clyde-built passenger steamer that had been pressed into service as a hospital ship in 1914 and then hastily converted to a troop ship in 1915 to help supply the beleaguered ANZACs (Australian and New Zealand Army Corps) in the Dardanelles Peninsula with reinforcements. Clarence finally joined the 2nd AIF Battalion at Gallipoli on 22 June after a two-month-long voyage, which seems to have been broken by prolonged stops in Ceylon and Egypt. Although he had mercifully missed the carnage of the Anzac's first beach landing on 25 April in which the 2nd Infantry Battalion lost around 500 men, killed, wounded or missing, the physical conditions he found in the tiny Allied enclave known as Anzac Cove would have been appalling, with disease and exposure claiming many more casualties than Turkish rifles and shells. Just over two months after arriving, Clarence suffered a hernia and was sent to recuperate at a military hospital in Mudros on the nearby Greek island of Lemnos. Ironically, his injury may well have saved his life. While he was receiving treatment the Anzacs launched an attack on a Turkish position known as Lone Pine, suffering more than 2,000 casualties, killed, wounded and missing. On 10 August Clarence was discharged from hospital, though rated as yet only fit class B. He was now sent to the Anzac's advanced base camp at Kephalos on the nearby Greek island of Imbros. Here he promptly acquired a stomach bug, which laid him low with gastro-enteritis, sending him straight back to hospital in Mudros. By the time he was fit enough to resume duty the Gallipoli campaign was all but over, the Allies having secretly withdrawn from the Peninsula in a meticulously planned and executed manoeuvre that left the Turkish Army facing empty trenches on the morning of 9 January 1916.

While all of this was going on Clarence had sailed from Lemnos to Egypt on board SS *Huntsgreen*, a captured German steamer, disembarking at Alexandria on 28 December 1915. From here he was moved to the Australian Army camp at Tel-el-Kabir, site of a famous battle fought 33 years earlier between British and Egyptian forces. This huge, tented city housed 40,000 battle-weary troops with little to do and nowhere to go. Unsurprisingly, discipline was a problem. On 24 January 1916 Clarence broke camp and went AWOL for 48 hours, for which he received seven days' Field Punishment No. 2. This comprised being manacled and shackled for up to two hours each day as well as extra fatigue duties and drill. Two months later

Clarence sailed from Alexandria with the 2nd Infantry Battalion, now part of No 1 Anzac Corps, on SS *Invernia* bound for Marseilles. Clarence's otherwise detailed Army Service papers now have a gap of nearly five months without any recorded incident. There was in fact plenty going on. The 2nd Battalion, which arrived in Marseilles on 28 March 1916, had embarked on a long train journey north, ending at Hazebrouck in French Flanders in early April.

After a fairly uneventful couple of months in the trenches, the time came in mid-July for the 2nd AIF Battalion to do its bit in the great Somme Offensive. On 23 July the Battalion went over the top at Pozières and during two days' hand-to-hand fighting lost more than 500 men, killed, wounded and missing. After being relieved, the 2nd Battalion began to rebuild its strength at Pernois. It was probably here that Clarence was appointed lance corporal, on 11 August, only 20 months after enlisting. With such huge losses, promotion was much more rapid that it had been in peacetime. A week later the 2nd Battalion was in action again, at Mouquet Farm. During this battle Clarence's hernia flared up again and he spent the next six days moving up the medical evacuation chain, from a RAMC Field Ambulance to Casualty Clearing Station No. 4 at Beauval, and then on to the 8th Stationary Hospital at Wimereux near Boulogne. From here he was discharged to the 1st Australian Divisional Base at Étaples. Five days of the harsh conditions here that would contribute to a riot and near mutiny a little over a year later, Clarence's hernia flared once again and he was admitted to No. 26 General Hospital at Étaples for a couple of days rest before being ferried over the English Channel and moved by train to the 5th Northern General Hospital in Leicester. Two months later, on 26 October 1916, he was considered fit enough to be discharged to No.1 Australian Command Depot at Sutton Veny on Salisbury Plain. From here in December he was granted his first period of extended leave since enlisting.

After about six weeks training with the 1st Australian Training Battalion, Clarence returned to France on 15 February 1917, rejoining the 2nd Infantry Battalion on 11 March. The 2nd Battalion had spent a long, wet winter in the trenches on the Somme but by March they were advancing over the destroyed landscape left behind by the German Army during its strategic withdrawal to the Hindenburg Line. On 9 April they went into action during the opening of the Arras Offensive in an attempt to capture and hold the village of Hermies. It was during this action that Clarence was wounded by shrapnel in his left foot and was transferred from the 3rd Field Ambulance at the Front to No.3 Casualty Clearing Station at Aveluy. After a couple of weeks' convalescence in Rouen he was transferred to the 1st Australian Divisional Base at Étaples before rejoining the 2nd Battalion on 2 May. Two days later he went into action in the Battle of Bullecourt and was wounded again, this time by a gunshot wound to a leg and forearm. For the sixth time in his short military career Clarence found himself being passed along the medical evacuation chain, from field ambulance to casualty clearing station to stationary base hospital and over the Channel to a general hospital in England, this time in Brighton. By mid-June the bullet wound in his forearm had healed though his calf wound had still not fully mended. Finally, on 16 August, he was deemed fit enough to resume duty and was transferred to the Australian Army's Overseas Training Brigade at Hurdcott, Wiltshire. A month later he sailed for France, disembarking at Le Havre on 18 September 1917 and rejoining the 2nd Battalion on the 28th just in time to take part in the Battle of Broodseinde on 4 October, a bitter fight under heavy rain in deep mud.

The 3rd Ypres offensive had been launched by the Allies on 31 July in an attempt to push the Germans out of the Flanders Salient and force a breakthrough into occupied Belgium. During the Battle of Broodseinde the 2nd Australian Infantry Battalion lost more than 150 men, killed or wounded, many as a result of mortar fire as they assembled for the attack. This was followed by the Battle of Poelcapelle on the 9th and the 1st Battle of Passchendaele on the 12th, in which both No. 1 and No. 2 Anzac Corps were engaged by Field Marshal Haig to push the front line towards Passchendaele Ridge, thought to be the key to breaking the German's hold on the Salient. The push eventually foundered under a combination of incessant rain, clogging mud and mustard gas. On 26 October another attempt to capture Passchendaele was launched, again under heavy rain, this time spearheaded by the 4th Division of the Canadian Army Corps along the Passchendaele Road, with the 1st Australian Division on its right. The following day the Canadian and Australian troops attempted to capture a position known as Decline Copse in an inadequately coordinated assault. It was finally captured later that night, then lost and then retaken in fierce hand-to-hand combat. Lance Corporal Clarence Neasham was killed in action here on 27 October 1917.

Clarence is buried at Belgian Battery Corner Cemetery, Ieper, Belgium, grave no. II.H.12. His Army Service papers note that the burial service was conducted by the Revd Johnson Redmond, chaplain to the AIF's 1st Infantry Brigade. Clarence is commemorated also on the Great War roll of honour at the Memorial Centre in Bathurst, New South Wales (where he appears to be listed twice, as 'C. F. Neasham' and as 'F. Neisham' – the latter name is not recorded as a casualty by either the Australian War Memorial or the Commonwealth War Graves Commission). An In Memoriam notice appeared in *The Bathurst Times* on 26 October 1918, presumably placed by his aunt. It includes the words: 'Until the day breaks and the shadows flee away'. Clarence's name also appears on the St Augustine's roll of honour. His photograph, taken by a Norwich photographer, William Bond, who had a studio in Magdalen Street close to St Augustine's, was placed in Norwich Library's Great War memorial collection by his brother Leonard. It shows him in the tunic and slouch hat of an Australian infantryman. He wears a lance corporal's single stripe on his right sleeve while his left sleeve bears what appears to be the patch of the 2nd Infantry Battalion. His left sleeve also has at its cuff long service and good conduct chevrons and three wound stripes, making it probable the photograph was taken in Norwich sometime between August and mid-September 1917 on a brief period of leave. Clarence was awarded the 1915 Star and the British War and Victory medals.

Clarence's father, Corporal Frederick Neasham, served with his old regiment, the King's Dragoon Guards as part of the General Service Dragoons, and saw action on the Western Front from October 1915. Clarence's brothers also joined up. Private Leonard Victor Neasham enlisted on 7 October 1914 and served with the Norfolk Regiment and the Royal Defence Corps until 5 February 1919, having been invalided out of front line service and awarded the Silver War Badge in recognition of his injuries while serving his country overseas. Clarence's obituary in *The Bathurst Times* provides these details: 'A brother, younger by five years [presumably Leonard], lost an eye and had his knee cap permanently injured in France.' Leonard married Ethel Mary Marshall of 14 Wingfield Road in St Augustine's church on 18 May 1918. Youngest brother, Private Ronald Leslie Neasham, also served in the Norfolk Regiment and later in the Army Service Corps. In 1924 Ronald followed in Clarence's footsteps and emigrated to Australia, settling in Kalgoorlie, Western Australia. In April 1940 he enlisted in the Australian Army only to be discharged six days later after the Army discovered that he was not in fact 35 years old but 40 and so above the upper age limit.

Private 17234 Ernest Denham, 1st Battalion, Norfolk Regiment

Ernest Denham was born in Norwich in 1878, the fourth child of William James Denham, a tobacco-cutter, and Sarah Denham née Smith. In 1881 the family, including Ernest's older siblings George, Emmeline and Frederick, was at 4 Britannia Terrace, New Catton. His mother died in 1882, aged 25. His father remarried in 1889 to a Miss Isabella Duffield. By 1891, the family had moved to 47 Albany Road, New Catton. While Ernest was still at school at this date his older siblings had started work: George as a clicker (leather-cutter) in the shoe trade, Emmeline as an upholsterer and Fred as a cabinet-maker. In 1899 Ernest married Sarah Ann Martha Kent (known as Martha). The couple then lived as boarders in the house of Ernest's father and stepmother, who by 1901 were at 65 Patteson Road, New Catton. Ernest was now a furniture-maker. He had two sons, Ernest William, born 1904, and Albert Philip, born 1908. By 1911, they were living in their own home at 14 Cross Street off Sussex Street, St Augustine's. Ernest was now a painter and paper-hanger.

Ernest enlisted in Norwich on 9 December 1914 aged 36 and was posted to the 1st Battalion, Norfolk Regiment. Although a portion of his Army Service papers have survived they contain very little detail about his military service. After a period of training in England he first went over to France on 25 May 1915. The 1st Norfolks, part of 15th Brigade, 5th Division, had been on the Western Front since the beginning of the war, a veteran 'Old Contemptible' battalion that had fought at Mons, Le Cateau, Marne, Aisne and the 1st and 2nd

Battles of Ypres. By the autumn of 1917, Edward had survived the Somme, Arras and the battles of Polygon Wood and Poelcapelle during the 3rd Ypres offensive. He was killed in action in Flanders on 28 October 1917, aged 39. On this day the 1st Norfolks were defending a fortified lookout position on the Menin Road known as 'Stirling Castle' (in reality, the remains of a French chateau almost totally obliterated by artillery). Here they were put to work repairing the defences. The surrounding landscape is described in the regimental history as 'nothing but a network of shell holes'. A painting by the war artist David A. Baxter depicts it as a depressing terrain of tree stumps, mud and flooded shell holes. A death notice, including the patriotic sentiment 'He answered his country's call' was placed by his family in the *Eastern Daily Press* 19 days after his death. Interestingly, his relatives gave his rank as 'pioneer' so perhaps his civilian skills as a furniture-maker, painter and decorator were used for building trench defences. Ernest is commemorated at the Tyne Cot Memorial, Zonnebeke, Belgium, and on St Augustine's roll of honour. He was awarded the 1915 Star and the British War and Victory medals.

1918 – Kaiserschlacht, Lys, Salonika, Last 100 Days

Corporal 240645 Ernest Henry Clarke, 1/5th Battalion, Norfolk Regiment, formerly Private 3044, 5th Battalion, Norfolk Regiment

Ernest Henry Clarke was born in Norwich in 1896, the sixth surviving child of Benjamin Edward Clarke, a shoemaker, and Mary Ann Clarke née Hoy, a shoe-machinist. *(For more on Ernest's background see p.102.)* Prior to the war Ernest worked as a clicker (leather-cutter) in the shoe trade. He enlisted in East Dereham, Norfolk, on 21 September 1914 and was posted to the 2/5th Battalion, Norfolk Regiment, a Reserve Territorial unit with its Depot in East Dereham. He was appointed lance corporal on unpaid promotion on 9 June 1915 and remained in England until 31 January 1916 when he embarked with the Mediterranean Expeditionary

Force to join the bulk of the 1/5th Norfolks, who were rebuilding their strength in Egypt after the disaster of Gallipoli. At this juncture his rank reverted to private, a common procedure for soldiers going overseas. On 13 March 1916 he was reappointed lance corporal, this time on paid promotion and was promoted to acting corporal on 29 August 1916 and finally to full corporal on 27 February 1917.

Ernest was taken prisoner in Palestine during 163rd Brigade's disastrous assault on the Turkish defences in front of Gaza on 19 April 1917. The 1/4th and 1/5th Norfolks lost between them over a thousand casualties killed, wounded and missing on this day. The conditions endured by British POWs in Turkish camps were notoriously harsh. It was an experience Ernest did not survive. Confusion subsequently arose about the date of Ernest's death. Due to a clerical error his father was informed as late as February 1919 that he had died while a prisoner in Turkey sometime between Christmas Day 1916 and 7 January 1917, in other words, before he had actually been taken prisoner. He was then informed his death had occurred sometime between Christmas Day 1917 and 7 January 1918. The date was not finally pin-pointed until March 1919 due to the testimony of a repatriated fellow POW, Chief Engine Room Artificer Harry Burton Broomhead, an Australian submariner who had sent a written report to the Infantry Records department at Warley confirming that Private 3044 E. H. Clarke, 21, had died at Bor camp near Nigde in Central Anatolia on 2 February 1918, the cause of death, dysentery. He has no known grave.

The story of Ernest's fellow POW, Harry Broomhead, is worth noting. A Yorkshireman by birth, he had transferred from the Royal Navy to the Royal Australian Navy in 1915 to help crew Australia's first submarine to go into active service, *AE2.* Her one and only voyage was to the Mediterranean to take part in the Dardanelles campaign. She was subsequently scuttled in the Sea of Marmara to prevent her falling into enemy hands. Chief Broomhead spent the next four years as a POW in Turkish camps. During his incarceration he managed to get a letter delivered to his mother in England, telling her that he was 'practically starving' and weighed just a few ounces under 5 stone. After the war he returned to active service with the Royal Australian Navy.

Ernest is commemorated at the Baghdad (North Gate) War Cemetery, Iraq, and commemorated also on the St Augustine's roll of honour, where his rank is mistakenly given as private. He was awarded the British War and Victory medals.

Private 34675 Ralph Victor Gant, 10th Battalion, Essex Regiment, formerly Private 24308 Norfolk Regiment

Ralph Victor Gant was born in north Heigham, Norwich, in 1893, the seventh and youngest child of Benjamin Gant, a self-employed painter, paper-hanger and builder, originally from Reedham, Norfolk, and Emma Gant née Beart. In 1891 the Gant family was at 7 Langley Street, Heigham. Ralph's older siblings, in descending order of age, were George, Ethel, Frederick, Alice, Bessie and Benjamin. By 1901 the family had moved to 30 Old Palace Road in the parish of St Bartholomew; all except George, who was now living with his aunt and uncle in Angel Road, New Catton, and Bessie, who was a patient at the isolation hospital in Earlham Road when the Census was taken. While Ralph and Benjamin were still at school, Ethel, Frederick and Alice were employed, respectively, as a tailor, a carpenter and a dressmaker. Frederick married in 1904 and Ethel in 1907, the year their father died, aged 48. By 1911, the family had moved again, to 67 West End Street, Heigham. Ralph, 17, was now a grocer's clerk and Benjamin a surveyor's clerk.

Ralph enlisted in Norwich, probably as a 1916 conscript. His Army Service papers have not survived. His first posting seems to have been to one of the Norfolk Regiment's Territorial battalions, probably to one of the second-line units held in reserve. On 27 August 1916 he married Gladys Lundy, spinster of the parish, at St Augustine's church. In the register his occupation is given as a private in the 2/5th Battalion, Essex Regiment, a second line Reserve Territorial unit based in Harrogate at this date. At some point he was transferred to the 10th Battalion, Essex Regiment, part of the 18th Eastern Division in France. Private Ralph Gant, 24 was killed in action on 21 March 1918. This was the day on which the German Army launched its massive spring offensive, the Kaiserschlacht. The 18th Division's defence of the British Front during the first three days

Frederick and Ralph Gant, *Norwich Mercury*, 25 May 1918

on this onslaught became known as the Battle of St Quentin. The 10th Essex lost more than 60 killed in action here. Ralph's widow placed a death notice in the *Eastern Daily Press* a month later. Ralph is commemorated at the Pozières Memorial, Somme, France, and on St Augustine's roll of honour. He was awarded the British War and Victory medals.

Ralph's brother, Rifleman Frederick Thomas Gant of the 11th Battalion, King's Royal Rifle Corps, died of wounds at Ypres in September 1917. Another brother, Sergeant George Gant, Norfolk Regiment, was wounded at Ypres, sufficiently seriously to be discharged from the Army as unfit for active service in October 1917. Two of Ralph's brothers-in-law, Alfred and Frederick Lundy, who are also commemorated on St Augustine's roll of honour, were killed in France in 1914 and 1915 respectively. *(See p.24 and p.55.)*

Private 3/10230 James William Stocks, 9th Battalion, Norfolk Regiment

The second panel from the right in St Augustine's roll of honour chancel screen lists a Private James Stock (without a final 's'), preceded, out of alphabetical order, by a Private William Stock. No one with these names who served in the British Army during the war appears to have any obvious Norwich connection or was a member of

169

the Norfolk Regiment. It is far from uncommon to find names misspelled on war memorials and this seems to have been the case with James and William, whose most likely identities are Norwich-born brothers James and William Stocks.

James William Stocks was born in the parish of St Martin at Oak, Norwich, on 15 April 1885, the eldest child of James Stocks, a bricklayer's labourer, and Alice Stocks, a silk-winder. A second child, Frederick (known as Fred), was born in 1888. Although James's mother and her sons are recorded with the surname Stocks in the 1891 Census, both boys' births were actually registered under their mother's maiden name, Parnell, as was her third son, William, born in 1892. The boys' parents would eventually marry in 1896, though to add to the confusion their father (if, indeed he was their biological father), James, was actually recorded as James 'Starks' by the General Register Office. In 1891 the Stocks/Parnell family was living in the household of Alice's widowed mother, Ann Parnell, a silk-weaver, at 6 Newbegin's Yard in the adjacent parish of St Mary Coslany. By 1901 the family had moved again, to 1 Chequers Yard off Coslany Street in the parish of St Miles Coslany, the next parish along going south. James, 16, was now a general labourer, while Fred and William were still at school. By 1911 James and Alice Stocks had moved again, to nearby Tuns Yard, though without their sons, who were all now in their twenties and had presumably left home. The whereabouts of James and Fred at this date is not known. Youngest brother William, however, is listed as a private in the West Yorkshire Regiment in barracks at Colchester.

On 16 October 1911 James's youngest brother married Mary Smith, described in the 1911 Census as a 'tailoress for the Army and Navy', at St Paul's church, Norwich. The couple's address was given as 10 Bennett's Yard, Cowgate, Norwich. Bizarrely, James would later declare to the Army that it was he who married Mary Smith that day and not his youngest brother. However, that the groom was indeed William Stocks and not James William Stocks seems to be corroborated by the fact that in the register the groom's age is stated to be 20 (William's age) and his profession soldier (William's profession). James would later also tell the Army, perhaps rather more truthfully, that he was father of at least three of Mary's children. At the time of her marriage to William, Mary Smith already had an 8-

month-old daughter, Ivy Harriett, born at her widowed mother's home in Philadelphia Lane on 15 February 1911. A second child, James Henry, was born in Barnard's Yard off Midlands Street on 19 July 1913. A third, Alice, was born in Starlings Yard off Botolph Street on 19 August 1914. While Ivy's father's name was not recorded in the Norwich Birth Returns, it is James William Stocks and not her legitimate husband William Stocks who is named as the father of James Henry and Alice. A fourth child, Jack Alfred, was born to Mary in Cromer in north Norfolk on 7 August 1918, over four months after James's death in action in France. According to James's Army Service papers, the Army Records Department were of the opinion that this child at least was probably fathered by Mary's legitimate husband William and not by James. One can only speculate that as the father of at least two of Mary's children, James was prepared to perjure himself by making a false declaration concerning his marital status in order that she receive a wife's allowance and a widow's pension should he die on active service.

James enlisted in Norwich on 8 September 1914. At this date he was lodging at 11 Rosemary Lane in the parish of St Mary Coslany and was a labourer. According to his Attestation papers he had previously served in the 2nd Battalion, Norfolk Regiment. No other details of this earlier period of military service are recorded in his papers, but the likelihood is that he had joined up as a teenager in 1901 or 1902 and may have seen action during the final year of the Boer War. His medical report notes that he was 5ft 4 in height and had light brown hair and grey eyes. On enlisting James was posted to the 9th Battalion, Norfolk Regiment, one of the new Service battalions set up by Lord Kitchener. He remained in Britain, training and waiting for equipment, until 29 August 1915 when the 9th Battalion embarked for France, landing in Boulogne on the 30th. The 9th Norfolk first saw action less than a month later during the Battle of Loos. On 6 December James was appointed lance corporal. The shortage of experienced NCOs meant that such appointments, which in peace time might take many years, happened now at an accelerated rate. His lance corporal stripe, however, would not remain on his arm for very long. On 15 January 1916 he went absent without leave while back in England. He was arrested by a military policeman on 2 February and returned to France a prisoner under escort. On 25

February he was tried by Field General Court Martial and found guilty of desertion. Because his offence had occurred in England rather than France, he escaped the more serious charge of desertion in the field (i.e. in face of the enemy), for which the penalty was death by firing squad. As it was he was reduced to private and sentenced to 90 days (the maximum allowable) Field Punishment Number 1 without remission, that is, for three months, being manacled and cuffed in the open for up to two hours each day to a fixed object such as a gun-carriage wheel as well as extra drill and fatigues.

In August 1916 the 9th Norfolks were engaged in the great Somme Offensive for the first time. Their first significant action took place on 15 September when they were ordered to capture a German stronghold known as the Quadrilateral near the village of Ginchy. The British tanks that accompanied their advance proved ineffective because of mechanical failure and the attacking companies encountered thick rows of uncut barbed wire and had finally to retire to their starting trenches. Casualties were high. James's Casualty Form notes that he suffered a gunshot wound to the right foot and was moved to a casualty clearing station before being returned to England for further treatment on 28 September.

On 2 March 1917, James was deemed fit enough to return to active duty in France, rejoining the 9th Norfolks in the field on 19th. The regimental history describes a series of trench raids undertaken and repelled by the Battalion throughout the spring of 1917 in the industrial landscape around Loos, an area of quarries, destroyed factories, shattered masonry and smashed machinery. The weather was bitterly cold but not cold enough to prevent a partial thaw of the frozen mud. On 26 April James sprained his left ankle, possibly during the fighting around the devastated coal mining village, Cité St Laurent. This seems to have put him out of action until August when he rejoined the Battalion in time to take part in the Battle of Cambrai in November. Private James William Stocks was reported missing in action on 21 March 1918, the day on which the German Army launched its last great offensive, the Kaiserschlacht. On this day the 9th Norfolks were in trenches near Lagnicourt. As dawn rose they were bombarded with gas shells followed by an intense heavy artillery bombardment that annihilated most of the Battalion's front line companies. At the end of the day they had lost 10 officers and 30 other ranks killed outright by the shelling, more than 150 men out of action with serious wounds and 170 missing presumed dead or taken prisoner. Eight days later Mary Stocks, still at this time regarded by the Army as his wife and next of kin, was informed by telegram that he was missing in action. Over a year later, on 8 May 1919, James's father, whom the Army now regarded as his legal next of kin, was notified that for official purposes his son was assumed to have died in action on 21 March 1918, aged 31. He has no known grave. James is commemorated at the Arras Memorial, Faubourg-d'Amiens Cemetery, Arras, France, and possibly also on St Augustine's roll of honour if he is indeed the 'James Stock' listed there. The Norwich Great War roll of honour in Norwich Castle Keep spells James Stocks' surname correctly. He was awarded the 1915 Star and the British War and Victory medals.

It is not known how the Army finally uncovered James's false claim to have a wife or what action they took, if any, to recover falsely claimed allowances, personal possessions or pension. That they did eventually discover the deception seems borne out by the fact that in 1920 the War Office wrote a memorandum instructing the Army's Medal Branch to ensure the medals of the late Private James W. Stocks be despatched to Mrs Mary Stocks of Philadelphia Lane (her mother's address), on the strict understanding that she act as guardian of James's son, James Henry, holding his medals in trust until he was 'of an age to appreciate their value' rather than in her own right as his widow.

Private 242050 Charles William Springall, 9th Battalion, Cameronians (Scottish Rifles), formerly Private 12082, Norfolk Regiment

Charles William Springall was born in the parish of St Augustine, Norwich, in 1885, the second child of Alfred Springall, a general labourer, and Sarah Springall née Gowen, a silk-winder. In 1891 the family, including Charles, his older brother Alfred and younger brothers James and Henry, was at 14 Baldwin's Yard in the parish of St Martin at Oak. By 1901 the family, which now included Emily and Maud, had moved to No. 18 in the same yard; all except Charles, 15, and Alfred, 17, who were living with their grandparents, Samuel

Gowen, a brick-carter, and Emily Gowen, a laundress, at Shipfields in Sprowston, a northern suburb of Norwich. The brothers were now shoemakers. Later that year their father died. Their mother remarried in 1905, to Edward Hogg, and by 1911 Charles was back living with his mother and stepfather at 1 Horton's Yard in St Martin's at Oak. Alfred, meanwhile had married Gertrude Margetson and set up home in Globe Row, Heigham, to the west of Norwich. While Alfred continued to make shoes, Charles, like his mother and stepfather, and younger brothers James and Henry, had become a wire-netting weaver, almost certainly for the nearby Coslany-based iron foundry of Barnard, Bishop & Barnard. During the war this company supplied the Army with thousands of miles of wire-netting for use as trackways across the deserts of North Africa and the Middle East. Emily and Maud, meanwhile, were employed as a silk-filler and a letterpress worker respectively.

Charles enlisted in Norwich. His Army Service papers have not survived. His first posting was to the 7th Battalion, Norfolk Regiment, and he was in France by 31 May 1915. It isn't clear when he was transferred to the 9th Battalion, Cameronians (Scottish Rifles), a 'Kitchener' Service battalion established in Hamilton, Lanarkshire, in 1914. In February 1918 the 9th Cameronians were attached to the 14th Division on the Western Front. Private Charles Springall, 32, died of wounds here, probably during the Battle of St Quentin, on 25 March 1918. He has no known grave. Between 20 and 25 March, during the opening onslaught of the German's spring offensive, the Kaiserschlacht, the 9th Cameronians lost more than 70 men killed in action or died of wounds. Charles is commemorated at the Pozières Memorial, the Somme. He appears in *Norfolk Roll of Honour* under the combined Norwich parishes of St Miles Coslany and St Martin at Oak. He is not listed on St Augustine's roll of honour. He was awarded the 1915 Star and the British War and Victory medals. His youngest brother, Private Henry Springall, served in both the 6th Battalion, Norfolk Regiment, and the Machine Gun Corps during the war.

Private 12/1794 William B. Park, 12th Battalion, King's Own Yorkshire Light Infantry

William Park was born in Norwich in March 1879, the eighth of twelve children of John Park, a cordwainer (a traditional shoemaker) and the son of a cordwainer, and Hannah Park née Andrews. In 1881 the family, including William's older siblings Hannah, Sarah, John, Alfred, Walter, Samuel and Charles, and younger brother Arthur, was at King Street in the parish of St Peter Parmentergate. William himself, aged then about 2, is absent from the Census. Living nearby in Obey's Yard at this date were his uncle William, aunt Bertha and six cousins. Uncle William was also a cordwainer, clearly a family trade. By 1891 William's parents appear to have moved into the unnumbered and vacated house of his uncle in Obey's Yard. Three of his older siblings were now absent from the household: Hannah, who had married William Shreve, a tanner, in 1881, and John and Alfred, who cannot be traced. There were now three more children: Eliza, Alice and George. The older siblings remaining at home, Sarah and Sam, were a tailor and an ostler (a stableman or groom) respectively. By 1901 the family home in Obey's Yard had been numbered (No. 6). William's father was now a widower and three more of his siblings, Sam, Arthur and Alice, had vanished from the Census. William, 22, was now a French polisher. Ten years later he had been forced by poverty to become an inmate of the Norwich Incorporation Workhouse in Bowthorpe Road.

William enlisted at Farnley Park Camp at Otley near Leeds. The 12th Battalion, King's Own Yorkshire Light Infantry (KOYLI), was one of Lord Kitchener's New Army Service battalions, raised in Leeds in September 1914 by the West Yorkshire Coal Owners' Association and chiefly recruited from local colliery workers. How William ended up in its ranks is a mystery. Perhaps his experience of the workhouse had driven him to Yorkshire's coalfields in search of work. The 12th Battalion began its basic training at Farnley Park, then moved to Burton Leonard Camp near Ripon; completing its training in October 1915 at Fovant Camp near Salisbury, Wiltshire. It was attached to the 31st Division as a pioneer rather than a light infantry battalion. Pioneer units were often used in the construction of military roads and railways, and also undertook the extremely dangerous task of excavation, a job deemed eminently suitable for miners. Bizarrely, the 12th Battalion's first overseas posting was to Egypt rather than France, arriving there on 22 December 1915. However, it was there for only a couple of months before being sent to bolster the 5th Army on the Western Front. It remained with the 5th Army until the end of the war, mainly engaged in building light-gauge military railways, although it also had to take part in front line defensive duties when called on. Private William Park, 38, was killed in action on 30 March 1918. The date suggests he was killed during the opening of the German spring offensive, the Kaiserschlacht. He has no known grave.

William is commemorated on the Arras Memorial, Pas de Calais, France, and on St Augustine's roll of honour, which seems to be the only place that records his second initial. He was awarded the 1915 Star and the British War and Victory medals. Curiously, the Commonwealth War Graves Commission records one Henry Park of 6 Bennett's Yard off Ber Street as his father. William's father, John, had died in 1913, aged 72. Henry appears to have been another of his uncles. *Norfolk Roll of Honour* includes a W. Park under the parish of St John de Sepulchre, an area that encompasses Bennett's Yard.

Company Sergeant Major (Acting Warrant Officer, 2nd Class) 220033 Frederick George Fox, 4th Battalion, East Yorkshire Regiment, formerly Private 4558, Norfolk Regiment

Frederick (known as Fred) George Fox was born Norwich in 1891, the third surviving child of Frederick George Fox, a shoemaker, and Ellen Jane Fox née Perrement. Another Frederick George had died in infancy in 1888. Although he enlisted under the surname Fox, Fred was registered at birth with his mother's maiden name. His parents, in fact, didn't marry until 1915 after having had at least 15 children, 13 of whom survived infancy. The 1891 Census records the Fox/Perrement family at 3 Chequers Yard behind the Chequers pub in Coslany Street. This is presumably were Fred was born a few months later.

At this date his mother and sisters, Ellen and Ethel, are described in the Census as lodgers of Frederick Fox senior, though there seems little doubt, given the subsequent family history, that Ellen Jane Perrement was his common law wife. In November 1897 Fred transferred from St Miles Infants School in Oak Street to the Old Meeting House School, a nonconformist school in the parish of St George Colegate. Here he was admitted under the name Fred Fox. Arthur Cannell *(see p.84)* was also a pupil there at this time and Fred's younger brother Albert went there too, in 1904. At this date Fred's home address was 23 Newbegin's Yard off St Mary's Plain. He was still there in 1901, when the Census recorded his mother for the first time as Ellen Fox rather than Perrement. The children Fred, Ellen and Ethel, were, however, still named Perrement, though newer additions to the growing family – Rosina, Ernest, Albert and Arthur – were named Fox. Fred left school on 27 July 1904, aged 13. By 1911 the family had moved to 18 Leonards Street, St Augustine, and had grown again with the addition of William, Maud, Hilda and Herbert. Two more children, Phyllis and Leslie, born in 1911 and 1915 respectively, completed the family. Fred, 19, was still living at home in what must have been an incredibly crowded house. These terraced houses, which still exist, were basically just two-up, two-downs, with an outside privy, shared with neighbours. Fred had followed his father into the shoe trade where he worked in the finishing department. In 1912 he married Leah Beatrice Brooks, the daughter of a chimney-sweep. A few months later their only child, another Frederick George, was born.

Fred enlisted in Norwich. His Army Service papers have not survived but his record in *Soldiers Died in the Great War* notes he served in the Norfolk Regiment before transferring to the East Yorkshire Regiment. Interestingly, Fred and his younger brothers Albert and Ernest have consecutive regimental numbers (4558, 4559, 4557 respectively), which suggests they joined up on the same day. As Albert's Service papers have survived, it is possible to date Fred's enlistment on 25 May 1915. He was initially posted to the 4th Battalion, Norfolk Regiment, like his brothers. It would be interesting to know how a Norwich shoemaker went from raw recruit in a Norfolk Territorial battalion in1915 to company sergeant major in a Hull 'pals' battalion in 1918; unfortunately evidence is lacking.

The next known fact is that CSM Frederick Fox, 26, died of

wounds on 31 March 1918. The 11th Battalion, East Yorkshire Regiment, also known as the 2nd Hull (Tradesmen) Battalion, was a 'pals' unit largely made up of men from the same close-knit background. In December 1915 it became part of the 92nd Brigade, 31st Division, and sailed initially to Egypt before being moved to the Western Front in March 1916. Toward the end of March 1918 it was caught up in the massive German spring offensive known as the Kaiserschlacht, in particular the attempt by General Otto von Below's 17th Army to capture Arras. The 11th Battalion's War Diary notes 'fairly heavy' casualties on 27 March – around 35 killed in action and several more who subsequently died of their wounds. Fred's place of burial suggests he died while receiving treatment at the 6th Stationary Hospital at Frévent.

A family death notice appeared in the *Eastern Daily Press* on 8 April 1918 with a verse which remembered both Fred and Albert, who had died in Palestine in 1917:

> *When last we saw their smiling faces*
> *They looked so strong and brave;*
> *We little thought how soon they'd be*
> *Laid in a hero's grave.*
> *Could we have raised their dying hands*
> *Or heard their last farewell,*
> *The blow might not have been so hard*
> *To those who loved them well.*

Fred is buried at St Hilaire Cemetery Extension, Frévent, Pas de Calais, France, grave no. B.2, and commemorated also on St Augustine's roll of honour. He is listed under the parish of St Philip, Heigham, in *Norfolk Roll of Honour*. He was awarded the British War and Victories medals.

Private G/24416 Sidney Howard, 11th (1st South Downs) Battalion, Royal Sussex Regiment

Sidney Howard was born in Norwich in 1899, the last born of the 11 children of John Howard, a general labourer, and Emma Woodlove Howard née Jay. His older siblings in order of birth were John,

Walter, Emma, Harriet, William, Freddy, Caroline (known as Carly), Clara, Maud and George. In the early years of their married life Sidney's parents lived in New Yard off Magdalen Street, but by 1891 the family had moved to 65 Fishergate in the nearby parish of St Edmund's. By 1901 they had moved again, to Long Yard in the same parish. Sidney's father died in 1904, aged 48. By 1911 his mother and those of his siblings still at home had moved to 62 Magpie Road. Apart from Sidney, who was still at school, his older siblings still at home were all employed in the local shoe-making trade: William as a shoe-finisher, Carly as a shoe-fitter, Clara and Maud as box-makers and George as a general shoemaker.

Sidney enlisted in Norwich. His Army Service papers have not survived, but given his date of birth it is probable he wasn't conscripted until 1917 when he was 18. He may, therefore, have received his first experience of war during the truly terrible 3rd Battle of Ypres. In *Undertones of War* the poet Edmund Blunden, who was a junior officer in Sidney's battalion at this time, vividly described this mud-drowned horror as 'the slow amputation of Passchendaele'. Curiously, although according to official sources Private Sidney Howard, 19, was killed in action during the Battle of St Quentin on 3 April 1918, death notices placed by his family in the *Eastern Daily Press* all say 21 March. This earlier date was the first day of the massive German spring offensive known as the Kaiserschlacht, during which the 11th Royal Sussex virtually ceased to exist. The discrepancy in dates is possibly accounted for by his being reported missing presumed dead and then declared officially killed in action. He has no known grave. The death notice placed by his widowed mother, sisters and brothers, included a verse that appears to have been chosen to express their grief at the loss of the youngest member of the family:

> *Oh! why was he taken, so young and fair,*
> *One of the best, we all loved do dear?*
> *Hard was the blow that compelled us to part*
> *With one so loving and dear to our hearts.*
> *Oh! God above, in Thy loving grace,*
> *Find for him a resting place.*

According to additional information in this notice, Sidney's brother

William was then serving in France. A private in the Royal West Surrey Regiment, he later transferred to the Labour Corps No. 91 Company. His sister Harriet's husband, Tom Denmark Nichols, was serving in Egypt. Sidney is commemorated at the Pozières Memorial, Somme, France, and on St Augustine's roll of honour. He was awarded the British War and Victory medals.

Lance Corporal 602291 Arthur James Howell, 24th Battalion (Victoria Rifles), Canadian Expeditionary Force, formerly Sergeant, 27th Lambton Regiment (Saint-Clair Borderers), Canadian Militia, and Private, 4th (Volunteer) Battalion, Norfolk Regiment

Arthur James Howell was born in Norwich on 23 April 1891, the eldest child of Arthur James Howell, a stone mason, and Charlotte Howell née Chilvers. He was baptised at St Augustine's church on 27 September by the Revd W. A. Elder. His father had lived in Bakers Road just north of St Augustine's parish since childhood. His grandfather, Henry Howell, is described in the 1881 Census as a 'well

sinker and pump maker'. Bakers Road, Wingfield Road and Green Hills Road just north of the City Wall, was only then being developed for housing on former farm land and an early 19th-century pleasure garden. An Ordnance Survey map of the early 1880s shows that numerous wells were sunk here, supplying the new dwellings before mains water became available. By 1891 Arthur's parents had moved to 63 Esdelle Street to the east of St Augustine's Street, another new development, built over former Church Glebe land. By 1901 the family had grown, adding George,

Lottie, Reginald and Mabel. Sometime around 1909, aged 17 or 18, Arthur joined the 4th Battalion, Norfolk Regiment, becoming a part-time soldier in the county's home defence Territorial Force. All the family were still in Esdelle Street in 1911 with the addition of Lily, Arthur's youngest sibling. According to the Census, Arthur, 19, was now employed as a coppersmith's apprentice.

In common with thousands of young men before the Great War, Arthur Howell seems to have taken advantage of one of the assisted-passage schemes set up by the Government of Canada to attract emigrants from Britain. On 26 April 1912 Arthur arrived in Portland, Maine, on board SS *Ascania*, a Cunard liner launched just a year earlier. The ship's usual port of destination was Montreal, reached via the St Lawrence River when free of ice. Presumably the unusually large amount of floating ice in the north Atlantic at this time and the sinking of the *Titanic* on 15 April had caused the *Ascania* to divert to the ice-free waters of Portland. Arthur's final destination was Brampton in the Greater Toronto area of Ontario, Canada. Brampton's economy at this time was largely based on horticulture – the mass production of hot-house blooms – and Arthur's trade as a coppersmith was put to use here by the area's principal employers, the Dale Estate, maintaining its many steam-heated greenhouses.

On 29 January 1915 Arthur signed Attestation papers in the town of Sarnia in Lambton County, Ontario, declaring his willingness to serve in the Canadian Overseas Expeditionary Force (CEF). The papers record he was by trade a coppersmith, was unmarried and his religious denomination was Church of England. He was 5ft 8in height and had a fair complexion, blue eyes and fair hair. He had a small scar on his right thumb. His birthday is recorded incorrectly as 27 April 1891. Arthur already had considerable military experience: three years with the Norfolk Regiment's 4th (Territorial) Battalion and more than two years in the Canadian Militia with the 27th Lambton Regiment (Saint-Clair Borderers) in Sarnia. An obituary published in the *Toronto Evening Telegraph* on 4 May 1918 noted: 'He had been promoted to sergeant, but gave up his stripes in order to get to France'. It was common for non-commissioned soldiers in the Canadian Militia to give up their rank voluntarily, a process called reversion, when they transferred to a Canadian Expeditionary Force (CEF) unit going overseas, most of which already had their full quota of NCOs. Arthur was now placed in the 24th Infantry Battalion (Victoria Rifles), which embarked for England on 11 May 1915. After a period of training it arrived in France on 16 September, where it formed part of the 5th Infantry Brigade, 2nd Canadian Division. The 2nd Division spent a long, cold winter in the trenches in Flanders. By the autumn of 1916 it was engaged in the Battle of the Somme: at Flers, Thiepval, Le Transloy and the Ancre Heights. The following April it took part in the Canadian Corps' famous capture of Vimy Ridge, and that autumn, 1917, the 3rd Ypres campaign and Cambrai. Lance Corporal Arthur Howell, 26, was killed in action at Bellacourt on 11 April 1918 during the second phase of the German spring offensive, the Lys. The 24th Infantry Battalion's War Diary records: 'At 6 a.m. enemy opened up heavy bombardment on our front line, support trenches and rear … same lasted all day.' Throughout the day they fought off repeated attacks by waves of German soldiers deploying the 'Hutier' tactic, developed by General Oskar von Hutier of the 8th Army, in which barrage was followed by repeated assaults by storm troopers on the perceived weak point in the Allies' front line. Due to their solid resistance all day the German attack failed to overrun the Canadians' line, though at a cost of 17 killed and 40 wounded.

Arthur is buried at the London Cemetery, Neuville-Vitasse, Pas de Calais, France, grave no. II.E.10, and is commemorated also on St Augustine's roll of honour. His name is inscribed in the book of remembrance in Brampton Great War Memorial, Ontario, and he is also commemorated on a brass plaque in Brampton's Anglican church Christ Church. He was awarded the 1915 Star and the British War and Victory medals. Arthur's younger brother Private George Howell was killed in action in 1915. *(See p.29.)* In 1935 their photographs in uniform appeared in a commemorative volume on the military men of Peel District of southern Ontario.

Private 23978 George Stephen Attridge, 4th Battalion, Grenadier Guards

George Stephen Attridge was born in the parish of St Miles Coslany, Norwich, in March 1886, the third child of Nelson Attridge, who was originally from the village of Willingale in Epping Forest, Essex, and

Mary Ann Attridge née Warnes, who was from the village of Old Catton just to the north of Norwich (Nelson Attridge's name was mistakenly recorded as Atteridge in the marriage register). George's father was a foreman carter, possibly for the Norwich brewers Bullards, whose St Miles Anchor Brewery was in Coslany Street. In 1901 the Attridge family, including George's sisters Elizabeth, Alice and Ethel, was living at 19 Distillery Yard off Oak Street in St Miles Coslany. By 1911 George's older sisters Elizabeth and Alice had left home, his younger sister Ethel was still at home and employed as a shoe-machinist, his father was now employed as a poultryman (which had also been his father's trade in Essex), and George himself, 25, was employed as a corn-carter. Four years later the family of John Abigail moved in next door. *(See p.263.)*

George was still living with his parents in Distillery Yard when he married Ella Edith Clayton on 21 November 1915. The wedding took place in the bride's parish church, St Matthew, in Thorpe Hamlet, a suburb to the east of Norwich. Ella's father is recorded in the marriage register as a nurse, an uncommon occupation for a man at that time except in what were then called lunatic asylums; there was a large one in nearby Thorpe St Andrews. After marriage the newly-weds lived at 8 Raynham Street, Heigham, a suburb to the west of Norwich. There was another wedding in the family on Christmas Day 1915, when George's eldest sister Elizabeth married Rifleman Albert Holmes of the King's Royal Rifle Corps in St Augustine's church. George, a witness, had enlisted in Norwich on 11 December 1915. While George's occupation given in the register at his own wedding was carter, his Army Attestation form records his 'trade or calling' as a game porter. Like thousands of men all over the country, George enlisted on the very last day of the Derby Scheme, a government-sponsored initiative to persuade more men to volunteer for the armed services before the introduction of compulsory conscription in 1916, asking them to commit to military service if required at some unspecified later date. Huge numbers gathered outside recruiting offices and barracks that Saturday morning eager to volunteer before what many perceived to be the less honourable alternative of compulsory conscription came in. Although he was placed in the Army Reserve, as a 29-year-old, employed married man, George would not have expected to be called up very soon. It was generally understood that younger, unmarried or unemployed men would be called up first, and so it proved as his mobilisation did not come until five months later. On 30 May 1916 he was ordered to report to the Grenadier Guards depot at Caterham Camp, Surrey. At almost 6 foot in height he was well above the average height of adult men of that period (around 5ft 6). The Foot Guard regiments, the British Army's elite infantry units, wanted their pick of the fittest, tallest recruits and often seem to have got them.

Private George Attridge (the rank 'Guardsman' was not officially adopted until after the war) crossed over to France for the first time on 14 November 1916, arriving during the final days of the Battle of the Somme. As a fighting force, the 4th Battalion, Grenadier Guards, took part in most of the major campaigns on the Western Front, including, over the 16 months of George's service, the 3rd Ypres Offensive (Passchendaele) from July to November 1917, Cambrai in November 1917, and the Somme battles of the German spring offensive, the Kaiserschlacht, in March 1918. In April 1918, during the second phase of the German spring offensive, the Lys, the 4th Grenadiers Guards found themselves engaged in a desperate rear-guard action that perfectly exemplified Field Marshall Haig's recent General Order that the British Army was to fight 'to the last man'. On 11 April the 4th Guards Brigade was ordered to hold the line and cover the retreating British and French forces. Believing that the best form of defence is attack, the 4th Battalion raided enemy-occupied positions near Pont Rodin, which were well-defended with machine-guns and artillery. During the assault the Grenadiers exhausted 70,000 rounds of small arms ammunition and used up all their rifle grenades, losing 15 other ranks and one officer killed in action. On 12 April all that remained of the 4th Battalion in the field, amounting to little more than two companies, was entrenched near the village of Vieux-Berquin, fending off what was estimated to be a whole German infantry division. Officer-in-command, Captain Thomas 'Tom' Tannatt Pryce, twice winner of the Military Cross, finding they had been cut off from retreat, decided to make a stand rather than surrender, in order to give the retreating British divisions time to regroup. The account of what followed came from a corporal, the only Grenadier to escape death or capture, who hid in a ditch until nightfall then crawled across no man's land until he came across a patrol of Australian troops.

At the end of the first day, after repelling repeated attacks, there were just 40 Grenadiers left alive. At first light on 13 April it was observed that the Germans had brought up three field guns to within 300 yards of their position. Realising they would soon be obliterated unless they could put the guns out of action, Captain Pryce ordered his men to give a battle cry and charge the enemy with fixed bayonets. Although they succeeded in driving the enemy off the guns, reinforcements in strength soon came up making their situation utterly hopeless. Only 17 Grenadiers were now left and they had run out of ammunition. Still refusing to surrender, Captain Pryce led his men in a second bayonet charge and was last seen in hand-to-hand combat against overwhelming numbers.

Private George Stephen Attridge, 32, was killed in action during this last stand on 13 April 1918. Between 11 and 14 April the 4th Grenadiers lost 4 officers and 115 other ranks killed in action. A survivor, taken prisoner, described being shown the bodies of his comrades piled up in massed heaps in front of the German guns they had twice charged. With only 40 men Captain Pryce had held up a whole German division for more than 10 hours. Field Marshall Haig said there had been no finer last stand in the history of the British Army. Captain Pryce was posthumously awarded the Victoria Cross for his part in this action, while Sergeant Buckle and Privates Gale and Longford, who were also killed, were awarded the Military Medal. George's widow was notified of his death on 29 April. On 5 May a death notice was published in the *Eastern Daily Press*. George's remains were not identified and he has no known grave. His role in this heroic last stand seems not to have been recognised until now. George is commemorated at Ploegsteert Memorial, Comines-Warneton, Hainaut, Belgium, and on St Augustine's roll of honour. He was awarded the British War and Victory medals.

Private 32858 James Henry Warminger, 18th Battalion, Welsh Regiment

James Henry Warminger was born in Norwich in 1882, the second child of James Henry Warminger and Mary Ann Warminger née

Chiperfield. His father was a shoe-finisher; his mother, born in Swanton Abbot in north Norfolk, was the daughter of an agricultural labourer. His parents married in Norwich in 1874. Their first surviving child, Agnes, was born in 1879. By 1891 the Warmingers were in Palace Yard, an over-crowded, insanitary courtyard of 50 two- and three-room dwellings near the cavalry barracks in the parish of St James Pockthorpe, by reputation the worst slum in Norwich. There were now five more children: James, Elizabeth, Sarah, Philip and Mary. On 26 February, only a few weeks before the 1891 Census was taken, these five were all baptised on the same day in St James's church, a not uncommon practice. In 1896 the family's seventh and final child, Arthur, was born. The following year Mr Warminger died, leaving 15-year-old eldest son James the family's sole breadwinner. In 1899 Agnes married Alfred Wigley, a shoemaker, and left home. By 1901 Mrs Warminger and her five other children had moved to 21 Fishergate in the parish of St Edmund. James, 19, now worked in the shoe trade, as did his brother Philip, 14. In 1902 James married Florence Beatrice Howard. They lived at 21 St Mary's Plain in the parish of St Mary Coslany. By 1911 James was back in St James Pockthorpe, at 52 Cavalry Street, with Florence and their seven children: Arthur, Henry, Florence, Alfred, Reginald, Bertie and Stanley. By 1916 they had moved back to St Mary's Plain.

James enlisted in Norwich and was posted to the 11th Battalion, The Welsh Regiment, a battalion known as the 'Cardiff Pals'. It would be interesting to learn how a Norwich shoemaker ended up in a Welsh Pals battalion but unfortunately his Army Service papers have not survived to offer any clues. Perhaps he was recruited for his shoe-making skills. Many infantry battalions had a boot specialist in their ranks. James first went to France on 3 September 1915, three days ahead of the bulk of the Battalion, which suggests he was part of an advanced party of support staff. Just over a month later the 11th Welsh sailed from Marseilles for the Macedonian Front, having seen no action on the Western Front. It seems unlikely James went with it. He probably now returned to Britain where he was transferred to the Welsh Regiment's 18th (Bantam) Battalion, which in July became part of the newly formed 119th Welsh (Bantam) Brigade. 'Bantam' battalions had been formed all over Britain in 1915 from recruits fit and willing to serve but below the Army's minimum height requirement, which had already been reduced to 5ft 3 for infantry at the war's start. After generations of under-nourishment in Britain's industrial centres, the average height of working-class men had fallen considerably. The Army Service papers of James's youngest brother Arthur record that he was 5ft 2¼ in height and weighed little more than 6 stone (38.1 kg) on enlistment. James's transfer to a Bantam battalion suggests he was of a similar height. For the remainder of the war the 18th Welsh served on the Western Front as part of the 40th Division. They took part in the Battle of the Ancre during the Somme campaign of 1916, the battles of Arras and Cambrai in 1917 and the battles fought to resist the German Army's spring offensives, the Kaiserschlacht and the Lys, in 1918. Between 12 and 15 April 1918 the Battalion was engaged in defending a strategically important railway junction at Hazebrouck. Over four days it lost more than 80 officers and men killed in action. Private James Henry Warminger, 36, was declared missing presumed dead on 13 April 1918. He has no known grave. James is commemorated at Ploegsteert Memorial, Comines-Warneton, Hainaut, Belgium, and on St Augustine's roll of honour, where he is listed as Henry J. Warminger rather than James Henry. He was awarded the 1915 Star and the British War and Victory medals.

James's brothers also served in the Army during the war. In 1916 Arthur was conscripted and was posted to the 29th Battalion, Middlesex Regiment, a non-combatant, labour unit that was re-designated the 5th Battalion, Labour Corps, in 1917. In 1918 Philip was briefly a member of the 25th Training Reserve, which had been formed from the Norfolk Regiment's 10th (Reserve) Battalion in 1916. After the war, James's widow married again becoming Mrs Florence Bowles.

Lance Corporal 28285 Herbert Francis Gooch, 1st Battalion, King's Own (Royal Lancaster) Regiment, formerly Driver T/27490 (Horse Transport), Army Service Corps

Herbert Francis Gooch was born in the parish of St Peter per Mountergate (also known as Parmentergate), Norwich, in 1889, the fourth of the ten children of Thomas Wade Gooch, a pastry cook and confectioner, originally from Great Yarmouth, and Harriet Frances Gooch née Storey, originally from Ludham, Norfolk. Herbert's older siblings, in order of birth, were Audrey, Arthur and Charles; his younger, Annie, Frederick, George, Edward, Ernest and Violet. Mr and Mrs Gooch, who had married in Great Yarmouth in 1880, were recorded in the 1881 Census at 6 Healds Buildings off Rose Lane in the parish of St Peter per Mountergate. They were still there in 1891, so this is probably where Herbert was born. By 1901 they had moved to 60 Beaconsfield Road in the parish of St James Pockthorpe. At this date Herbert was still at school. His older brothers were working for the Great Eastern Railway, Arthur as a telegraphist and Charles as a telegram messenger.

Herbert enlisted in Norwich on 10 April 1909. His Army Service papers have survived and as he enlisted before the war these provide details about his life between the 1911 Census and the war which are hard to come by for most Great War servicemen. Prior to enlisting he had been employed as a clicker (leather-cutter) for a major Norwich shoemaker, Howlett & White (later known as the Norvic) at its factory in St George's Plain in the parish of St George Colegate. Herbert had served a five-year apprenticeship, starting at the age of 14 in 1903 and ending on 1 February 1908. According to a reference written by his foreman, George Worthington, Herbert had left the firm at the conclusion of his apprenticeship, aged 19. The firm was actually expanding at this period, so it is unlikely he had been laid off. While his character was rated as sober and honest and his conduct satisfactory, his reason for leaving is given rather opaquely as 'Change necessary', which suggests he was not satisfied with making shoes for a living. The recommendation of his recruiting officer, a major in the Norfolk Regiment, appears to support this assumption, describing Herbert as:

A very respectable & intelligent man, above the ordinary standard. Has been accustomed to driving, is very anxious to join the ASC [Army Service Corps]. *Has a 7th Standard Education.*

The medical officer, passing him fit for service, noted he was 5ft

3¼ in height (two or three inches below the average adult British male at this period), with a fair complexion, light brown hair and blue eyes. He had a number of tattoos on his left arm and ring finger.

Herbert signed on with his chosen arm of the British Army, the Army Service Corps, for only two years 'with the colours' and ten years in the Reserves. The Cardwell reforms of the 1870s had brought in the option of enlisting for 12 years (known as Short Service) rather than 21 years, which had been the norm since the Napoleonic era. With so small a standing, professional army, the bulk of which was serving in remote outposts of the Empire, it was thought prudent to have a reserve of fit, trained men to call upon in times of national emergency. Reservists were obliged to attend training 12 times a year and be ready to return to the colours in the event of a general mobilisation. The ASC was formed in 1869 to unify the various Army supply formations that had previously come under the command of the Commissariat and the Military Train. Herbert's first posting was to No. 2 Company. This was a Horsed Transport Depot company based in Woolwich, Kent, used for the induction and training of recruits. Two years later, the 1911 Census records Driver (equivalent to Private) Herbert Gooch at Southill Barracks in Chatham, Kent, with No. 48 Company, his duty specifically defined as 'Driving a pair of horses'. Although motorised transport was in use by this date, the horse-drawn wagon was still the Army's principal method of transport.

On 9 April 1911, the two-year component of his service complete, Herbert was transferred to the Reserves and returned to civilian life. A record among his Army Service papers notes that almost exactly a month earlier he had been admitted to hospital in Chatham with a common enough ailment of soldiers and sailors of that era, gonorrhoea. He was diagnosed as having only a mild contagion, indicating the infection had been detected early. Nevertheless, Herbert would have had to endure a very uncomfortable week and a half undergoing the standard treatment of the day before antibiotics of flushing out the bladder with an antiseptic solution via a catheter and scraping the urethra internally. Despite this minor blot on his record, his Commanding Officer noted that his conduct had been very good and there had been 'no instance of drunkenness in whole service of two years' and he was accordingly issued with a Sobriety

Certificate, presumably for presentation to any potential employer. His wish was to work as a groom or coachman using the skills and experience he had gained in the ASC in the care and management of horses. It is not known whether Herbert obtained civilian employment in this sphere or whether he returned to Norwich, although a note among his Service papers, that some sort of medical report had been sent to a doctor in Prince of Wales Road, Norwich, possibly notifying him of his treatment for venereal disease, suggests he returned there at least initially. Older brother Arthur, who had married in 1908, was now living in Ipswich where he was still working for the Great Eastern Railway, while Charles, who had been promoted from telegram messenger to telegraphist, was living in a boarding house in Bury St Edmunds with several other railway employees.

At the beginning of August 1914, as war became inevitable, Reservists were recalled to the colours. Herbert was mobilised at Woolwich on 5 August. By the 11th he was at Avonmouth waiting for a ship to take him to France, landing, probably at Le Havre, on the 12th. By the 13th he was in Rouen where the ASC was assembling a massive depot of horses and supplies, part of the Lines of Communication, the vast logistic operation that maintained the British Expeditionary Force (BEF). It is reckoned it took seven men, not counting medical support, to keep one soldier at the Front supplied. Nothing more is recorded in Herbert's Service papers until he was granted leave in April 1915. On 10 June 1915 he was appointed acting corporal and on 15 August he was posted from Rouen to a railhead supply detachment at Chocques near the Béthune Front. Here on 12 September, being 'surplus to establishment', he reverted to the rank of driver. After seven days' leave in December, Herbert was back in France, moving supplies by horse-drawn wagon from the railhead at Chocques to the Front.

In April 1916 Herbert was posted again, this time to a B.H.T.D. (Base Horse Transport Depot), and on 22 June he was posted yet again, this time to the 32nd Divisional Train, an ASC supply column attached to the 32nd Division, a New Army division made up of locally raised Service battalions from all over Britain and Ireland that was then preparing for the 'Big Push' on the Somme. Eight days later he was posted again, to the 90th Field Ambulance, one of three mobile Royal Army Medical Corps units attached to the 32nd Division, presumably to help manage their horses or motorised transport. The five months during which the Battle of Somme dragged on, from July to November, would have been among the most stressful that Herbert had ever faced. It is little wonder that on 25 August he went absent without leave when on active service from his billet (temporary civilian lodgings) until apprehended by the Military Police at about 10 p.m. This was a serious offence for which the ultimate sanction was death by firing squad. However, if the Army shot everyone who went AWOL for a few hours for a drink at the local estaminet or a visit to a brothel, it wouldn't have had many men left to fight the Germans. In Herbert's case he was punished with the humiliation and discomfort of four days' Field Punishment No. 1, being manacled to a post or wagon wheel in the open air for up to two hours each day.

Nothing more is known of Herbert's movements until September 1917 when he was, in the words of his active service sheet 'Compulsorily transferred in the interests of the Service' to the 11th Battalion, King's Own Royal (Lancashire) Regiment, a Service battalion which had been formed in 1915 as part of the 40th Division, a formation composed of so-called 'Bantam' battalions, that is, of soldiers below the Army's minimum height requirement of 5ft 3. Herbert, as we know from his medical report, was a quarter of an inch above this standard. He was transferred retaining his ASC rate of pay, which was 2d (two old pence) a day higher than that of an ordinary infantryman because of the skill required to manage teams of horses or maintain motor vehicles. His transfer does not appear to have been a punishment. The Army was simply short of men due to the enormous losses it was then suffering in Flanders during the 3rd Battle of Ypres, commonly known as Passchendaele.

On 10 November 1917 Herbert married Alice Armes of 30 Magpie Road, the daughter of Philip Armes, a shoemaker, at St Augustine's church. The rector, the Revd J. H. Griffiths, officiated. Their married life stated at 38 Magpie Road, though Herbert was not destined to spend much time there. On 5 February 1918 he was posted to the 1st Battalion, King's Own (Royal Lancashire) Regiment, a Regular battalion, part of the 4th Division then based in the Arras sector. Two days later he joined the Battalion's 'A'

Company and two weeks after this, on 21st, he was appointed lance corporal, a temporary, unpaid position. On 28 March, the 4th Division met the full onslaught of the first phase of the German Army's spring offensive, the Kaiserschlacht, at Arras. Having survived this, Herbert's Battalion was flung into the breach on 18 April to try to halt the second phase of the spring offensive, the Lys, at Béthune. Here Private Herbert Gooch received a gunshot wound to the head. He was evacuated to Field Ambulance No.12 and then to General Hospital No. 4 at Camiers where he died on 20 April, aged 29. His personal possessions, which were returned to his widow in December, comprised 17 postcards, 1 marriage license, 5 greeting cards, 1 cigarette case, 15 photographs, a pipe and a gold ring. Herbert is buried at the Étaples Military Cemetery, grave no. XXXIX.K.4A, and is commemorated also on St Augustine's roll of honour. He was awarded the 1914 Star and the British War and Victory medals.

Private 57162 Thomas Stephen Crosskill, 20th Canadian Infantry Battalion (Central Ontario Regiment), Canadian Expeditionary Force, formerly Private, 12th Regiment (York Rangers), Canadian Militia, and Gunner, Royal Field Artillery, [British] Territorial Force

Thomas Stephen Crosskill was born in Peckham, Camberwell, London, on 23 June 1890, the fourth surviving child of Walter Peter Crosskill, a shoemaker and later a tinsmith and iron-worker, and Elizabeth Ann Crosskill née Daynes. His parents, both Norwich born, had married in Norwich in 1877 but by 1881 were living in Bermondsey, London, leaving behind their first born, Robert, born 1878, with his grandparents, Robert and Susannah Daynes, licensees of the Turkey Cock pub in Elm Hill. After moving to London Thomas's parents had at least six more children: Charles (born 1882, died 1886), Water (1883), Elizabeth (born 1885, died 1894), Susannah (1887), Thomas (1890) and a second Charles (1892). By 1891 the family, still without Robert, was living in Vaughan Place, Peckham. By 1899 the family seems to have moved back to Norwich, as Thomas was admitted to Bull Close Boys School on 22 August that year. His home address was now 10 Bull Close Road in the parish of St Paul. The family was still there in 1901 and now included three more children: David (born 1896), William (1898) and a second Elizabeth (1902). Thomas left school on 22 June 1904, the day before his 14th birthday. By 1911 the family had moved again, to 12 Leonards Street in the parish of St Augustine. Their elder children, including Thomas, had left home by this date, leaving only the three youngest at home. During and after the war, Mr and Mrs Crosskill lived at 8 Gildencroft, part of a row of then rather dilapidated 16th-century cottages opposite St Augustine's churchyard.

Thomas emigrated to Canada on 29 April 1910, departing from Liverpool on SS *Virginian* and arriving in Quebec on 7 May. Assisted-passage schemes enabled young men and women to seek adventure and hopefully better employment prospects in the outposts of Empire. According to the ship's immigration manifest Thomas's final destination was the town of Bradford, Ontario, where he was going to work as a labourer. His former occupation in England was given as shoemaker. The 1911 Census of Canada locates Thomas (or Tom as he now seems to have been called) lodging in the Peel District of southern Ontario, working on the roads as labourer. He had become a naturalised Canadian citizen by dint of length of residency. Curiously, the 1918 Norwich Absent Voters Register lists Thomas as resident at his parent's home, 8 Gildencroft, which might indicate he was on leave there when the roll was taken. Thomas signed his Attestation papers in Toronto on 8 January 1915, having previously enlisted in Aurora in the 12th Regiment (York Rangers), an Ontarian militia unit. He was posted to the 20th Infantry Battalion, part of the second contingent of the Canadian Overseas Expeditionary Force (CEF), which was then preparing to be sent to France. His papers record that he was now a shoemaker again, rather than a labourer, unmarried and his religious denomination Baptist. He had been recorded as Church of England when arriving in

Canada in 1910 so he had perhaps become a Baptist while there. He was 5ft 6¾ in height, with a dark complexion, brown hair and brown eyes. His papers also reveal that he had been a member of the Royal Field Artillery's Territorial Force in England, presumably the East Anglian Brigade.

The 20th Canadian Infantry Battalion was established in Toronto in October 1914 through an amalgamation of several Ontarian militia units, including the York Rangers. However, it did not begin to assemble as an operational unit until May 1915, shortly before sailing for Britain, where it remained in training until September before going over to France as part of 2nd Canadian Division, fighting at Loos, the Somme, Vimy Ridge and Passchendaele. Private Thomas Crosskill, 27, was killed in action on 23 April 1918. At this date the Allies were under severe pressure on the Western Font during the second phase of German Army's massive spring offensive, the Lys. The 20th Battalion's War Diary records that they were entrenched at Neuville-Vitasse near Arras at this date. The day's work mainly consisted in routine probing of no man's land for enemy movements. There is no mention of Thomas's death and he seems to have been the only casualty in the Battalion that day. It is possible indeed that his death resulted not from enemy action, but from 'friendly fire'. Enemy action that day was 'very quiet, very little hostile shelling'. The Diary notes, however, that at 11.35 p.m. shells from their own batteries and 18 pounders 50 yards behind their line fell short onto their positions. Two weeks after his death his parents, brothers and sisters placed a death notice in the *Eastern Daily Press*. It included the verse:

> *A devoted son, a faithful brother,*
> *One of God's best towards his mother;*
> *He bravely answered duty's call,*
> *His life he gave for one and all.*
> *But the unknown grave was the bitterest blow,*
> *None but an aching heart can know.*

In fact his grave is not unknown. He is buried at Wailly Orchard Cemetery, Pas de Calais, France, grave no. II.B.24, and commemorated also on St Augustine's roll of honour. His name is inscribed in the Book of Remembrance in Brampton Great War

Memorial in Brampton, Ontario, Canada. He was awarded the 1915 Star and the British War and Victory medals. On 14 May 1918 the *Toronto Evening Telegram* published an obituary notice based on information supplied by his elder brother:

> *Robert Crosskill has received word that his brother Pte. Thomas Crosskill, was killed in action in the recent German drive. He enlisted in Aurora with the York Rangers and went overseas with the second contingent. He was at the front for fifteen months. Beginning with the battle of Loos, he fought at St. Eloi, the third battle of Ypres, the Somme and Vimy Ridge, where he was blown up by a shell. After five months in England he returned to the firing line. He was a first bayonet man and a bomber.*

In 1935 his photograph in uniform was reproduced in a commemorative volume on the military service of men of the Municipal District of Peel, Ontario.

Four of Thomas Crosskill's brothers served in the armed services of the British Empire during the war. Eldest brother Robert had served 17 years as an able seaman in the Royal Navy between 1893 and 1910, some of it on board the battleship HMS *Glory.* In November 1914 he enlisted in the 4th Battalion, Norfolk Regiment, but was dismissed after just six days as being physically unfit for military duties. He was 36. He seems then to have emigrated to Canada with his wife Nellie and enlisted in Brampton, Ontario, as a private in the 126th (Peel) Infantry Battalion, a Reserve unit, but did not go overseas. Older brother Walter served on the Western Front from late 1914 right through to 1919 as a private in the 1st Battalion, Norfolk Regiment. Younger brother, Charles, was a Leading Stoker in the Royal Navy, serving in submarines in the Adriatic campaign against the Austro-Hungarian Imperial and Royal Navy, and in monitors off the coast of Belgium, as well as in the Dardanelles campaign. Youngest brother William enlisted as a private in the 9th Battalion, Queens Royal (West Surrey) Regiment during 1918. All survived the war.

Private 27049 Bertie George Crosskill, 2nd Battalion, Duke of Edinburgh's (Wiltshire Regiment), formerly Private 36349, Essex Regiment

Bertie George Crosskill was born in the parish of St Augustine, Norwich, in 1898, the only known child of Maria Crosskill née Bone. His mother had married a William Hubbard Crosskill in Norwich in 1889 but no other record of this man has been found. Had he perhaps married under a false name? In the 1901 Census, 3-year-old Bertie is recorded living with his mother, described as a widow, in the home of his grandmother, Maria Bone (also widowed), at 3 Eagle Opening, a small yard near the Spread Eagle pub on Sussex Street, St Augustine's. Both women were employed in shoemaking. The attendance register for Bull Close Senior Boys School notes that Bertie was admitted as a pupil on 8 April 1907, having previously been a pupil at Bull Close Juniors until the age of 8 or 9. At this time his home address was 27 Palace Yard, possibly St James's Palace Yard off St James's Street in the parish of St James Pockthorpe. Bertie left school on 1 March 1912 aged 14. By 1911 he and his mother were back with his grandmother in Eagle Opening, though then at No.4. Bertie's mother was now described as a shoe-trimmer.

Bertie Army Service papers have not survived and there is no record of when or where he enlisted; however, given his age – he was not 18 until 1916 – and the fact that he was not awarded the 1915 Star, he was almost certainly a 1916 conscript; indeed his Essex regimental number suggests his first posting was to a Service battalion in 1917. Private Bertie Crosskill was killed in action on 8 May 1918, aged 19 or 20. The War Diary entries of the 2nd Battalion, Wiltshire Regiment, for this week give the impression this was a notably quiet period. On the 9th, however, it notes that a party attached to the 2nd Battalion, Bedfordshire Regiment re-joined them in the evening and it was only then that it was discovered that the detachment had been in action with the 2nd Battalion, Bedfordshire Regiment, on the 8 May and had suffered heavy casualties. The War Diary of the 2nd Bedfordshires rounds out the story. The British and French armies in Flanders had been severely weakened by the German's second spring offensive, the Lys, in early April. On 19 April, the British 30th Division put together a composite brigade composed of companies drawn from the best remaining fighting men of the 2nd Bedfordshires, 2nd Wiltshires, 16th and 17th Manchesters and 2nd Yorkshires. This Brigade was then put in to hold the line between Vlamertinghe and Reninghelst against further anticipated attacks while the rest of the Division regrouped. Two companies each drawn from the 2nd Bedfordshires and 2nd Wiltshires composed No.1 Composite Battalion, which was placed under the overall command of the 2nd Bedfordshire Regiment's HQ staff. Fighting was particularly intense between 25 April (2nd Battle of Kemmel) and 29 April (Battle of Scherpenberg), with more than 100 casualties. On 8 May the Germans briefly resumed their offensive, starting with a heavy barrage of trench mortars and gas shells before storm troopers and special pioneer companies armed with *Flammenwerfer* (flamethrowers) forced French troops on their right flank to retreat, which in turned forced the Beds and Wilts Composite Battalion to withdraw to their support trench to avoid being outflanked. A counterattack by the Allies to try to recapture their original front line failed and the German guns kept up a heavy bombardment until evening. Casualties were high. The two Wiltshire Regiment companies on detachment lost 23 killed in action and many more wounded or missing. Bertie's remains were never identified and he has no known grave. He is commemorated on the Tyne Cot Memorial, Zonnebeke, Belgium, and on St Augustine's roll of honour. He was awarded the British War and Victory medals. He does not appear to have been closely related to Thomas Crosskill. *(See p. 192)*

Second Lieutenant Gordon Robert Lovelace Jode, 12th (Yeomanry) Battalion, Norfolk Regiment, formerly Squadron Sergeant-Major 1273, 1/1st Battalion, King's Own Royal Regiment, Norfolk Yeomanry

Gordon Robert Lovelace Jode was born in the London borough of Sutton on 3 June 1885, the third child of William Lovelace Jode and Kate Emily Jode née Jeary. His father, the son of a Camberwell jeweller and goldsmith, was a travelling salesman in fancy stationery who later ran his own retail printing and stationery business. His mother, who grew up in the village of Eaton south of Norwich, was the daughter of a Norwich bookseller, Herbert Jeary. They married in Norwich in 1881. Gordon was baptised in Sutton parish church on 28 June 1885. Gordon was a popular Christian name at this time; the death of General Gordon at Khartoum in January 1885 had produced an upsurge of patriotic emotion. Curiously, however, for some unknown reason, Gordon's wife and in-laws usually called him Peter. The surname Jode almost certainly indicates Jewish ancestry at some indeterminate point in the past. Versions of the name, possibly derived from Yehuda or Joshua, are found in English records as early as the 13th century. Gordon's direct ancestry, however, has only been traced with any certainty to a William Jode born in Suffolk in 1778.

Between 1881 and 1890 Gordon's parents lived in London, first in

Camberwell, where their first child Kathleen was born in 1883; then in Sutton, where Albert (1884), Gordon (1885), Stella (1888) and Hilda (1889) were born. Another child, Stanley, died when just six weeks old in 1886. By 1891 the family had moved to St Albans, Hertfordshire, where it was now prosperous enough to employ a domestic servant. Here the last two members of the family, Mabel (1891) and Bertha (1894), were born. All the Jode children except Stanley, who seems to have died before he was baptised, were given the additional surname Lovelace in order to benefit from an endowment established by the will of a wealthy 18th-century ancestor on their father's side of the family. Girls were entitled to a sum of money towards a dowry, boys a contribution towards the cost of their education. Gordon and Albert, who died of meningitis in 1897 aged 13, probably received small educational grants from the Lovelace Trust though this cannot be verified as the Trust's records for this period are lost.

Sometime before 1900 the family moved to Norfolk, settling at 'Glenview', 72 School Road, Drayton, a village on the north-west outskirts of Norwich. Gordon's father now owned his own stationery printing and retail business. Missing from the Jode household in the 1901 Census were Kathleen, 17, employed as a lady's help by a landed proprietor in Penge and Gordon, 15, lodging with his aunt, Miss Lucy Jeary, above the family's stationery shop in St Giles Street where he was working during the day as a sales assistant. Later in 1901, possibly after his 16th birthday in June, Gordon was engaged as a junior clerk by Norwich Union Life Insurance Company, a position he retained until the outbreak of war in August 1914.

On 11 February 1911, Gordon, 25, enrolled in the Norfolk Yeomanry on a four-year term. His medical examination reveals that he possessed an above average physique for a young man of that era, being 6ft tall, 'fit and of good physical development'. The Norfolk Yeomanry, more formally known as the King's Own Royal Regiment of Imperial Yeomanry, had been established in 1901 at the personal direction of King Edward VII, who was its first honorary colonel-in-chief. Its royal association set it apart from other yeomanry regiments. Rather than the standard-issue khaki, its officers and men wore a well-cut royal blue tunic with yellow facings and a black metal helmet with yellow plumes that would not have been out of place in the Crimean War 50 years earlier. In addition, unlike other yeomanry regiments, its troopers and not just its officers were issued with cavalry swords as well as Martini–Enfield carbines. Within the county's military hierarchy the Norfolk Yeomanry was regarded as a select unit with membership, even for other ranks, restricted to gentlemen from good county families who had riding experience or, at the very least, demonstrated an aptitude for looking smart on a horse. In 1908 it joined the new Territorial Force set up under the Haldane Reforms. This brought in more recruits from the urban middle-classes, young, upwardly mobile men such as Gordon. Seeking recruits in February 1915 the Regiment placed a notice in the *Eastern Daily Press*: 'Recruits wanted of good class who are willing to serve abroad. Good horseman preferred'. By October, still short of suitable recruits, the Regiment sought to modify the image it had largely fostered itself that it was officered by scions of the aristocracy and manned by the sons of yeoman farmers. An editorial in the *Eastern Daily Press* noted:

> *The very name Yeomanry suggests farmers, and they are well represented in the ranks, but there are no restrictions as to class. It must not be supposed that only the sons of farmers and country people are eligible: all are welcomed who are physically fit, but naturally it is an advantage if the recruit knows something about horses.*

The continued emphasis on the need for recruits to have some degree of horsemanship is ironic given that the Regiment would do all of its fighting on foot during the war and would eventually be absorbed into an infantry regiment. As a Territorial Gordon would have continued in his full-time civilian occupation at Norwich Union during the week. He would attend a set number of drill sessions per year including training in musketry and horsemanship in the evenings after work and on Saturdays, hence the Terriers' nickname of 'Saturday Night Soldiers'. He would also have attended a summer camp for a fortnight each year. In 1912 it was held at Northrepps Hall Park near Cromer and in 1913 at Beccles in Suffolk.

Two months after enrolling as a Territorial, the 1911 Census reveals the Jodes had left Drayton and moved to 5 Angel Road, a street of modest terraced houses just to the north-east of St Augustine's in the suburb of New Catton. Among those absent from the household at this date were Kathleen and Hilda. Kathleen was a nurse at St Luke's Hospital, London, while Hilda was a milliner for a draper in Holt in north-east Norfolk. Also absent was their father, who had gone to South Africa in 1903 to set up a new stationery and bookselling business. For Afrikaners a man named Jode would probably have been immediately classified as a *Boere Jode*, an Afrikaans-speaking Jew whose Yiddish-speaking ancestors had emigrated from Europe in the early 19th century. The idea was for the rest of the family to join him once the business was established. In January 1914 Kathleen and Mabel did just that, but neither Gordon nor his mother were keen to leave England. Mrs Jode had her roots in

Norfolk and Gordon was by now engaged to be married. On 8 May 1914 he wrote to Kathleen in the Cape with news from home. He had been coaching a rowing four on the river, playing tennis at a new club called the Pickwicks in Salhouse, weeding the lawn with his fiancée Maud and viewing the recently fire-damaged pavilion on Great Yarmouth's Britannia Pier, where he hoped the Pierrots would soon be playing again. (It had been put about in the press that the fire had been caused by a bomb planted by Suffragettes angered at being refused permission to hold their meetings there.) A horse for use at the Norfolk Yeomanry's summer camp, which began that year on 26 May at Holkham Park in north Norfolk, had suddenly been made available to him due to the death of its owner, a friend of his fiancée's family, farmers in Rackheath. As the Regiment compensated each man who provided his own horse at camp with the not inconsiderable sum of £5 this was a major boon.

On 5 August 1914, the day after Britain declared war on Germany, Gordon was embodied as a full-time trooper in the Norfolk Yeomanry, taking leave of his civilian life for the duration of the national emergency. When he had joined the Territorials in 1911, he had sworn an oath to make himself available for full-time active service in the event of a war, though as a Territorial he was not obliged to serve overseas like a Regular. Another Norfolk Yeomanry trooper, a sanitary inspector from Swaffham named William Johns (later known as W. E. Johns, author of the Biggles stories), wrote of his exuberance at finally having a foe to fight:

> *A yeoman, I led my mare from the stables, and, slashing with my sword at imaginary foes, galloped down the drive to what, in my youthful folly, I supposed to be death or glory. I had yet to learn that in war there is plenty of death but little glory: that in war only death is real: that the glory is simply gilt and tinsel to wrap around the other so that it looks less like what it really is.* [*Flying*, 13 August 1938]

With three and half years' experience in the Yeomanry, including attendance at four summer camps, Gordon was clearly regarded as prime NCO material, as only a month after the Regiment went on to a war footing he was promoted to corporal, agreeing at the same time to serve overseas if called upon to do so. Six weeks later, on 24

October, he was appointed acting sergeant, a temporary extension of his non-commissioned authority though without additional pay.

Over the following 11 months the Norfolk Yeomanry undertook coastal defence duties and training with the Essex and Suffolk Yeomanry as part of the 1st Eastern Mounted Brigade, operating from a base at Rendlesham in Suffolk. But this wasn't proper war and there was tremendous excitement when finally in September 1915 the Regiment was given orders to proceed overseas. In the days leading up to embarkation rumour spread that they were being sent to France, in fact their destination was the Dardanelles. The Regiment had to leave their horses behind, which was a blow as it probably meant they would be fighting on foot as infantry unless remounts were to be supplied, which seemed unlikely given the extremely circumscribed battle zone they were being sent to. On 25 September they sailed from Liverpool on the White Star liner RMS *Olympic*. Few on board, not even the majority of the officers, knew as they steamed south to Gibraltar that the Gallipoli campaign had ground to a halt and plans were even then being laid to withdraw the Anglo-French force there from the Peninsula.

The sea was rough throughout much of the voyage, which was otherwise without incident apart from picking up the shipwrecked crew of a French collier sunk in the Med by a prowling U-boat, whose periscope was spotted at one point and fired at. By the time they reached Gallipoli on 10 October the Dardanelles expedition, which had begun barely six month earlier with high hopes of a rapid victory and a march on Constantinople, knocking Turkey out of the war, had degenerated into a fly-blown, pestilential stalemate. The 1st Eastern Mounted Brigade (though 'Mounted' was now redundant) was attached to the 54th (East Anglian) Division. On disembarking it was immediately dispatched to front line trenches near a position known as Norfolk Street in the ANZAC (Australian and New Zealand Army Corps) sector. Here they served alongside the 1/4th Battalion, Norfolk Regiment, who had been there since August and were thus able to pass on their hard-won know-how of the local terrain and the hazards and discomforts of trench warfare. Part of their stretch of the front line had been dug in the dry season, six feet below the bed of a dry watercourse which flooded in wet weather. For the men fighting in these cramped and squalid conditions there was no rest and no place of safety from shells and snipers. In November the weather suddenly turned very wintry, which provided relief from the heat and the flies but added the risk of frostbite and exposure.

Writing to Kathleen from Egypt on 21 January 1916, Gordon recalled his experiences at Gallipoli. The safe landings she had heard about were anything but:

> We had a pretty rough time of it for three months as no doubt you have heard ere this, & in a climate that bred dysentry [sic] like wild fire. More than half the regiment were in hospital before we left, – mostly from disease, & my own troop actually diminished from 36 to six, but has grown to 14 again since we have been here.

The Regiment had left England with 25 officers and 504 other ranks. It left Gallipoli three months later with just 13 officers and 221 other ranks fit for duty. Six men had been killed and 20 wounded by enemy action, but the vast majority of casualties resulted from disease and exposure. Sparing his sister the gruesome details Gordon's letter goes on with an account of the Mediterranean Expeditionary Forces' brilliantly executed evacuation of the Peninsula, undertaken over several days without the Turks suspecting a thing.

> It was a wonderful piece of work, splendidly organised, & completed without a hitch. I was one of the last to leave & it was exciting leaving the trenches empty with the Turks still firing away.

The Norfolk Yeomanry were evacuated in four parties over two days. The last to leave, a hand-picked party of 21 men, all crack shots, remained in the trenches firing on the Turkish positions until 1.40 a.m. on 20 December, when they too slipped away. Gordon was presumably a member of this party.

> We walked on blankets & sacks & anything that would deaden the sound of our feet. The camp & store dumps were all destroyed, carts smashed, stores destroyed, & in fact as little left for the Turks as possible. We reached the beach at three in the morning in a slight haze, & were away before they knew we

were gone. We went on an Arctic trawler to Mudros harbour [a nearby Greek island], *transferred to a P&O boat, the Beltana, a sister ship to yours* [Kathleen had sailed to the Cape on SS *Berrima* – both ships had subsequently been pressed into service as Australian troop transports], *11,000 tons & reached Alexandria harbour Xmas dawn in a storm.*

Gordon ends his letter to his sister with an account of his present situation in Egypt, hinting that a parcel or two would not be unwelcome. Thousands of packages from home intended for the troops at Gallipoli had never got to them, though some had been picked up at Mudros and Malta during the voyage to Alexandria. Their contents had really helped, he said, to make them look less like 'the haggard wretches who came away from the Peninsula'. He hoped to get a month's leave if a billet could be found on one of the crowded ships sailing for England. From their camp at Sidi Bashr just outside Cairo he expected to move shortly to Tel el Kebir, 'a fort 140 mile up country, which looks like being pretty dull'. Here he believed the Regiment would get back to full strength. Seventy recruits, he had heard, were ready to come out but had got measles and were replaced by 35 men of lower quality who had been hastily 'raked up' from various holding depots. To set against this disappointment, there was at least the exciting prospect of the Regiment acquiring 'gee gees' in Cairo next month, putting an end to the tedium of drilling as infantry and getting them mobile again. In fact no horses materialised and in February the Norfolk Yeomanry along with five other yeomanry regiments was incorporated into the 3rd Dismounted Brigade.

The Norfolk Yeomanry would remain in Egypt during the whole of 1916. In this situation, far from home and short of men, the promotion of experienced NCOs was considerably accelerated compared to peacetime. On 11 February 1916, the fifth anniversary of his joining the Regiment, Gordon was promoted to full sergeant, at the same time agreeing to four years' re-engagement (or less if the war ended sooner) in the Territorial Force. On 6 March he was promoted yet again: to squadron sergeant-major, a warrant officer rank. Soon after this promotion he was finally granted leave to return home, having been on active service overseas continually for six months.

On 6 April 1916 Gordon married his 24-year-old fiancée, Maud, eldest daughter of Rackheath farmer Thomas Goodley, in All Saints church, Rackheath. Their marriage was by licence because they did not have time during Gordon's leave to have the banns read. Instead a notice of their marriage appeared in the *Eastern Daily Press*. The bride's parents acted as witnesses. The wedding would have been a memorable one in the village as there would not be another one held there for almost two years, although the bride's mother was disappointed they couldn't have the wedding breakfast she'd planned because of food shortages. The day before the wedding Gordon made his will leaving all his property to Maud. His address now formally became that of his wife's parents: Manor Farm, Rackheath, Norfolk.

Back in Egypt on 28 August 1916 Gordon wrote again to Kathleen in South Africa. Hopes of a permanent post in England had not materialised and he had travelled back to Egypt with ten other sergeants, sailing from Devonport on SS *Oriana* in April. A stop at Malta gave him the chance to practice the haggling skills he had learned in Alex on Valetta's street hawkers, buying his bride some Maltese lace. Between Malta and Alexandra they were intercepted by a Royal Navy torpedo boat and warned that a U-boat was operating in the area, forcing them to divert round the north of Crete. After a week stuck in Alex waiting for transport, during which time he went to the races and admired the horses, knowing now he would probably never ride one into battle, he rejoined his Regiment at El Kubri, a place he found very hot and dusty with temperatures of up to 125 F in the shade. Here the troopers were employed building defences for the Suez Canal. Such was the intense heat during the day that work could only be carried out between 4 and 5 in the morning before the sun became too intense. Nevertheless, he felt they had done a good job in the circumstances and during the hours of enforced idleness many of the men had at least learned to swim in the Canal, which was so salty it was difficult to sink. At the end of June the Regiment moved to El Ferdan, about 80 miles to the north, then to El Ballah, where they were held in reserve during a Turkish raid on the Canal Zone, losing them ten days of their allotted two weeks' leave before they were released to continue to Alex in open trucks, observing the nightly breaking of fasts after sunset during Ramadan around the mosques as they travelled to Alexandria.

At the end of July the Regiment sailed about 300 miles west of Alex to the town of Sollum (As Sallum) on Egypt's border with Libya. They had been sent here to defend the town against marauding Senussi tribesmen, members of an Islamic sect financed by Germany and Turkey to harass British-occupied Egypt. Sollum had been occupied by the Senussi as recently as March but had been driven out and very considerately, as far as Gordon was concerned, kept away the whole time he was there. According to the regimental history life here was 'decidedly pleasant'. These were the Regiment's salad days; the horrors of Gallipoli were now more than half a year behind them and the even greater horrors of the Somme then unfolding on the Western Front were two thousand miles away. Here beside the Med the climate was generally good and the men were kept happy and in good health with sports, swimming and exercise. In a letter to Kathleen written in Sollum Gordon described the view from his guard post atop a cliff 600 feet above the shore. From here it was possible to see 40 miles out to sea and 10 miles inland:

> *The air up there is just so great. Down below the Med. is as blue* [as] *Reckitts paint is in their adverts & where we moored it was 49 feet deep & we could see the bottom as if there had only been a couple of inches.*

For an athlete like Gordon life was good. There were inter-regimental water polo matches, all of which Gordon rather boastfully claimed had been won by the Norfolk Yeomanry except on one occasion when he was sick and couldn't take part. Indeed, as he freely admitted to his sister, he didn't care if he remained there until the war ended. All the letters from England he had received lately were full of the news of another old friend who had 'gone west in France'. At least a dozen had either been killed or wounded, most on the Somme. 'I think I'm jolly lucky to be here, don't you?' he concluded.

In January 1917 the Norfolk Yeomanry were transferred to the 230th Infantry Brigade and renamed the 12th (Yeomanry) Battalion, Norfolk Regiment, thus completing their transformation from a mounted Territorial yeomanry regiment to an infantry Service battalion. In early March the Brigade HQ at Alexandria received a new draft of troops from England. Short of experienced junior officers the new Battalion began to look among its senior NCOs for officer material. On 13 March Gordon was granted a commission in the field (without having attended Officer Cadet School) and the rank of temporary second lieutenant. The 12th Battalion's War Diary notes that on 26 March 2nd Lieutenant Jode returned to Sollum from Alexandria with a new draft of troops. It seems to have been a pointless journey as a few weeks later the Battalion received orders to leave Egypt and moved into Palestine as part of the 74th Yeomanry Division. Here it took part in the campaign that would eventually drive out the Ottoman Empire from the Holy Land only to replace it after the war with British and French colonial masters under the terms of the secret Sykes–Picot Agreement.

On 3 May 1917 Gordon began a long letter to Kathleen from Palestine. His first impressions were favourable:

> *The Holy Land is quite a relief after the desert, but give me old England. There is a lot of barley about getting trodden out of existence & it seems a pity in view of the shortages at home. It's a rolling country, broken up with dry wadis or deep river beds, which make it difficult for transport. There are no hedges or trees except in the isolated gardens, then its prickly pear & olives & figs.*

In the same letter he describes watching the Second Battle of Gaza unfold below him while the 12th Battalion was held in reserve. The battle, fought between 15 and 19 April, was hugely costly to the British Army, which lost around 6,000 men for little material gain. St Augustine's men Albert Fox, Ernest Jolly and William Mason were killed in action here. On the 17th the 12th Battalion were entrenched at Wadi Ghuzze near a position dubbed 'Raspberry Hill':

> *I went upon a hill & watched the last battle & it seemed scarcely real, but more like a game. I could see our fellows advancing but could not see them falling. Through my glasses I could tell where they were held up & where they were pushing on. When I heard how many casualties there were I was awfully surprised. Loynes' lot were in it & one lot got strafed, but he is all right I'm glad to say.*

Major James Loynes was a charismatic Australian cavalry

commander. His regiment, the 11th Light Horse, took a prominent part in the battle and Major Loynes was in fact severely wounded. As a dismounted cavalryman, Gordon would no doubt have taken a special interest in the exploits of the still mounted Australian cavalry. On the 19th, still held in reserve, the 12th Battalion followed the attacking force:

> *A lot of shells go over us here, but they are mostly duds. We got one fellow laid out this morning, hit in his head & legs & I suppose he is on his way to civilization by now.*

After the battle, during which the 12th Battalion had been called upon to do nothing more than march up and down hot, dusty *wadis*, the troops went back to their familiar duty of digging defences. In a section of a long letter to Kathleen written shortly after his birthday that June, Gordon reflects on the fact that he was now 32. While his age didn't yet weigh upon him he was conscious he ought to be attending to business instead of 'spending three years picnicking in the sunny lands on the edge of the Mediterranean'. His father's business in South Africa was not thriving and his mother in Norwich was experiencing real financial hardship. Those of his surviving friends in the forces were scattered across the world, some wounded and some he had lost touch with. Feeling perhaps that he was concluding his letter on a melancholy note Gordon wrote a P.S. around the margins of the last page on 'the cutest little gentleman donkey' that the Regiment had adopted as its mascot. This was presumably Abdul, a baby donkey that had been found in May at El Gamli beside its dead mother. According to the regimental history it survived on a diet of tea, soapy water and shaving soap and accompanied the 12th Battalion through Palestine and France before being taken to England at the end of the war and given a home on the farm of one of the Regiment's officer, Major Barclay, at Brent Pelham, Hertfordshire. Unfortunately, a cow captured at the same time as Abdul had charged at an officer, got through their barbed wire and returned to the Turkish lines.

Between late October and mid-November the 12th Battalion was engaged in attacks on strategically important Turkish positions at Beersheba and Sheria in southern Palestine during the Third Battle of Gaza. From 4 December 1917 to 9 February 1918 Gordon held the rank of temporary captain while commanding a company in the field as part of the 74th Yeomanry Division, which took part in the capture of Jerusalem on 8 December and fought off repeated Turkish sorties throughout the remainder of the month. January and February were spent in road-making and training near Rahm Allah. At the end of his period of temporary promotion Gordon resumed the rank of 2nd lieutenant. During March 1918 the 12th Battalion fought its last major battle in the Middle East, the capture of Abu-el-Auf and the high ground behind it; an engagement that involved hand-to-hand fighting among the hills astride the Nablus road.

In April 1918, the German's massive spring offensive on the Western Front – the Kaiserschlacht – necessitated the withdrawal of two whole divisions, including the 74th Yeomanry, from General Allenby's command in Palestine to reinforce the beleaguered forces in France. The 12th Norfolks, with 35 officers and 835 other ranks, sailed from Alexandria on SS *Caledonia* on 1 May 1918, reaching Marseilles on the 7th. During May and June the Battalion was much preoccupied with training and equipping for the new fighting environment they now found themselves in: with gas alert drills, bayonet practice, rifle and Lewis gun instruction, and training in trench warfare and field manoeuvres at battalion, brigade and divisional level. Its War Diary records that while it was bivouacked at Nouvion in the Ardennes in May, 2nd Lieutenant Jode attended a bayonet fighting course at 230th Brigade HQ along with four NCOs. On the 25 May the Battalion moved into billets at Izel-les-Hameau where training continued. In June all of the Battalion's officers and a select group of NCOs were treated to a demonstration by the Tank Corps on how to coordinate tanks and infantry in battle. On the 20th news arrived that the Battalion was being transferred from the 74th Yeomanry Division, which had to reduce its brigades from four to three, to the 31st Division, a unit mainly composed of battalions from Lancashire and Yorkshire-based regiments. The 12th Norfolk's yeomanry credentials were maintained, however, by its inclusion in the 31st Division's reconstituted 94th Brigade, now designated the 94th (Yeomanry) Brigade. Here it was placed alongside the 12th Battalion, Royal Scots Fusiliers (formerly the Ayrshire and Lanarkshire Yeomanry) and the 24th Battalion, Royal Welsh Fusiliers (formerly the Denbighshire Yeomanry). Ominously, on June 1918, the 12th Battalion noted its first cases of influenza, a harbinger of the 'Spanish flu' pandemic that was then beginning its sweep around the globe, with 200 cases reported by their medical officer in one week alone. On 21 June 1918 the 12th Norfolks were moved closer to the Front in preparation for the planned big push that it was hoped would drive the German Army back over the Hindenburg line and out of France and Belgium. On the 25th the Battalion entered trenches near Nieppe Forest; its first active duty since Palestine. Here it was engaged in blowing up bridges and destroying enemy posts along the River Becque opposite the German front line. In August the Battalion began probing raids against German positions east of the river around the village of Vieux-Berquin, which was located in a farming area to the west of Armentières that had been overrun by the Germans in April.

It was during these final struggles of the war that 2nd Lieutenant Gordon Robert Lovelace Jode, 33, was killed in action, on 19 August 1918. He died leading his platoon as it secured the hamlet of Labris, a collection of enemy-occupied farm buildings on the road between Vieux-Berquin and Outtersteene. The 12th Battalion had begun its advance towards Labris in the early evening and at first met little opposition. Soon, however, German troops who had survived the creeping barrage, harried them with sniper fire and grenades thrown from their hiding places in the surrounding cornfields and shattered buildings. In such a situation it was the officers in their distinctive uniforms leading their platoons who tended to be picked off by snipers first. On 21 August the *Eastern Daily Press* published the text of an official report on the action at Labris:

> *A successful operation was carried out yesterday evening* [i.e., Monday 19 August] *between Vieux-Berquin and Outtersteene, on the right of our recent advance in that sector. Our line has been brought forward to the neighbourhood of the Vieux-Berquin and Outtersteene road, and 183 prisoners have been taken by our troops.*

What the official report could not mention due to censorship was that the 12th Norfolks suffered here their heaviest casualties in a single day during the entire war to date, losing eight officers and 38 other ranks killed in action and more than 100 wounded. The Battalion captured 12 machine guns, took 60 prisoners and counted more than 100 enemy dead on the battlefield, which suggests the fighting was intense with hand-to-hand combat in close quarters. It is not recorded precisely how Gordon died, indeed, unusually, his name and those of the other seven officers killed that day cannot be found in the Battalion's War Diary; they were, however, later recorded in the regimental history. As the Diary notes that their advance moved close behind the creeping barrage, it is possible Gordon was killed by a shell fired from a British gun rather than an enemy sniper

Gordon had survived almost to the end. Apart from a few minor skirmishes in September and October, this was the last major action in which the 12th Norfolks took part during the war. One week after his death, his widow, mother and sisters, and his in-laws, Mr and Mrs Goodley, placed death notices in the *Eastern Daily Press*. His mother's and sisters' included the words 'God knows why', which might be read two ways. His widow's was addressed simply 'From his heart-broken wife'. In his Army will, made on 5 April 1916, the day before his wedding, Gordon left Maud his entire property. This was settled by Probate in 1919 with his estate amounting to £243/4s/1d. Gordon is buried at Outtersteene Communal Cemetery Extension, Bailleul, Nord, France, grave no. II.C.56. He is commemorated also on the Norfolk Yeomanry Memorial in Norwich Cathedral; on the Norwich Union Great War Memorial in the vestibule of the Marble Hall in Surrey Street, Norwich; and on St Augustine's roll of honour. His

photograph was included in Norwich Union's Great War Book of Remembrance album. A trophy, the Jode Cup, was instituted to his memory by Norwich Union Staff Rowing Club and is still competed for annually. He was awarded the 1915 Star and the British War and Victory medals.

Maud Jode

Gordon's widow Maud later lived at Belaugh Grange, Wroxham, Norfolk, and remarried in 1922. In 1924 Gordon's older sister Kathleen, who had been a teacher in South Africa, returned to England to live with her mother and spinster sister Bertha in Gorleston on Norfolk's coast.

Mabel seems to have settled permanently in the Cape. In 1928 Gordon's father, having retired in South Africa, also returned to England. He died in Gorleston in 1931. Gordon's mother died four years later.

Private GS/72688 John James Fuller, 4th Battalion, Royal Fusiliers (City of London Regiment), formerly Private TR/9/10498, Training Reserve Battalion No. 9

John James Fuller was born in Norwich in 1899, the sixth of the eleven children of Robert Fuller, a corporation carter, and Ann Elizabeth Fuller née Williams. In 1891 the family was in Angel Road, New Catton, a suburb just to the north of St Augustine's. By 1901 they had moved to 35 Magpie Road. They were still there in 1911. John's older siblings were Elizabeth, James, William, Ester and Robert; his younger Ernest, Herbert, Mary, Ada and Arthur.

John enlisted in Norwich, probably as a conscript in 1917 when he was 18. He was first posted to one of the Army's new Training Reserve battalions, TR9, which had been formed in September 1916 from an amalgamation of the Norfolk Regiment's 10th (Reserve) Battalion with the Reserve battalions of three other East Anglian regiments: the Bedfordshires, Northamptonshires and Suffolks. At this stage of the war recruits were transferred after training to front line battalions often with little or no connection to their place of origin. In John's case he was posted to the 4th Battalion, Royal Fusiliers (City of London Regiment). The GS prefix to his new Service number (meaning General Service), indicates he had joined up for the duration of the war only. John was killed in action on 31 August 1918 during the Second Battle of Bapaume, aged 18 or 19. This following account of the 4th Battalion's costly part in the battle from the regimental history is closely based on the Battalion's War Diary:

On August 31st the 4th Battalion, who had moved up to positions south-east of Ecoust, attacked eastwards. Ten minutes before zero the assembly positions were subjected to a heavy shell and machine-gun fire, and there were many casualties; and when our barrage began, five minutes later, it missed the chief obstacles in the way of the Royal Fusiliers' advance. As a consequence, while the battalions on both flanks advanced with little trouble, the 4th Royal Fusiliers were decisively checked by machine-gun fire from the sunken road, about 250 yards to the east. Z Company made several most gallant attempts to reach these guns, but the men were mown down, and all the officers but one became casualties. [Source: *The Royal Fusiliers in the Great War,* p.302.]

John Fuller is buried at H.A.C. (Honourable Artillery Company) Cemetery, Ecoust-St Mein, Pas de Calais, France, grave no. 1.B.32, and is commemorated also on the St Augustine's roll of honour. He was awarded the British War and Victory medals. John's older brother William served as a driver in the 1st East Anglian Brigade, Royal Field Artillery, on the Western Front during 1917 and 1918 and survived the war.

Private 475135 Frederick Herbert Hall, 2/3rd Home Counties Field Ambulance, formerly Private 1920, East Anglian Field Ambulance, Royal Army Medical Corps (Territorial Force)

Frederick Herbert Hall was born in Norwich on 21 January 1892, the third child of Arthur William Hall, a stone mason, and Harriet Hall née French. Frederick had an older brother Edgar, born 1888. Another brother, Sidney, died at the age of four in 1894. In 1891 the family was at 1 Hammond's Yard between St Augustine's Street and the newly built Leonards Street. Another name for this yard was Stone Yard or Stone Mason's Yard (known today as Stone Mason's Court). Henry Hammond ran a monumental masonry business there in the 1870s and 80s, producing headstones and other funerary monuments. This business appears to have been taken over by Frederick's father in the 1890s. (A faded advertisement for 'Arthur Hall marble, stone and granite mason' can still be seen painted on a wall above Stone Mason's Court.) An Arthur Hall, stone mason, possibly the same man, is listed among those who worked on the re-building of Glandford church in north Norfolk between 1899 and 1906. The family was still in Hammond's Yard in 1901, grown by the addition of Frederick, Jessie, Gertrude and Sidney Frank (known in the family as Frank). By 1911 the family's address was 55 St Augustine's Street, which probably doesn't indicate a change of dwelling but the reassignment of their main address from Hammond's Yard to the area's main high street. Frederick and his older brother Edgar, aged 19 and 22 respectively, were now stone masons in the family business while their sisters Jessie and Gertrude were dressmakers. In 1909 Frank, also died prematurely, of meningitis aged 11.

Frederick enlisted in Norwich as a Territorial, probably in the East Anglian Field Ambulance. These mobile units of the Royal Army Medical Corps (RAMC) travelled with the troops up to the Front, providing first aid to the sick and wounded, moving those who needed more treatment on to casualty clearing stations. Frederick served as a stretcher-bearer as did his brother Edgar. The coincidence is noteworthy and may possibly indicate they had a conscientious objection to serving as combatants. Although Freddie's Army Service papers have not survived, Edgar's have and these note that he was a nonconformist in religion, almost certainly a Baptist, judging by the fact that he married in a Baptist church. Although English Baptists traditionally held strongly pacifist views their ministers generally left it to an individual member's conscience whether or not he enlisted prior to compulsory conscription in 1916. The explanation may, however, simply be that stretcher-bearers needed to have great upper body strength, something stone masons like Edgar and Frederick would have had in abundance. Frederick's Medal Roll Index card notes his first overseas theatre of war was Gallipoli; the accompanying date, 16 August 1915, suggests he was part of the 2nd or 3rd East Anglian Field Ambulance (EAFA) attached to the 54th (East Anglian) Division, the bulk of which had disembarked at Sulva Bay a week earlier with, in the words of the official report of the Dardanelles Commission, 'no artillery, no divisional signal corps, no field ambulances, no ammunition, and no mules'. Nothing of Frederick's personal experiences at Gallipoli are known though the hazards and discomforts there are well documented. One of the campaign's most famous figures was, like Frederick, a stretcher-bearer. Jack Simpson Kirkpatrick, nicknamed Murphy, was an English-born private in the Australian Army Medical Corps who, regardless of his own safety, brought down hundreds of wounded men from the killing fields above Anzac Cove on the backs of donkeys before being killed himself by enemy machine-gun fire in May 1915.

The 54th Division and the 3rd EAFA spent the remainder of the war in the Middle East. As Frederick was killed in action serving in the 2/3rd Home Counties Field Ambulance (HCFA) in France, he had clearly been transferred, perhaps during 1916 when the HCFA was first attached to the 58th (London) Division, or in 1917 when the 58th Division first went to France. Frederick's older brother Edgar, who had enlisted in the 2nd EAFA in July 1915 just as Frederick sailed for Gallipoli, was transferred to the 2/3rd HCFA on 18 May 1917 having been in France for less than a month. It is possible, therefore, that from then until Frederick's death Edgar and Frederick served as stretcher-bearers together. The surviving records disagree on the date of Frederick's death. The Commonwealth War Graves Commission (CWGC) has 1 September 1918, while *Soldiers Died in the Great War* and Frederick's Medal Roll Index card both have the 7th, as does his death notice in the *Eastern Daily Press* placed there by his parents. Family legend has it that Edgar was wounded in the same attack that killed Frederick. Private Edgar Hall's Army Service papers, unlike his brother's, have survived and these support this story, noting as they do that he received a gunshot wound to the scalp on 7 September but after treatment at a Field Ambulance was discharged the same day. Frederick and Edgar had only just returned from special leave in England. On 28 August Edgar married Rose Hilda Brown at the Silver Road Baptist Church, Norwich. The witnesses were his sister Jessie and his brother Frederick. Edgar's Service papers note that he returned to the Front on 2 September, presumably accompanied by his brother. A letter written to Frederick's father in 1920 by the Imperial War Graves Commission (the former name of the CWGC), notes that while his son was originally buried in Moislains churchyard in the Somme region, his remains had been exhumed and re-interred in Peronne Communal Cemetery. The CWGC's notes say that the remains of four soldiers were moved from Moislains to Peronne with the agreement of the French and Belgian governments. Interestingly, a watercolour painting by war artist David A. Baxter in the Imperial War Museum depicts stretcher-bearers from a Field Ambulance moving the wounded near Moislains in September 1918. Frederick is buried at Peronne Communal Cemetery Extension, Somme, France, grave no. V.F.28. and commemorated also on St Augustine's roll of honour. He was awarded the 1915 Star and the British War and Victory medals.

Information received by the author from the Hall family suggests that Edgar's comparatively early death in 1931, aged 42, was due to injuries he received alongside his brother on the Somme in 1918. His Army pension record confirms that the scalp wound he received on the probable date of Frederick's death was fairly slight. More serious and longer lasting was mustard gas poisoning, which reduced his lung capacity by 20 per cent, causing chronic bronchitis. It was possibly this injury which brought about his discharge from the RAMC on 24 March 1919 and the issue of a Silver War Badge.

Private (First Class) James Cooke, 'G' Company, 2nd Battalion, 307th Infantry Regiment, 77th 'Liberty' Division, United States Army

James Cooke was born in Norwich on 11 June 1895, the fourth

surviving child of James Henry Cooke, a fishmonger, and Blanche Cooke née Barker who came from the village of Postwick south of Norwich. Four years before James's birth the 1891 Census recorded his parents and their two young daughters, Alice and Lily, at 3 Compass Street in the Norwich parish of St Etheldreda. Mr Cooke was a shoemaker at this period. By 1901 the family had moved to 2 Roache's Court off Elm Hill in the parish of St Simon and St Jude, and had grown with the addition of Emily, William, James, Florence and Thomas. Absent was eldest daughter, Alice, 15, who was now a domestic servant in Thorpe Hamlet. An eighth child, Sydney, was born in 1906. By 1911 the family had moved to 44 Leonards Street, St Augustine's. James, 15, was now a shoe-heeler. Sisters Lily and Emily were also working in the local shoe trade. In June 1911 James's older brother William, 18, emigrated to Canada, sailing on SS *Royal Edward* from Bristol to Quebec. His final destination was Smith Falls, Eastern Ontario, where he was going to work as a dairyman. The next big event in the Cooke family occurred on Christmas Day 1912 when second daughter Lily married Edward Larkman in St Augustine's church. Exactly a year later third daughter Emily married Frederick Tungate in the same church. In the meantime, James had emigrated to the United States to join William, who by this time had left Canada and moved about 500 miles due south to the city of Rochester, New York, on the other side of Lake Ontario.

Ellis Island immigration records note that James, 18, first entered the USA via New York City on 11 July 1913. He had travelled third class (steerage) on SS *Adriatic* from Liverpool. Built in 1907, the White Star liner carried 2,825 passengers on this voyage, 1,900 in steerage. The ship's manifest records a number of personal details about James: he was 5ft 4 in height (a couple of inches below the average British male height for the period), had fair hair, grey eyes and a light complexion. He could read and write and was a shoemaker. His ticket had been paid for by his brother William. His destination was Rochester, where he intended to join his brother to work as a labourer. His mother is named as his next of kin, even though his father was still alive. He was to die of cancer of the oesophagus on 31 December 1916, aged 51, 'after a patiently born illness' according to his death notice in the *Eastern Daily Press*.

Virtually all US Infantry Service records of the First World War were lost in a fire at a St Louis record depository in 1973, making it difficult to discover very much about James's time as a 'doughboy', as US soldiers were known colloquially. Some scattered facts do, however, make it possible to trace the outline of his brief military career. The US publication, *Soldiers of the Great War*, which records, state by state, the names of all who served in the American Expeditionary Force during the war, lists only one soldier named 'Private James Cook' (but no one called James Cooke) in its New York State volume. This soldier was from Victor, a small town about

15 miles south-east of Rochester. Happily, the Ontario County Department of Records has published a transcription of 20th-century naturalisations in Ontario County online. This includes a 'James Cooke' of Victor, who in 1915 made a declaration of intent at a court of law to become a naturalised US citizen, having had the minimum two years' residency needed in order to qualify. It also lists a William Cooke of Victor, presumably James's older brother, who made his naturalisation declaration of intent two years later. By this time William was married, his wife's name Harriet. The corroborating proof that the 'James Cooke' of Victor who sought US citizenship in Ontario County in 1915, the 'James Cook' of Victor in *Soldiers of the Great War* and the James Cooke who emigrated from Norwich, England, are the same man is provided by the Army Draft registration card of 'James Cooke' of Victor, which gives his place of birth as Norwich, England. Another piece of the jigsaw is contained in the records of the American Battle Monument Commission (ABMC), the US equivalent of the Commonwealth War Graves Commission. Its Honor Roll of American servicemen who died in the war (1917–18) and are buried or listed among the missing in overseas cemeteries records just one soldier named 'James Cook' with a New York State connection: Private (First Class) James Cook of the 307th Infantry Regiment, 77th Infantry Division. The 77th Division was known as the Liberty Division because of the image of the Statue of Liberty worn as a badge on its soldiers' tunics. It was established by the US War Department at Camp Upton, Long Island, New York State, on 5 August 1917. Its personnel were almost exclusively draftees from New York City and State. The ABMC notes that Private 'James Cook' entered the US Army in New York.

The Liberty Division sailed for France in a series of convoys between 28 March and 13 May 1918. The 307th Infantry Regiment sailed in the 7 April convoy, arriving in Liverpool on 17th. It was then transported by train to Dover. A history of the Regiment published in 1920, *From Upton to the Meuse with the 307th Infantry*, notes bluntly that 'nobody liked England', the little they saw of it from their chilly, over-crowded train being shrouded in mist and coated in frost. This was probably the last James ever saw of his home land. In France, the 77th Division formed part of the US 2nd Army Corps. From late August through to October 1918 the 2nd Corps

218

was engaged in the Oise–Aisne offensive, fighting its way north through France towards the Aisne Canal. The history of the 307th mentioned above (which lists 'James Cook' in its 2nd Battalion's 'G' Company) records that on 5 September 'G' Company re-joined the Battalion having lost its way during the night and inadvertently advanced into enemy-held territory. It was then sent to guard an outpost on a ridge above the village of Merval, the Liberty Division's next objective. The area, known as the Marais–Minard wood, was covered in forest and swamp. The regimental history continues:

> *September sixth and seventh passed without notable event beyond a slow but steady drain of casualties from artillery and machine gun fire, and constant drenching of gas where 'G' lay stretched across the swampy land.*

It was presumably here that Private James Cooke, 22, was killed in action on 6 September 1918. An obituary published in an Ontario County local newspaper under the headline 'Victor Boy Makes Supreme Sacrifice' provides intriguing additional details of James's life in the USA. Noting he was born in England, it says he had been about eight years in America when in fact he had lived there only four before enlisting. 'He was a young man of sterling qualities – "a good little fellow"'. At 5ft 4 he would indeed have seemed particularly diminutive next to most doughboys, whose average height was 5ft 8. An aunt is mentioned, a Mrs Alice Concanon, with whom James had been lodging and who looked upon him as her son. Mrs Concanon, a younger sister of his mother, had emigrated to the USA in 1897. The 1910 US Census records her in the town of Manchester in Ontario County married to Edward Concanon (or 'Canconon', as he is spelled in the Census), a New

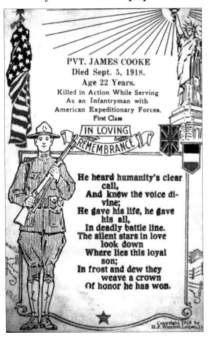

PVT. JAMES COOKE
Died Sept. 5, 1918.
Age 22 Years.
Killed in Action While Serving
As an Infantryman with
American Expeditionary Forces.
First Class

IN LOVING
REMEMBRANCE

He heard humanity's clear call,
And knew the voice divine;
He gave his life, he gave his all,
In deadly battle line.
The silent stars in love look down
Where lies this loyal son;
In frost and dew they weave a crown
Of honor he has won.

Copyright 1918 by
H.F. Wendell, Leipsic, O.

Yorker of Irish descent. James was inducted into military service by the Second District Draft Board of Ontario County and went from Victor to Camp Devens on 25 February 1918. He was only the fifth man of that contingent to be reported on the casualty list. Aunt Alice had received a letter from James shortly before news of his death reached her by telegram. He was stationed 'not far from Paris', getting ready 'to go into the big fight' and hoped to be home for Christmas. The obituary goes on to note that the family of James and his brother William (then living in Hathaways, a small settlement near Victor) had 'suffered heavy loss in the cause of freedom and justice', as both of their brothers-in-law had been killed in the war. One was presumably their younger sister Emily's husband, Private Frederick Tungate of the 8th Battalion, Royal Fusiliers, who was killed in action on the Somme on 6 August 1916. It is not known who the other was. None of James and William's other three sisters lost a husband. The obituary is a little ambiguously worded and it may be that the other brother-in-law was a brother of William's wife Harriet and therefore possibly either a Canadian or a US service-man. James Cooke (recorded as 'James Cook' in the ABMC's roll) is buried at the Oise-Aisne American Cemetery, Fère-en-Tardenois, France, and is commemorated also on St Augustine's roll of honour. In his home town of Victor, James is still remembered as the only US servicemen from the town to have died in combat during the First World War (two others died of disease). The town's American Legion post, No. 931, is named in his honour the James Cooke Post.

Private S/307337 Edward James Sizer, Army Service Corps

Edward James Sizer was born in Canning Town near Plaistow, Essex, in September 1891, the fifth surviving child of George Fickess Sizer, an excavator, originally from Barrington, Cambridgeshire, and Bessie Ann Sizer née Wotton, a dressmaker, originally from the village of George Nympton, Devon. His parents were married in Edmonton, Middlesex, in 1882. The family seems to have moved about a great deal if the children's places of birth are anything to go by: Alice, the first born (Cirencester, 1879); a first Edward (born and died Walthamstow, 1882); Ada (Holloway, 1885); Kate (Isleworth, 1888);

Rose and Edward (Canning Town, 1890 and 1891); Bessie (Dorking, 1894) and finally Agnes (Cromer, 1895). Their father's work presumably necessitated going where the excavation contracts took him. By 1901 the family had moved to Norwich, to 8 Primrose Road, Thorpe Hamlet. A few years later Edward was a pupil at the Boys Model School in Princes Street. In 1911 the family was still in Thorpe Hamlet, though now at 15 Chalk Hill Road. Edward, 19, was absent and cannot be found in the Census. He was perhaps at teacher training college; his Army Service papers state that his civilian profession was school teacher. Two of his sisters, Alice and Kate, were elementary school teachers at this date, employed by Norwich Town Council Education Committee, while younger sister, Bessie, was a student teacher, a not inconsiderable achievement when one considers that their father was illiterate and had started work as an unskilled labourer.

Edward enlisted or was conscripted in Norwich on 2 March 1916 but was not called up for military service until a year later, on 5 March 1917, aged 25. His address at this date was 15 Chalk Hill Road, his parents' house. At almost 5ft 10 he was well above the average male adult height for that era. His medical report notes that he needed glasses as his vision without them was poor. His weak eyesight and higher than standard educational attainment may have influenced the Army's decision to employ him as a clerk in a non-combatant unit, the Army Service Corps (ASC), which had a not altogether affectionate nickname in the Army of 'Ally Sloper's Cavalry' after a well-known newspaper comic strip character who was always finding ingenious ways of dodging work and creditors. Members of the ASC were better paid than their equivalent ranks in the infantry, did not normally face the dangers front line troops endured, and on the whole had better rations and more comfortable billets. Naturally, this led to resentment.

On 26 June 1917, three months after call up, Edward boarded a troopship at Southampton bound for Cherbourg. From here he travelled by train to Taranto in Italy. On 10 July he embarked from here on SS *Saxon* for Salonika (Thessaloniki) in north-east Greece. The Anglo-French expeditionary force based in Salonika had been sent there at the invitation of the officially neutral Greek government in the autumn of 1915 to bolster the beleaguered Serbian Army on the Macedonian Front. Edward arrived in Salonika on 15 July 1917, a little over two weeks after Greece had finally ended its neutrality and declared war on the Central Powers (Germany, Austria-Hungary, Bulgaria and Turkey). He now joined the 3rd Base Horse Transport Depot, which supplied the Army with pack horse and mule companies for moving supplies over the largely trackless terrain.

On 28 July 1917 Edward was transferred to 228th Brigade's Supplies Train. The 228th Brigade was created in the field in 1917 from a number of miscellaneous garrison units and was attached to the 28th Army Division. On 18 September 1918 the 28th Division was ordered to support the Cretan Division, a mainly pro-Allied Powers section of the highly factionalised Greek Army, in an assault on Bulgarian forces along a heavily defended ridge above Lake Doiran. The 3rd Battle of Doiran or Dojran Lake was an utter disaster for the Anglo-Greek force, which lost more than 7,000 men in the battle. On 21 September Edward was admitted to the 21st Stationary Hospital, Salonika, with pneumonia. Private Edward James Sizer, 27, died on active service in Salonika, Greece, on 22 September 1918, aged 27. He seems to have been a victim of the 'Spanish flu' pandemic, the first known St Augustine casualty to succumb. Edward is buried at Sarigol Military Cemetery, Kriston, Greece, grave no. A.140, and is commemorated also on the Boys Model School Memorial in Norwich Cathedral, as well as on St Matthew's roll of honour, Thorpe Hamlet, and on St Augustine's roll of honour. He also has an individual memorial on the east face of St Augustine's Great War roll of honour chancel screen, where a panel beside the choir stalls is inscribed in gilded lettering:

Sacred / To the memory of /
Edward J Sizer RASC
Teacher / And an esteemed member / Of this choir
Who died on Active Service / at Salonika
On the 22nd September 1918

Although the inscription says RASC (Royal Army Service Corps), the Corps did not receive the royal prefix until after the Armistice, two months after Edward's death. He was awarded the British War and Victory medals.

Private G/29587 Herbert Edward Fevyer, 7th Battalion, The Queen's (Royal West Surrey) Regiment

Herbert Edward Fevyer was born on 7 August 1899 in the Plomesgate Union Workhouse, Wickham Market, Suffolk, the son of Jessie Petra Fevyer. His father's identity is unknown. His mother, a dairy worker from Sudbourne, Suffolk, would have been 15 or 16 when she became pregnant. She was the daughter of George and Anna Fevyer. Her father was a mariner and Jessie spent some of her childhood in Hull where he was working as a seaman. In the 1901 Census she is recorded as a domestic servant in the home of a schoolmaster in Wickham Market. Herbert, however, aged 20 months, is recorded living at 39 Bevan Road, Lowestoft, with a 60-year-old widowed tailor, Elizabeth Beck, occupying one room in a house shared with another family. Although Mrs Beck is described as Herbert's grandmother, her real identity is a mystery, perhaps the mother of the Herbert's father, perhaps a foster mother. By 1911 Herbert's mother had married and moved to another part of the country. Of Herbert himself there are no more traces until the war.

Herbert Fevyer enlisted in Norwich. His Army Service papers have not survived, though given his age he was probably conscripted in 1917 when he was 18. The 7th Battalion, The Queen's Regiment, was a 'Kitchener' Service battalion that had been raised in Guildford in 1914. It formed part of the 55th Brigade, 18th (Eastern) Division, and served on the Western Front throughout the war. Private Herbert Fevyer, 19, was killed in action on 1 October 1918. The 7th Battalion's War Diary for this day records that its men spent the day cleaning the trenches and waiting to be relieved by another battalion. They had just fought in the Battle of St Quentin Canal, part of the Allies' struggle to break through the Hindenburg Line, and were looking forward to a bath and a rest away from the Front. 'The day passed quietly' the War Diary notes. 'Casualties O.Rs [other ranks] killed – 1. Wounded – 4'. Presumably, Herbert was the one. Even when nothing much was going on, there was always the danger of becoming the target of a sniper or the unlucky victim of a shell 'with your name on it'. He has no known grave. Herbert is commemorated at the Vis-en-Artois Memorial, Pas de Calais, France, and on St

Augustine's roll of honour where his name appears out of alphabetical order, suggesting it was added after the memorial screen was erected in January 1920. *Norfolk Roll of Honour* lists him under the nearby combined parishes of St Miles Coslany and St Martin at Oak, though he doesn't appear on the roll of honour board in St Miles and St Martin didn't have one.

Private 14737 Harold Alfred Victor Miller, 'C' Company, 9th Battalion, Norfolk Regiment

Harold Alfred Victor Miller was born in the town of Acle, Norfolk, on 11 May 1897, the second child of Harry Denton Miller, a baker and confectioner, and Alice Kezia Miller née Pollard, who was originally from Castle Acre, Norfolk. In 1901 the family was at 239 Raglan Street, Lowestoft, where Harold's father ran his own bakery business. In addition to Harold, the family included at this date older brother Denton and 9-month-old Dorothy, who died later that year

before her first birthday. At some point before 1911 the family seems to have moved to the Pulham Market area, as Harold was a pupil at the school there. By 1911 the family had moved again, to 121 Ber Street, Norwich, and had added three daughters, Annie, born 1902, Beatrice (1904) and Gracie (1905). At this date Harold's older brother, Denton, was working as an errand boy for a harness-maker, while Harold, 13, was a pupil at Surrey Street School. His parents later lived at 13 Angel Road, New Catton, just outside St Augustine's parish boundary, but probably not until after the war.

224

Harold enlisted in Norwich on 1 September 1914, aged 17. His Service papers have not survived, but the Norfolk Regiment's Wound Book notes that he was wounded on 7 October 1917 and hospitalised at the West General Hospital at Newport, Monmouthshire. The nature of his wound is not recorded. At this date the 9th Norfolks were in the front line near the town of Lens in northern France. Whether he was back with the 9th Norfolks by time of the Battle of Cambrai in late November 1917 is not known. He would almost certainly have been back in France to experience the German spring offensives of 1918. Having survived almost the entire war, Private Harold Miller, 21, was killed in action on 8 October 1918. He has no known grave. In the final weeks, the 9th Norfolks were advancing through the St Quentin area with the 2nd Battalion, Sherwood Foresters, on their right and the 118th American Infantry Regiment on their left, supported by Whippet mini-tanks, when they were ambushed by machine-gun fire from the direction of Brancourt and Jonnecourt, suffering such heavy losses (more than 60 were killed in a few minutes) that they were forced to withdraw in order to regroup.

Harold is commemorated at the Vis-en-Artois Memorial, Pas de Calais, France, and on St Augustine's roll of honour, as well as on St Mark's roll of honour in Hall Road, Lakenham. His name on the St Augustine's roll of honour has been added out of alphabetical order, which suggests it was a late addition, perhaps reflecting his parents' move after the war from Ber Street to Angel Road. He is listed under St Mark's parish in *Norfolk Roll of Honour*. His photograph was donated to Norfolk Library's Great War Memorial collection by his mother. It shows him with a lance-corporal's stripe on his upper right sleeve. He was awarded the 1915 Star and the British War and Victory medals.

Gunner 875510 Herbert Robert Powell, Royal Field Artillery (Territorial Force), formerly Acting Bombardier 1589, Royal Field Artillery (Territorial Force)

Herbert Robert Powell was born in Norwich in 1892, the sixth child of James William Powell, a general labourer, and Mary Ann Elizabeth

Powell née Perfect, who was a maker of pill boxes before marriage. Herbert's eldest brother, James William, was born out of wedlock in 1873 and bore his mother's maiden name. After marrying in 1874 his parents had six more children: Leah, Sidney, Claude, Violet (known as Daisy), Herbert and Olive, the last of whom was born in 1896. During this period and for years after, the family lived at 21 Mousehold Street in the parish of St James Pockthorpe. In 1896 Leah's newly wedded husband, William Sayer, came to live with them. Their first child, Sidney Sirdar (an Urdu word for a military leader), was born in 1900. They also had a paying lodger so it must have been a rather crowded household. In 1897 Herbert's eldest brother James, a shoemaker, married Emily Greaves and moved to Rose Yard, St Augustine's, where they began a family of their own. In 1901, just before the Census, Herbert's mother died, aged 48.

Ten years later, at the time of the 1911 Census, the Powell and Sayer families were still at 21 Mousehold Street, though without Sidney, who had died in 1907, aged 26, and Daisy, who had married Robert Green, a builder's labourer, in 1909. Like James she had moved to Rose Yard. Leah and William Sayer now had three more children, Samuel, Sarah and William, bringing the total head count in the household up to ten. Herbert was now a fitter and labourer, while younger brother Claude was in the shoe trade and their widowed father a labourer at a sewage works. In the autumn of 1912 Herbert married Ethel Loome, possibly Edward Loome's sister *(see p.89)*, a weaver of braces. It is not known where Herbert and Ethel lived. Their first and only child, Herbert, was born a few months later. At the same period Herbert's younger brother Claude died, aged 27.

Herbert enlisted in Norwich. His Army Service papers have not survived but his Medal Roll Index card notes he first went to France on 16 November 1915. The Commonwealth War Graves Commission records that Herbert held the rank of gunner and served in the 54th (East Anglian) Division's Ammunition Column. When the bulk of the 54th Division left England for the Dardanelles in July 1915 it left its artillery and supply train behind. It remained in Norfolk at Brandon and Thetford until mid-November when it was shipped over the English Channel to Blaringhem in northern France. Here, most of the Division's artillery officers and men were transferred to other brigades on the Western Front, while the guns and ammunition were sent to the Middle East. Herbert, who at one point held the rank of acting bombardier, seems now to have been transferred to the 153rd Brigade, Royal Field Artillery, then attached to the 36th (Ulster) Division. The Ulster Division and its artillery brigades fought on the Somme in 1916: at Messines, Langemarck and Cambrai in 1917 and through the German spring offensive of 1918 to the final 100 days of the war.

Gunner Herbert Powell, 26, died on 17 October 1918. The exact circumstances of his death are not known. By the autumn of 1918 the war in France had become mobile, as it had last been in 1914, but this time with the roles reversed and the Allied armies driving the retreating German Army before it. Such a rapid advance caused serious problems for the supply columns and artillery trying to keep up with the infantry and cavalry, having to move in the open, in daylight, over devastated roads within range of the enemy's howitzers. Herbert, however, is buried not in Flanders or northern France but over 400 miles away at St Germain-au-Mont-d'Or Communal Cemetery Extension near Lyon, grave no. B.71. There was a small British military hospital near here between 1917 and 1919; little is known about it but it may have been established to treat the sick or injured from the supply columns that passed through Lyon en route between the port of Marseilles and the Western Front.

Herbert is the last casualty (whose date of death is known) commemorated on St Augustine's roll of honour to have died on active service before the Armistice was signed on 11 November 1918. It is not known whether he lived in the parish but at least two of his siblings did: his sole-surviving brother James Perfect and older sister Mrs Daisy Green both lived in Rose Yard off St Augustine's Street. His widow Ethel may have been a sister of Private Edward Loome. Herbert was awarded the 1915 Star and the British War and Victory medals.

1918–1921 Spanish Flu

Private 40029 Edward Charles Betts, 12th Battalion, Suffolk Regiment

Edward Charles Betts was born in Norwich in 1876, the second surviving child of Edward Betts, a mustard miller, and Mary Elizabeth Betts née Pye. In 1881 the family was at 125 Wilderness Terrace off King Street in the parish of St Peter Southgate. Colman's famous mustard was made nearby at its Carrow Works and at least two, possibly three generations of the family worked for the company. Edward's grandfather, William Betts, was an agricultural labourer in the village of Shotesham, Norfolk, near Jeremiah Colman's original mustard mill at Stoke Holy Cross. By 1861 grandfather William, his wife Ann and their five children had moved to the parish of St Etheldreda, Norwich, just at a time when Jeremiah James Colman was building a new mustard works nearby in Carrow. Edward's father was a mustard miller there all his working life and Edward himself and his brothers and sisters also worked there. Mr and Mrs Betts had 11 children, five of whom died in infancy. Edward's surviving siblings were older brother Alfred and Ellen, Sydney, Lily and William. In 1911 the family, excluding Alfred, Ellen and Lily who had left home, was still at Wilderness Terrace (a precipitous, wooded hillside above Carrow Works was formerly known as the Wilderness Pleasure Gardens). On Christmas Day 1913 Edward married Ethel Maria Hicks, a widow, at St Augustine's church. After marriage he lived at his wife's home 63 Botolph Street, St Augustine's.

Edward enlisted in Norwich on 20 July 1916. His Army Service papers have not survived but the record of his award of the Silver War Badge in 1918 gives the dates of his enlistment and discharge. The Silver War Badge was awarded to serviceman who had been discharged from active service due to a disablement acquired as a result of their war service overseas. The need for such a badge had arisen early in the war when men with no obvious wounds or disability who had been discharged because they were no longer fit for military service were given white feathers, accused of cowardice or of being a shirker in public places because they were not in uniform.

Edward was posted to the 12th Battalion, Suffolk Regiment, which was established in Bury St Edmunds in July 1915 as a 'Bantam' battalion. Bantam units were made up of men below the Army's revised, wartime minimum height requirement of 5ft 3in. This does not necessarily mean Edward was of short stature, as by 1916 Bantam units were taking men of almost any height. Interestingly, the poet Isaac Rosenberg served briefly as a private with the 12th Suffolks while it was stationed at Bury St Edmunds in 1915. He found his fellow recruits, mainly Londoners like himself, 'a horrible rabble' and the Battalion itself 'the most rascally affair in the world'. The 12th Suffolks landed at Le Havre on 6 June 1916, part of 121st Brigade, 40th Division (known as the 'Bantam Division'). Nothing is known of Edward's movements between July 1916 and his discharge from the Army on 7 August 1918, although, presumably, he was with the 12th Suffolks at the Battle of the Ancre in November 1916, at Cambrai in November 1917 and the battles of the German spring offensives between March and May 1918. The reason for his discharge is given simply as 'wounds'. Immediately prior to this he was attached to the Suffolk Regiment's Depot, so had presumably been back in England for a few weeks or even months recuperating before he was medically assessed as no longer fit for active service.

Edward, 42, died in Norwich on 4 November 1918, a victim of the Spanish flu pandemic. In common with a small number of soldiers commemorated on St Augustine's roll of honour, Private Betts is not recorded in national rolls of honour as an official war casualty – in his case because he died after he was discharged. He was living on his Army pension at the time of his death, so presumably had not yet found work or was unable to work. An interesting consequence of his death appears in the Army Service papers of his younger brother Sydney John Betts, who served as a private in the Labour Corps in England, France and Ireland between 1917 and 1919. In October 1918 he was hospitalised for ten days in Norwich Military Hospital with influenza. On 14 November, only a month after leaving hospital, he overstayed his leave pass and had to be ordered by Norwich police to rejoin his unit. He had perhaps been detained by his brother's funeral arrangements; if so a degree of compassion seems to have been shown by the Army on this occasion as his only punishment, the deduction of three days' pay, was comparatively slight. A further bereavement struck the Betts family a few weeks later. Colman's *Carrow Works Magazine* noted that former employee, Edward Betts (Edward and Sydney's father), had died at the age of 68, another victim, perhaps, of Spanish flu. Edward junior's place of burial is not known. Having died after discharge from the Army, Edward was not entitled to a Commonwealth War Graves Commission headstone. He is commemorated on St Augustine's roll of honour and on Colman's Carrow Works Great War Memorial. He was awarded the British War and Victory medals and the Silver War Badge.

Air Mechanic (2nd Class) 219116, Frank George Brighty, Royal Air Force, formerly Royal Naval Air Service and Royal Navy

Frank George Brighty was born in the parish of St Mary Coslany, Norwich, on 28 July 1890, the first child of George Alfred Brighty, who ran his own coach-building business, and Matilda Brighty née Child. Frank was baptised at the church of St Miles Coslany on 22 October 1890. His only sibling, Marjorie Mabel, was born in 1898 and baptised at the same church. The family lived at 18 Pitt Street, St Augustine's, throughout Frank's life. In 1901 they shared their home with Mrs Brighty's widowed mother, Mrs Mary Ann Child, and another lady lodger. In 1908 Frank's father died and was buried in the family plot in the Rosary Cemetery, Thorpe Hamlet. Mrs Brighty was evidently a woman of resourcefulness and determination for she kept her late husband's coach-building business going and is described in the 1911 Census as head of the household and a coach-builder in her own right, while Frank, not yet 21, is listed as 'Assisting in the Business'. On 29 April 1915 Frank married Gertrude E. Green in Norwich. The couple lived with Frank's mother in Pitt Street, renting one of her upstairs rooms. Frank was registered here as a paying lodger in the 1914/15 Norwich Register of Electors. They had two children, Maurice Frank, born 2 December 1916 and Joan, born 21 June 1918.

On 12 August 1916 Frank enlisted in the Royal Navy as a rating. His Navy Service papers record that he was 5ft 7in height, and had brown hair, brown eyes and a fresh complexion. His skills as a motor mechanic and coach-builder were soon recognised and put to use in the Royal Naval Air Service (RNAS), into which he was formally transferred on 1 September 1917 with the rank of acting 1st class air mechanic on pay of 3 shillings a week. His first official RNAS posting was to HMS *Daedalus*, a shore-based naval seaplane training school at Lee-on-Solent, Hampshire. Prior to this he was briefly stationed at the RNAS training school at Crystal Palace, then at seaplane stations in South Shields and Fishguard as a naval rating (2nd class air mechanic) with the trade of engineer-fitter. HMS *Daedalus* was established on 30 July 1917 under the command of seasoned aviator, Squadron Commander Douglas Evill DSC, who would rise to the rank of Air Marshall of the RAF during the Second World War. The process of launching seaplanes here was slow and cumbersome. South Shields and Fishguard had slipways, but here the delicate aircraft had to be wheeled from their temporary, canvas-roofed hangars to the cliff edge where a crane carefully lowered them 30 feet onto a trolley on rails on the beach below. The aircraft were then floated into the waves and the engines started. Achieving take-off in the often choppy waters wasn't easy and the nearby pier presented pilots with a sizeable hazard. Bands playing on the end of the pier were well used to being buzzed. Presumably, Frank would have been involved in the construction of the permanent hangars and slipway that eventually replaced it.

On 1 April 1918 Frank was transferred to the newly established Royal Air Force, which combined the RNAS and the Royal Flying Corps into a single military air service. At this date he was posted once again to the seaplane base at Fishguard, his rank reverting to air mechanic 2nd class. The 1918 'Absent Voters' Register for Norwich records Frank Brighty as a resident of 18 Pitt Street and enlisted in the RAF. Interestingly, the register records that a close neighbour, Joseph Milne, was also serving as an air mechanic in the RAF at this time. On 18 February 1919, Frank was transferred to an RAF Dispersal Unit at Thetford, Norfolk, where a medical board assessed him fit grade A. From here he was granted a demob furlough and returned to the family home in Norwich. Just 10 days later, on 28 February 1919, aged 28, he died in Town Close Ward at the Norfolk and Norwich Hospital of heart failure brought about by pneumonia, another victim of the Spanish flu pandemic.

Frank was buried in the Brighty family plot (no. N2325) in the Rosary Cemetery, Thorpe Hamlet, on 5 March 1919. Although he died while still a serving member of the RAF within the qualifying post-war period, he does not have a Commonwealth War Graves Commission headstone, presumably because he was buried in the family plot with its own headstone. Words from the Lord's Prayer, 'Thy will be done', are engraved directly beneath his name. Frank is also commemorated on the St Augustine's roll of honour and he is the only non-Army serviceman honoured there. He was awarded the British War medal; strangely, there is no record of his being awarded the Victory medal also. His widow, Gertrude, also died young, in 1922, aged 33.

Private 442644 George Pye, 940th Area Employment Company, Labour Corps, formerly Private 17282, 7th Battalion, Norfolk Regiment

George Pye was born in Norwich in 1872, the eldest of the ten children of George Pye, a gasworks labourer, and Harriet Pye née Hood, who was from the village of Moulton, Norfolk. From 1881 to 1901 the family lived at 157 Bull Close Road in the parish of St Paul. George's siblings were Robert, Ernest, John, Rebecca, William, James, Harriet, Henry and Benjamin. George was a jobbing labourer. He married Annie Elizabeth Meeks in Norwich in 1902. They lived at 1 Springfield Court off St Martin's Lane in the parish of St Mary Coslany. By 1911 they had three children: George, Annie and Harriet. At this date George was a labourer at Norwich waterworks.

George's Army Service papers have not survived and as he died after the Armistice he is not recorded in *Soldier Died in the Great War*, it is therefore not possible to say where or when he enlisted, though it is likely to have been in Norwich. George first went to France on 30 June 1915 where he joined the 7th Battalion, Norfolk Regiment. He was 42 or 43 and therefore older than the upper age limit for recruits, so, presumably, lied about his age in order to get in. It is not known when he transferred to the Labour Corps so he may well have seen front line action with the 7th Norfolks at Loos in 1915 and the Somme in 1916. He was 45 in 1917; it may have been then he was transferred to the new Labour Corps, which was formed in January

1917 to meet the pressing demand for men to carry out essential, non-combatant military work on the Home Front and overseas, such as constructing and maintaining military harbours, roads and railways. Its members were mainly drawn from men deemed either too old or otherwise unfitted for service in combatant units. Despite its non-combatant role the Labour Corps lost over 9,000 men during the war, carrying out its work in often very dangerous circumstances. George's unit, the 940th Area Employment Company was based in the Oise area of northern France near St Quentin.

George, 49, died in England on 11 March 1919, a victim of the Spanish flu pandemic. He is buried in a Commonwealth War Graves Commission grave at Norwich Cemetery, Bowthorpe Road, Norwich, grave no. 54/176. His headstone bears an inscription requested by his next-of-kin: 'Peace, perfect peace now that a loved one is laid to rest'. He is commemorated also on St Augustine's roll of honour where his name appears out of alphabetical order, suggesting it was added after the memorial was erected in January 1920. He was awarded the 1915 Star and the British War and Victory medals. By a remarkable coincidence another soldier with the same name, Driver 875573 George Pye of the 53rd Divisional Ammunition Column, Royal Field Artillery, is buried in the next grave to George's. He also died in England, on 2 April 1919. By a further coincidence, he appears to have lived in the same area of Norwich as George's parents. His widow, Mrs J. Pye, lived at 19 Little Bull Close in the parish of St Paul. A George Pye is listed among St Paul's war dead in *Norfolk Roll of Honour*, but which one is not known.

Private 35308 George Alfred Wiseman, 3rd Garrison Battalion, Bedfordshire Regiment

George Alfred Wiseman was born in the parish of St Augustine, Norwich, on 8 May 1891, the second youngest surviving child of John and Rosina Wiseman. Neither of George's parents were Norwich-born, though both came from Norfolk: his father from the village of Saxlingham, his mother from the town of Pulham Market, near the home of the famous 'Pulham Pigs' RNAS airships. Married in Norwich in 1875, they first lived in St Saviour's Lane off Magdalen Street, where in 1881 the family included children Ellen, Walter and

Alice. By 1891 they had moved to 102 Calvert Street, a street which then lay partly in St Augustine's parish. The family by this date had grown with the addition of Arthur, Bertie and Ada. They were all still there in 1901 with the further addition of George and Percy. The 1911 Census records that Mrs Wiseman had ten children, seven of whom were still living (Ada had died in 1903, aged 15; two others, names unknown, presumably died in infancy). By 1911 George and his younger brother Percy were the last two children still living in the family home in Calvert Street. George, 19, was now a grocer's assistant. In 1915 he married Florence (known as Florrie) Green. Given George's commemoration on St Barnabas's rather than St Augustine's roll of honour (where his brother Percy is commemorated), it is likely the couple set up home after marriage in the Norwich suburb of Heigham.

George enlisted in Norwich on 8 May 1916. His Army Service papers have not survived but his Medal Roll Index card and other sources confirm that he served in the Bedfordshire Regiment. He

seems to have been a 1916 conscript. In November 1917, on the second anniversary of his brother Percy's death at Gallipoli an In Memoriam notice was placed in the *Eastern Daily Press* by Mrs Florrie Wiseman, noting that her husband was with the Army in India. His unit was the Bedfordshire Regiment's 3rd Garrison Battalion. Formed in Bedford in January 1917 the Battalion arrived in India in June 1917. In March 1918 it moved to Burma as part of the Indian Army's Rangoon Brigade. Largely composed of 'walking wounded' from several regiments that had served on the Western Front, his presence in this unit may indicate he had been wounded in action, perhaps during the Battle of the Somme, and was considered no longer fit for combatant duties. Ironically, given his brother's death at Gallipoli, the 3rd Garrison Battalion's primary duty was guarding Turkish prisoners of war.

Private George Alfred Wiseman died of acute pneumonia while a serving member of the 3rd Garrison Battalion, Bedfordshire Regiment, on board the troop transport ship *Aeneas* on 18 April 1919 and was buried at sea. Built in 1910 this Holt Blue Funnel passenger liner had been commandeered for use as a troopship for the Salonikan Front by the Australian Government between 1915 and 1917. By 1919, returned to civilian ownership, it was under contract to move troops back and forth between Australia, Burma, Ceylon, India and Britain. It would seem probable George was a victim of the Spanish flu pandemic, which in the confined conditions below decks on a crowded troopship in the Tropics would have spread easily. George seems to have died on the Arabian Sea somewhere between Bombay and Aden as the *Aeneas* headed for England. For some reason notice of his death does not appear to have reached the Commonwealth (then known as the Imperial) War Graves Commission (CWGC) and was not commemorated by them. In April 2013 the author asked the CWGC and the MoD whether George is entitled to official commemoration as a British war casualty. In May 2014 the CWGC confirmed that the National Army Museum had decided Private George Wiseman's sacrifice should indeed be remembered, 94 years after his death, and he is now commemorated at the Hollybrook Memorial, Southampton, which honours service personnel of the two world wars who were lost or buried at sea. George Wiseman appears in *Norwich Roll of Honour* and is also listed, under the parish of St Barnabas, Norwich, in *Norfolk Roll of Honour*. His name also appears on the Great War memorial in St Barnabas's church. His photograph was donated to the Norfolk and Norwich Library's Great War commemoration collection. George Wiseman was awarded the British War and Victory medals, which for some reason were not received by his widow until 1922. His younger brother Edward Percy died during the Dardanelles campaign in 1915. *(See p.53.)*

Rifleman 388011 Edward Charles Halfacre, 8th Battalion (Post Office Rifles), City of London Regiment, formerly Private 2183, 6th (Cyclist) Battalion and Private 43632, 8th Battalion, Norfolk Regiment

Edward Charles Halfacre was born in the parish of St George, Tombland, Norwich, on 2 April 1895, the only surviving child of Edward Halfacre, a coachman and chauffeur, and Elizabeth Mary Ann Halfacre née Joyce, a brush-maker from the parish of St Saviour. Edward's father was born in Wokingham, Berkshire, in 1857. By the age of 15 he was a labourer for the Ordnance Survey, a job that entailed a great deal of moving around the county. He seems to have settled in Norwich by the late 1870s, having married Elizabeth Joyce there in 1877. Their first child, Rosanna, died in infancy in 1878. By 1881 they had moved to James's Yard off Bethel Street in the parish of St Giles. Mr Halfacre was now a coachman, driving carriages for a private household. By 1891 he and his wife had moved to 2 Kerrison's Yard in the parish of St George Tombland and it was presumably here that Edward was born, 17 years after his sister Rosanna's death. Both parents were in their late thirties so it may be that Edward was an unexpected arrival. He was baptised at St George's on 5 May 1895.

In 1901 Edward and his parents were still at 2 Kerrison's Yard; his father still a domestic coachman, presumably for one of the families of professional men who lived in the large town houses that surround Tombland opposite Norwich cathedral. Kerrison's Yard itself was formed out of a jumble of outbuildings and stables behind the grand Georgian façades facing Tombland, wedged in beside the north wall of the church of St Mary the Less, then being used as a place of worship by members of a Spiritualist sect known as the Catholic Apostolic Church or the Irvingites. Edward attended the Boys Model School, situated a stone's throw away in Aldred's Court off Princes Street. The family was still living in Kerrison's Yard in 1911. Edward's father was now described as a domestic chauffeur, his employer's horses having presumably been replaced by a motorcar. Edward, 16, was now an ironmonger's apprentice.

Edward enlisted in Norwich on 19 May 1915. Although his Army Service papers have not survived, four pages from his Army pension record are still extant. These reveal that in the almost four years he served in the British Army he was posted to at least six different units. His first was the Norfolk Regiment's 6th (Cyclist) Battalion, a Territorial unit that provided coastal defence along the East coast. On 3 February 1916, while Edward was waiting for his first overseas posting, his cousin, James Halfacre of Bull Close Road, Norwich, a Private in the Army Service Corps, died in an Army hospital in Malta from the effects of dysentery contracted at Gallipoli. Aged 46, he had been the only other member of the Halfacre family to move from Wokingham in the wake of Edward's father's move to Norwich in the late 1870s. Edward, meanwhile, seems to have kept in touch with St Augustine's church, where he had been a Sunday School teacher. The parish magazine for April 1916 notes that he had donated the cost of a chair for the newly built parish hall. When the Norfolk Cyclists were disbanded in July 1916, Edward was posted to the 1/1st Battalion, Hertfordshire Regiment. He then went overseas for the first time, embarking at Folkestone on 26 July and landing at Boulogne the next day, arriving at No.17 Infantry Base Depot, the vast Army camp at Étaples, on 28th. From here he was transferred on 10 August to the 8th Battalion, Norfolk Regiment.

During the first phase of the Battle of the Somme in July 1916 the 8th Norfolks had suffered enormous casualties at Montauban and Delville Wood. When Edward joined the 8th Battalion on 1 September it was training and rebuilding its strength in the Monchy-Breton area prior to going into action again at Thiepval on 26 September and then at the Schwaben Redoubt on 5 October, where, mercifully, its casualties were comparatively light. The remainder of the year was spent in and out of cold, muddy trenches in the Albert area of the Somme. On 19 January 1917, Edward was sent to the 55th Field Ambulance for treatment for 'Pediculosis' (lice infestation) and on 13 March to the 54th Field Ambulance with leg wounds, possibly from shrapnel. He remained with the 8th Norfolks throughout 1917, fighting right through the hellish 3rd Ypres campaign otherwise known as Passchendaele until the 8th Norfolks was disbanded in February 1918. He was then posted to a holding unit, the 18th Entrenching Battalion, which took men from disbanded units of the 18th (Eastern) Division and held them in readiness for duty in other front line battalions. In Edward's case he was transferred in quick succession to the 8th Battalion, London Regiment; the 9th Battalion, Norfolk Regiment; the Rifle Brigade; and, finally, back to the 8th London Regiment in May 1918. Known as the Post Office Rifles, the 8th Battalion's origins lay in a Volunteer regiment founded in London in 1868. The majority of its recruits, as the name suggests, were London Post Office workers. It fought with distinction on the Western Front throughout the war, losing 1,800 killed in action and 4,500 wounded. When Edward joined, it was rebuilding its strength after the onslaught of the German's spring offensive, known as the Kaiserschlacht.

In June 1918 Edward succumbed to influenza, an early sufferer of the pandemic that was then beginning to sweep around the globe. This was presumably a milder strain of the virus as he was out of action for only ten days before returning to his unit. At the end of July he got into trouble for complaining about an NCO's order, for which he received seven days Field Punishment No. 1, which normally involved being tied spread-eagle to a fixed object like a stake or gun carriage wheel, exposed to the elements for up to two hours each day, not perhaps the best recuperation for a man recovering from influenza. During August and September the war become one of fluid movement again and the Post Office Rifles were engaged in the battles of Amiens, Albert, Ephey and in the Final Advance to Artois

On 1 February 1919, Edward Halfacre sailed for England via Dunkirk and was discharged from the Army on 17 March on health grounds. He had survived the war but in a weakened state and when a more virulent influenza strain caught up with him his body was not able to resist it and he died, ostensibly of a diseased heart, on 21 May 1919. On the 23 May the *Eastern Daily Press* printed the following brief obituary:

> *Halfacre, May 21, at 2, Kerrison's Yard, Tombland, Norwich. Edward Charles, the beloved only child of Edward and Elizabeth Halfacre, aged 24, late of the 8th London Post Office Rifles. His end was peace.*

He died in the house in which he had been born. It is not known where he is buried. Edward is commemorated on the Model Boys School Memorial in Norwich Cathedral and the St Augustine's roll of honour. St Augustine's church also has an individual memorial to him on one the east-facing panels of the roll of honour chancel screen. On this is inscribed in gilt lettering:

Sacred / To the memory / of /
Rfle. Edward C. Halfacre
8th London P.O. Rifles
One of our Sunday School Teachers
Who passed away / 21st May 1919

Private Halfacre was awarded the British War and Victory medals. The Silver War Badge, granted to those who were invalided out of active service was finally posted to his father in January 1920, nearly 10 months after his death.

Private 32862 George William Skipper, 7th Battalion and 1/4th Battalion, Norfolk Regiment

George William Skipper was born in Norwich in December 1898, the eldest son of James William Skipper, a shoe-finisher, and Sarah Skipper née Mann, a starch hand (a job in the confectionery trade) originally from Hackney, London. His parents were married in Norwich in 1887 and lived first at 21 Rose Yard off St Augustine's Street with George's grandmother, Emily Skipper, a charwoman. George had three older sisters, Emily, Honor Amelia (known as Emilia) and Beatrice, and two younger brothers, Leonard and Sydney. By 1901 the family had moved to 6 Crown and Anchor Yard off St George's Street. Ten years later poverty had riven the family apart. The 1911 Census records that while George's mother remained in the family home (now known simply as Anchor Yard) with Emily (22), Emilia (16) and her youngest, Sydney (4); his father had accepted parish relief and gone into the Norwich Incorporation Workhouse in Bowthorpe Road, while Beatrice (13) and Leonard (10), who were at least kept together, were placed in the Incorporation's new Mixed Children's Home, opened at 83–85 Pottergate Street in 1904 in order to segregate children from the adults in Bowthorpe Road Workhouse. Twelve-year-old George, meanwhile was at the Incorporation's Boys School in St Faith's Lane. What happened to him between 1911 and 1917 when he joined the Army is not known, though his Service papers do record that at the time of enlisting he was again living at 6 Anchor Yard, unmarried and working in the shoemaking trade.

George was conscripted in Norwich on 9 March 1917, aged 18 and 4 months. His medical report notes that he was just 5ft 2 in height, an inch below the Army's revised, wartime minimum height requirement, and was generally in poor physical condition. He was first posted to the Norfolk Regiment's Training Reserve (3rd Battalion), where he remained until the end of October. His Service papers record that during this period he was confined to barracks twice for minor offences, once for being briefly absent from duty and once for having a dirty rifle on parade. On 1 November 1917 he was transferred to the 7th Battalion, Norfolk Regiment, and sent to France to join his unit there a week later. The 7th Norfolks formed part of the 35th Brigade, 12th (Eastern) Division, and had been engaged in trench warfare on the Arras Front since the beginning of the year. A few weeks before he joined them, the Battalion had taken part in a particularly bloody raid on German trenches. The official history of the regiment notes with a hint of embarrassment that 'little quarter was given' to a large number of surrendering German soldiers during the raid. The men, it says, were 'particularly exasperated by a long series of trench mortar bombardments'. This and the fact that several of its platoon commanders had been killed during the action suggests that discipline broke down and a spree of revenge killings took place. It was in the aftermath of this atrocity, among battle-weary comrades, that George, an 18-year-old raw recruit, now found himself. Two weeks later, on 20 November, George had his first taste of battle at Cambrai. The 7th Norfolks' role in the early stages of the battle was minimal and its casualties low, however, initial British successes failed to be consolidated and on 30 November the Germans launched a devastating counter-offensive. On several occasions during the day the 7th Battalion was almost completely surrounded. Fearing capture, the Battalion's War Diaries were destroyed to prevent them falling into enemy hands. Casualties were very high and included the Battalion's CO, Lieutenant Colonel Gielgud.

The 7th Norfolks spent part of the winter of 1917/18 at Merville near Hazebrouck rebuilding its strength after Cambrai. In March 1918 they were sent south to the Albert Front to help stem the German's massive spring offensive, the Kaiserschlacht. On 27 March the Battalion came under attack by overwhelming numbers of German troops near Aveluy and was forced to retreat, sustaining heavy casualties, including more than 200 reported missing in action, among them George. It would be over a month before his next of kin was notified that he was a prisoner of war at Langensalza camp in Thuringia in eastern Germany. Conditions there were brutal. The camp was basically no more than an insanitary, badly drained field with a series of cold, damp, ramshackle huts housing over 12,000 men, including French, British, Russians and Italians. There were over 3,400 British POWs there in the autumn of 1918. One British soldier, captured in 1916 and held at a number of camps in Germany, described the guards at Langensalza as the most ferocious he ever encountered. *(Source: the Mulford collection, Imperial War Museum.)* George was not finally released until 23 January 1919, two months after the Armistice.

Following liberation George was hospitalised for three weeks, part of the time at the Norfolk War Hospital in Thorpe near Norwich where he was treated for chronic diarrhoea. After this he was granted 28 days furlough, due to all released POWs. It was during this period of leave, on 9 March 1919, that he was officially demobbed from the 7th Norfolks and placed in the Army Reserves. On 7 June 1919 he was called back to the colours, posted to the 1/4th Battalion, Norfolk Regiment, and sent out to join the Egyptian Expeditionary Force in Cairo, which he reached on 23 June. An uprising, occasioned by Britain's suppression of the independence movement there, had erupted in March and raged on throughout the year with riots, strikes and attacks on British military installations and personnel. George had been in Cairo barely more than two weeks when he fell sick and was admitted to the Citadel Military Hospital with fever and shivering, which were subsequently diagnosed as symptoms of severe double pneumonia. He had almost certainly become a victim of the Spanish flu pandemic. A telegram was dispatched to his father as next-of-kin informing him that George was dangerously ill. His father had in fact died in 1918 while George was still a POW in Germany.

Private George Skipper died a few days later on 21 July 1919. According to the medical officer's report his death had been 'aggravated by service during the present war'. Considering the weakened condition he was in when he was released from Langensalza prison camp, it is astonishing the Army should have considered him fit enough to be sent out to reinforce Britain's beleaguered forces in Egypt. Telegrams and forms concerning his death, burial and the disposal of his death plaque and scroll continued to be addressed to George's late father throughout the year. George is buried at the Cairo War Memorial Cemetery, Egypt. Although his name appears in *Norfolk Roll of Honour* under St Augustine's, his name does not appear on the parish's roll of honour. He was awarded the British War and Victory medals.

Lance Corporal 339823 William Stocks, Labour Corps, formerly Private 9207, 2nd Battalion, West Yorkshire Regiment

William Stocks was born in the parish of St Martin at Oak, Norwich, in 1892, the third child of James Stocks, a bricklayer's labourer, and Alice Stocks née Parnell, a silk-winder. *(For more on William's unusual family background see p.169.)* By 1911 William was a private in the West Yorkshire Regiment, living in barracks at Colchester. On 16 October 1911 he was married in St Paul's church, Norwich, to Mary Smith, described in the Census that year as a 'tailoress for the Army and Navy'. The couple's address in the register was 10 Bennett's Yard, Cowgate.

As William's Army Service papers have not survived it is not possible to give a very detailed account of his military career. He had been a Regular in the Prince of Wales's Own West Yorkshire Regiment since at least 1911 and was with its 2nd Battalion when it landed in France to join the BEF on 5 November 1914, having returned to England from Malta in September. On 14 November the Battalion came under fire on the Messines Ridge, its first taste of action. This qualified William for the award of one of the rarest of the Great War service medals, 1914 Star (also known as the Mons Star), which was only awarded to soldiers and airmen who came under enemy fire in France or Belgium between 5 August and 22 November 1914. At some point during the war William was appointed lance corporal and transferred to the Labour Corps. Transfers to this non-combatant unit, especially by a pre-war Regular still only in his twenties suggests he had suffered a serious enough injury to bar him from active service at the Front, though not disabling enough to warrant his discharge or prevent him doing labouring work. Unlike his brother James he survived the war and was demobbed. During the April–June quarter of 1919, William's death was registered in Norwich. Aged 27, he seems to have succumbed to the Spanish flu. Having died after discharge from the Army of an illness unrelated to his military service, he is not commemorated in any national, regimental or civic roll of honour. His place of burial is not known. He was awarded the 1914 Star and the British War and Victory medals.

Private 43197 Herbert Victor Forster,
1st Battalion, Norfolk Regiment

Herbert Victor Forster was born in Norwich in 1894, the fourth surviving child of William Forster, a shoemaker, and Emma Sophie Forster née Rudd. In 1901 the family was at 8 Bakers Road just north of St Augustine's. By 1911 it had moved to 8 Leonards Street off St Augustine's Street. The Census records that Mrs Forster had 15 children, seven of whom were still living. By this date Herbert's eldest brother William was living on the other side of the city in the parish of St John de Sepulchre, having married and left home the previous year. Two other older brothers, Walter and Albert, were still at home and working as shoemakers. Herbert, 17, was an errand boy for a shoe shop. Younger siblings Alice, Freddy and Hilda completed the family.

Herbert enlisted on 11 January 1915 and served as a private in the Norfolk Regiment, first in its 1st Battalion, then at the Regiment's Depot at Britannia Barracks, Norwich, until 28 August 1918 when he was discharged as no longer physically fit for war service, having been wounded while serving abroad. He was awarded a Silver War Badge, which the Government had made available since 1916 to discharged wounded servicemen out of uniform so that people didn't accuse them of shirking their patriotic duty. Private Herbert Forster died on 6 May 1921. His death was clearly considered to be directly attributable to his war service as he was buried in the military section of Norwich Cemetery with a Commonwealth (or Imperial as it was then known) War Graves Commission (CWGC) headstone on which his relatives inscribed: 'God takes our loved ones from our home but never from our heart'. Men and women who died of wounds or illness attributable to their time in the Armed or Auxiliary Forces of the British Empire before 31 August 1921, whether or not they had been discharged, were entitled to have a burial or commemoration maintained by the War Graves Commission. Whether Herbert was another victim of Spanish flu is not known, possibly not, as other victims who died after discharge were not commemorated by the CWGC. Herbert is very possibly the last Norfolk Regiment casualty of the Great War buried in a CWGC-maintained grave. He was awarded the British War and Victory medals and the Silver War Badge. He is not listed on St Augustine's roll of honour.

Herbert's eldest brother, Private 16442 William Samuel Forster of the 10th Battalion, Essex Regiment, was killed in action on the Somme on 26 September 1916. Death notices placed by his relatives in the *Eastern Daily Press* included one placed on behalf of Private Albert Forster, 'then serving abroad'. Albert appears to have served in both the Norfolk Regiment and Machine Gun Corps and survived the war.

Two unknown soldiers

Private R. Brown

It has not proved possible to identify this soldier with any certainty. The position of his name, out of alphabetical order at the bottom of the second from left panel of St Augustine's roll of honour chancel screen, suggests it was added after the memorial was erected in January 1920. The inferior quality of the carving and a contemporary photographic souvenir of the memorial, showing an empty space in the position now occupied by this name, seem to prove this assumption. More than 200 British soldiers with this surname, initial and rank died on active service during the First World War. While *Norwich Roll of Honour* and *Norfolk Roll of Honour* both list a Robert Brown without details of rank or regiment, the latter under the parish of St Giles, Norwich, no casualty with this name directly associated with the parishes of St Augustine or St Mary Coslany can be found. The late addition of the name on the roll of honour may indicate Private R. Brown died after discharge from the Army, like a small number of other men listed there. The use of an initial rather than a forename suggests the name was added by someone who did not know the individual personally. Given all of this, a possible candidate is Private 372657 Robert Brown, Labour Corps, formerly Private 17125, 7th Battalion, Norfolk Regiment. Fortunately, his Army Service papers have survived and these give his address on enlisting as 1 Fox and Goose Yard off St Martin's Lane in the parish of St Martin at Oak, a small parish which lies between St Augustine and St Mary Coslany. His nominated next of kin was his father, 'Joshuah' Brown of the Bishopsgate Street Hospital (more usually known today as the Great Hospital of St Helen's), a medieval foundation which by the 20th century had become more of a retirement home than a hospital. Robert's stated age on enlistment on 7 December 1914 was 37 years and 5 months. This was almost certainly untrue. Census records from 1881 to 1911 contain only one Robert Brown within the right age range with a father named Joshua or 'Joshuah' living in Norwich. This Robert Brown's date of birth, as calculated by his stated age in census returns, would make his age on enlisting in 1914 as nearer 41 than 37. At this early period in the war the upper age limit for recruits was 38, so presumably he lied about his age in order to get in.

This Robert Brown was born in Norwich in July 1873, the fourth child of Joshua and Caroline Brown. His father was a shoemaker. His older siblings were Joshua, Caroline and William; his younger, Charlotte, Johnny, Eliza, Harriet, Rachel and Emma. Each census from 1881 to 1911 records the Brown family resident at 18 Fullers Hole, an address that no longer exists, located then beside the River Wensum off St Martin at Oak Street. Robert, who is described as a shoe-riveter in 1891 and a general shoemaker in 1911, cannot be found in the 1901 Census. This may be explained by a note on his Army Service papers that he served 12 years in the Rifle Brigade and so was perhaps overseas at this date. Presumably later a Reservist, his first posting on being recalled to the colours in 1914 was to the Norfolk Regiment's 3rd (Reserve) Battalion. He remained in England until 30 June 1915, when he was posted to the 7th Battalion, Norfolk Regiment, which was already in Flanders and just about to go into the front line for the first time at Ploegsteert ('Plug Street') Wood in the Ypres Salient. He remained with the 7th Norfolks until 10 October 1917 when he was transferred to the Labour Corps' Area Employment Company No. 747, which was then attached to General Byng's Third Army on the Western Front and tasked with battlefield salvage collection.

Robert was now 44, double the age of the average infantry-man. He had just survived two very tough years at the Front, serving throughout the battles of the Somme and Arras. In the light of his subsequent conduct it would probably be fair to say that both physically and mentally he had had enough of soldiering. It was after about seven months in the Labour Corps that the trouble seems to have begun. He was up on charges four times in May 1918: for being absent from roll call twice, and twice for being drunk and breaking out of camp. In August he was found to be drunk on the 2 p.m. parade and in September he broke out of camp again. His punishments included deductions of pay and Field Punishment No. 1 (being tied to a fixed object such as a post or a gun carriage wheel for up to two hours each day for up to three weeks, with extra duties and drill). In December he was tried by Field General Court Martial for again being found drunk on duty and was sentenced to 21 days Field Punishment No. 2 (being fettered or handcuffed but otherwise able to walk about or march, again with extra duties and drill). In February 1919 he was deprived two days' pay for being absent from 'Police duty' for most of one day. On 2 April 1919 he was finally transferred into the 'Z' Army Reserve – in effect demobbed. His home address now was given as the Great Hospital in Bishopsgate, Norwich, his father's retirement home where he could not have resided himself, meaning that he was in effect homeless. What became of him is not known. Possibly he died sometime in 1919 or the early 1920s and a relative requested that his name be added to the St Augustine's memorial, there being no memorial in St Martin at Oak's parish church. No church records have been discovered to account for the name's late inclusion. Whether the Private R. Brown on the St Augustine's roll of honour is this soldier or another man may never be known.

Lance Corporal C. Wills

The identity of this soldier, listed on St Augustine's Great War roll of honour, is unknown. The fact that C. Wills is listed with an initial rather than a full forename, one of only four men so listed on the roll of honour, suggests that the person or persons who drew up the final list of names to be carved did not know him. No serviceman named C. Wills appears in either *Norwich Roll of Honour* or under a Norwich parish in *Norfolk Roll of Honour*. No one named C. Wills of an age to have served in the armed services in the First World War appears in any of the censuses taken in Norfolk between 1870 and 1911. Fourteen soldiers named C. Wills (19 if one includes Royal Navy, Australian and Canadian personnel) are recorded as casualties of the First World War by the Commonwealth War Graves Commission, while *Soldiers Died in the Great War* has 15. None appears to have had any connection with Norwich or to have served in the Norfolk Regiment and only two are listed with the rank of lance corporal: Charles Wills from Homerton, London, who served in the 10th Battalion, London Regiment, a Territorial Force unit known as the Stockbrokers' Battalion, and Charles Jeffrey Wills of the 2nd Battalion, Devonshire Regiment and Machine Gun Corps, who came from Brixham, Devon. Again, neither man appears to have had any Norfolk connections.

It may be that C. Wills is in fact a chimera – that he never existed and his inclusion on St Augustine's roll of honour is due to a misunderstanding. Could it be significant that the name of the person who donated a photograph of the late Private Willsea to Norwich Library after the war, was a Mrs L. C. Willsea? It is not too far-fetched to imagine the parish clerk at a crowded parishioners' meeting trying to write down the names of those to be commemorated and in the hubbub Mrs L. C. Willsea's name being minuted as LC [i.e. Lance Corporal] Wills, C.

Four survivors' stories

Although the death toll of servicemen from the parish of St Augustine with St Mary Coslany in the Great War was considerable and terrible – possibly as high as 17 per cent of those who served their King and Country – the majority did survive. These are the stories of four of them.

The Submariner

Engine Room Artificer (ERA) M. 742 John Henry Bowles DSM, Royal Navy

John Henry Bowles was born in Norwich on 24 September 1893, the eldest child of Samuel and Charlotte Bowles. He had three brothers, Christopher, Bertie and George, and four sisters, Violet, Ivy, Elsie and Gladys. His parents worked in the local shoemaking industry. In the 1901 Census the family was recorded at 20 Sussex Street, St Augustine's. By 1911 John's parents had moved to Bishop's Court, Stumps Cross, in the parish of St Saviour.

John joined the Royal Navy in 1911 on his 18th birthday, signing on for 12 years. His Navy Service record notes that he was just under 5ft 2 in height. Being short was a distinct advantage in the cramped conditions of the new submarine service towards which his naval career gravitated. Prior to becoming a submariner, John served with the submarine depot ships, HMS *Dolphin* and HMS *Maidstone*. His first sub, *E19,* was built by Vickers in Barrow-in-Furness in 1915. E-Class submarines were 181 feet long with a beam of 22½ feet. They were propelled by two screws powered by diesel engines and were armed with five torpedo tubes and a 12-pounder deck gun. *E19* had a crew of three officers and 28 ratings. In the autumn of 1915 *E19* was ordered to proceed to the Baltic under the command of Lieutenant Commander Francis Newton Allen Cromie RN, a clean-cut, square-jawed naval officer, straight out of the pages of an Edwardian schoolboys' yarn. *(Photo below.)* In the Baltic, *E19* joined a flotilla of five other E-class and four C-class subs. Their main task was to harry merchant shipping supplying German ports, in particular freighters carrying iron ore from neutral Sweden, raw material vital to Germany's armaments industry. On 11 October 1915 members of the crew boarded and then scuttled four ore-carrying German freighters bound for German ports and forced another to run aground, all without the loss of a single life. The freighters' crews were given time to transfer onto passing vessels before their ships were sunk, a feat unequalled in the annals of submarine warfare up to that time. The impact on the Baltic iron ore trade was immediate; it virtually ceased overnight and forced the German High Sea Fleet to divert ships from the North Sea to the Baltic to provide convoy protection. On 7 November *E19*'s torpedoes sank the German battle cruiser *Undine* off Trelleborg in the western Baltic. It then went into Revel (Tallinn) in Estonia, then part of the Russian Empire, to over-winter before the ice closed in.

Captain Cromie

The successful operations of the Royal Navy's Baltic submarine flotilla were irresistible material to the British propaganda machine. John's photograph appeared in the *Eastern Daily Press* in October 1915 above the caption: 'Now serving on the Submarine E19, whose successful exploits in the Baltic have recently been reported. Bowles is the eldest son of Mr & Mrs S. J. Bowles of 20 Sussex

Street'. The publication of such information was technically an offence under the Defence of the Realm Act of 1914, but newspaper editors appear to have been given special dispensation if the story was deemed to be good for national morale. John was also mentioned in the November issue of St Augustine's parish magazine: 'We are proud to know that one of our choir boys is engaged in submarine work in the Baltic'. In July 1916 the *Eastern Daily Press* reported that John Bowles, along with his fellow submariners, had been awarded the Imperial Russian decoration, the St George's Cross.

Although the flotilla remained in the Baltic, continuing to operate throughout the ice-free months of 1916 and 1917, it had become a victim of its own success. Merchant shipping was now heavily guarded by German naval convoys and there were no longer the easy pickings of 1915. The perils of submarine operations were nevertheless ever present. *E19*'s sister sub, *E18*, was lost with all hands in May 1916, probably after striking a mine. The Bolshevik Revolution in October 1917 and the subsequent Treaty of Brest-Litovsk in March 1918 took Russia out of the war, leaving the Baltic flotilla with no friendly allied port to refuel and refit. Cromie, who by 1918 had been promoted to acting captain and placed in command of the entire Baltic flotilla, moved it to Helsingfors (Helsinki) in Finland, where much of the former Imperial Russian fleet lay at anchor. Here the British submariners found a state of near anarchy. Several Russian naval officers had been murdered by their own crews and there was a real danger the British subs would be sold to the Germans by the revolutionary government. In April 1918, as the Germans closed in, fearing the flotilla would fall into enemy hands, Captain Cromie ordered his seven surviving submarines to sail out of Helsingfors harbour into the icy Gulf of Finland behind a Russian ice-breaker, where their crews were transferred to tugs before the subs were blown up and sunk.

After this John Bowles returned to Britain and resumed work with the submarine depot ship HMS *Dolphin*. A special issue of the *London Gazette* devoted to 'Honours for the Submarine Service' published 23 April 1918 lists ERA John Henry Bowles RN among those awarded the Distinguished Service Medal. Captain Cromie, meanwhile, had been appointed senior naval attaché at the British Embassy in Petrograd. Here, on 31 August 1918, he was shot dead at the foot of the grand staircase during an attack by, depending on which version you read, a drunken mob intent on looting the Embassy's wine cellar or members of the Cheka (Soviet secret police) looking for the Embassy's telegram code books.

John Bowles served on HMS *Dolphin* until the end of June 1918 when he received a temporary promotion to the warrant officer rank of acting mate and was posted to the battleship HMS *Ramillies*, based in Devonport. After the war he received the 1915 Star and the British War and Victory medals to go alongside his DSM and Imperial Russian decoration. John married Vera Walker in Dorset in 1919. He left the Navy in 1923 and died in Norwich in 1972.

From Policeman to Prisoner of war

Private 6622 Joseph Herbert Graves, 1st Battalion, Norfolk Regiment

Joseph Herbert Graves was born in Norwich in 1886, the third son of Joe and Emily Graves of 5 Rose Yard, St Augustine's. According to the 1901 Census Joseph was employed as a mustard-packer, presumably at Colman's Carrow Works in Norwich. From 1903 to 1911, however, he was in the Army and from then until the war in the police force. In 1914 his father became the landlord of the Britannia, a Morgan's Brewery-owned pub that once stood near the junction of Botolph Street and St Augustine's Street.

In January 1916 the *Eastern Daily Press* published a group photograph of five of Mr and Mrs Graves's sons, all currently in the armed forces. *(See p.252 below.)* They were, in descending order of age, Robert *(top left)*, a sergeant in the East Anglian Brigade, Royal Field Artillery; George *(top right)*, a chief petty officer in the Royal Navy; Joseph *(centre)*, a private in the Norfolk Regiment; Sidney *(left)*, a private in the Canadian Expeditionary Force; and Arthur *(right)*, a private in the 2nd East Anglian Field Ambulance, Royal Army Medical Corps. The newspaper noted that Mr and Mrs Graves's youngest boy, Edward, 14, was also doing his bit for King and Country in the Boy Scouts. They also had two daughters, Edith and Hilda, who were no doubt doing their bit too. Accompanying the photograph was a long article detailing Joseph's experience of being wounded at the Battle of Mons in August 1914 and of being taken prisoner.

The Graves brothers from the *Eastern Daily Press* 15 January 1916

Joseph enlisted in the Norwich Regiment's 2nd Battalion as a Regular on 13 August 1903 and served in South Africa and Gibraltar before leaving the Army in 1911 to join the Metropolitan Police. At the outbreak of war in August 1914, now aged 30, he was allowed to leave the police in order to re-join the colours and was posted to the Norfolk's Regiment's 1st Battalion. Because of his age and experience he was selected for special duties as a motorcycle despatch rider on the staff of the Commander-in-Chief of the British Expeditionary Force, Field Marshal Sir John French. On 23 August 1914, during the Battle of Mons, the first major battle of the war, he was wounded and taken prisoner. That morning he and another despatch rider had been ordered to ride from Bruges to Mons, make observations and report back to HQ. While making their way back they encountered what he thought were Austrian troops (there were in fact none in the battle) and Uhlans (mounted lancers), whom they attacked with their machine-guns, probably Vickers .303s, which could be used mounted on a motorcycle-sidecar combination. During the fire-fight Joseph's comrade was shot and killed instantly. Maintaining a cool head, he laid his fallen comrade's body beside a wall, removed his ammunition and papers, set fire to his motorcycle and destroyed his weapons so that they could not be used by the enemy. Unfortunately, just as he was riding off he was shot through the arm, which he said felt as though someone had struck him with an iron bar. After this he had great difficulty in controlling his machine. A shell then burst nearby, showering him with red hot shrapnel and throwing him off his bike. With a shattered arm and badly cut about and burnt he lay where he had fallen, unable to move, awaiting capture or death. As he waited he managed to extract the despatches from his pouch, tear them up and roll them into pills of paper, which he swallowed.

After a while some German soldiers came up to him, called him an English swine and began beating him. While this was happening one of the soldiers smashed his rifle on the road, which accidentally went off killing or wounding him. A German officer then came up and questioned him about the British Army's strength and position. Refusing to answer he was stripped and beaten with a horse whip until a second officer came up and stopped the torture. Naked, bleeding and dying of thirst, he was then left beside the road, passing in and out of consciousness until discovered by a unit of the German Army's medical corps, who provided first aid and a drink from a flask, which he thought would be water but turned out to be coffee and brandy. The memory of that drink would, he said, remain with him for the rest of his days.

Joseph was taken first to a German field dressing station at Badour and then to a hospital at Mons, where he was nursed by a Belgian lady named, he thought, Madame Vanderton. In October he was moved to Düsseldorf, where he joined 100 other British prisoners of war. Here he experienced an Allied air raid that destroyed two gasometers near where they were being held. The next day they were put into cattle trucks and moved to Hamelin in Lower Saxony. For three days they were given no food or water, and had to perform all their bodily functions in the same over-crowded, fetid trucks in which they were huddled, some of the worst injured having no option but to lie on the filthy floor. At each station where they stopped guards came into their truck, swore at them, insulted them and struck them with their rifle butts and the flats of their swords. At Hamelin they were moved into what he called a 'tamboo' (Army slang for a small dugout): a long, narrow, wooden hut about 60 feet long by 13 feet across with a canvas roof. The hut adjoined a small compound surrounded by electrified wire. Here one day, while exercising, two American ladies came to the fence and threw over food parcels. They were all starving by now, having had to subsist on a daily ration of a slice of black bread, a bowl of thin soup and some weak coffee. Excruciatingly, the parcels were confiscated by the guards while the ladies, whom they were never able to thank, were led away, shouting back to them 'God bless you boys, you'll be home soon. Look out, it's coming.' On Christmas Day 1914 the prisoners' only festive treat was a tiny white roll of bread.

During 1915 conditions improved somewhat due to the arrival of Red Cross parcels and to the intervention of the American Consul in Hamelin, who managed to get them some tobacco and other comforts. Before this, cigarettes had been forbidden and they had been forced to smoke a mixture of coffee grouts and dried moss. They were finally allowed to write home, which was a relief as Joseph had heard that he had been reported killed and then missing in action. In August 1915 he was moved to Soltau camp on Lüneburg Heath in Lower Saxony, the largest POW camp in Germany at that time. On 1 October he was told that he was being repatriated along with 120 other wounded British POWs whom the Germans no longer considered fit for active service and therefore no longer a threat to the Fatherland. The lack of proper medical treatment, the beatings and the malnutrition he had suffered had left his wounded arm and hand shrunken and useless. On being returned to England he had a spell in a London hospital before being moved to the Police Convalescent

Home in Hove; moving finally to the Norfolk Regiment's 3rd Reserve Battalion at their Depot in Norwich.

Private Joseph Graves was discharged from the Army on 5 June 1916, having been assessed as no longer physically fit for active service due to injuries caused by a gunshot wound. He was awarded the Silver War Badge to show people that he had been honourably discharged from HM Forces, the 1914 Star with Bar to show that he had been under fire overseas in 1914, and the British War and Victory medals. All of his brothers survived the war. Joseph Graves died in Norwich in 1947.

The twice shipwrecked sailor

Leading Seaman J. 22110 John Harlow, Royal Navy

John Harlow was born in Norwich on 17 August 1895, the third child of John and Alice Harlow. His family lived at 34 Leonards Street, St Augustine's, Norwich, before the war. John's father was a baker and

he had four brothers: Walter, Arthur, James and Sidney. His Navy Service Record notes that he was a dresser of leather prior to joining up.

John entered the Royal Navy in 17 August 1913 on his 18th birthday, signing on for 12 years. Apart from training vessels and shore establishments his first Grand Fleet berth was HMS *London*, a Formidable-class battleship on which he served for just three weeks during September and October 1913 before being returned to a shore establish-

ment. Finally, on 20 January 1914 he joined the crew of HMS *Formidable* herself.

In January 1915 the *Eastern Daily Press* reported that John was home on leave, staying with his parents in Leonards Street, following the sinking of HMS *Formidable*. Completed in 1901, the *Formidable* was one of the Royal Navy's so-called 'pre-Dreadnought' battleships: small, slow, under-gunned and thinly armoured compared to the mighty *Dreadnought* and her sister battleships. Acting as the flagship of Vice Admiral Sir Lewis Bayly, the *Formidable* was steaming in the rear of a convoy through the English Channel off Portland Bill in the teeth of a storm in the early hours of New Year's Day 1915, when she was twice struck by torpedoes from the German submarine *U-24*, which had been lying in ambush for just such an opportunity. HMS *Formidable* immediately began to sink.

John had finished his watch at midnight as the old year passed and had retired to his hammock below deck. At around 2.30 a.m. he was

Captain Loxley and Bruce, from a painting by Charles Padday

woken by the noise, not of the first torpedo exploding, but of the commotion as his shipmates scrambled through the dimly-lit and cramped lower deck compartments. Not stopping to dress, he blew up his swimming collar, tied it around his neck and clothed only in a blue Guernsey sweater fought his way onto the upper deck. Here he saw that the ship was listing to starboard. The skipper, Captain Noel Loxley, in true stiff-upper-lip manner, could be seen standing on the sloping bridge with his fox terrier, Bruce, by his side calmly directing operations. The night was pitch black and the sea very rough. What with this and the heavy listing of the deck the crew had difficulty lowering the lifeboats, a task John lent a hand to. Several boats capsized or where smashed against the hull. Anything wooden that could be wrenched away from the decks was thrown overboard, including the ship's piano. The men then huddled together sharing cigarettes and singing 'It's a long way to Tipperary' and 'Get out and get under' to keep their spirits up, awaiting the order to abandon ship. Everyone now seemed to be remarkably calm, John thought, as though resigned to his fate.

John clung on to the steeply sloping deck until Captain Loxley gave the order 'every man for himself', when he jumped over the stern, a drop of 25 feet into a cold, black, stormy sea. He was one of the last to leave the ship, which may very well have saved his life as it meant he was in the icy water for a shorter time than some of his unfortunate shipmates. Luckily, he was picked up by one of the ship's lifeboats fairly quickly and they were soon spotted by a cruiser from the convoy some way off. These escorting cruisers had been ordered not to turn round and approach the sinking battleship for fear that they too would be torpedoed. One of the cruisers was HMS *Tipperary*, which suggests the sailors' choice of song had a certain grim humour. Other survivors were rescued by a Brixham trawler that happened to be in the vicinity. Another boat drifted for almost a whole day until spotted and brought to shore; only 48 of the 70 men on board survived the ordeal. In the heavy swell John's boat was smashed against the side of the rescuing cruiser and the 40 survivors on board were thrown into the sea; they had to swim to the ship's side and climb up the ropes thrown to them. Finally, reaching safety, suffering from exposure and shock, he passed out, only regaining consciousness in the sick bay.

A total of 547 men out of a crew of 780, including Captain Loxley, lost their lives that night. His body was never recovered though the body of his dog, Bruce, was found washed up on shore. Bizarrely, another dog features in accounts of this tragedy. Lassie, a border collie owned by the landlord of a pub whose cellar was used as a temporary mortuary for some of the sailors' bodies, is said to have licked the face of one sailor who then revived. John Harlow's comment on the tragedy was stoical: 'It's all in the business of war. You can't blame the Germans for torpedoing us if they get the chance. We should do the same to them. I still like the sailor's life, though I did not expect I should ever have any more of it when I stood on the *Formidable* during those last few minutes.'

A year later John had another lucky escape. He was now serving on HMS *Natal*, a Warrior-Class cruiser built in 1905, anchored in Cromarty Firth off the west coast of Scotland. On 31 December 1915, on the eve of the first anniversary of his deliverance from HMS *Formidable* and the tragic loss of so many of his shipmates, his new berth suddenly exploded and sank with the loss of 404 out of a crew of 703. Those killed included a number of civilians, among them women and children, who had been attending a cinema party on board that afternoon. The sinking this time was not the result of enemy action, but was thought to have been caused by the accidental detonation of a faulty cordite charge. The disaster was reported in the *Eastern Daily Press*, which also republished John's photograph. A list of survivors of the explosion and sinking was produced by the senior medical officer of the hospital ship HMHS *Plassy* the day after the disaster. Curiously, this does not include John's name. The *Eastern Daily Press*, however, noted that his name appeared 'in the list of the saved'. It seems that several of the ship's ratings were either playing in or watching a football match at Invergordan at the time of the explosion. Whether John was on shore leave at the match or was accidentally missed off the *Plassy* list isn't known.

John's next ship was the Royal Sovereign-class battleship HMS *Royal Oak*, on which he served throughout the remainder of the war. He joined her on 18 April 1916 and would therefore almost certainly have been on board at the Battle of Jutland (31 May–1 June 1916), during which the *Royal Oak* escaped damage. In 1939, long after John had retired from the Navy, HMS *Royal Oak* was sunk by the German U-boat *U-47* in Scapa Flow with the loss of 833 lives. Tragedy seemed to follow every ship he sailed on. John Harlow retired from the Navy with the rank of Leading Seaman on 16 August 1925. It is not known when or where he died.

From Grocer's Boy to War Hero

Captain Herbert Flood Pitcher MC, 1st Battalion, Northampton Regiment

Herbert Flood Pitcher was born in Norwich in 1878, one of the 12 children of James Pitcher, a bricklayer and pub landlord, and Lydia Diana Pitcher née Huke. Herbert's parents were married in Great Yarmouth, his mother's home town, in 1867. His father was the licensee of the Whip & Nag pub in Tooley Street (part of present-day Pitt Street) in the parish of St Mary Coslany, Norwich, from 1871 to 1884, when he died at the age of 41, so Herbert was probably born on the premises. His unusual middle name commemorates the Norwich floods of November 1878 when low-lying streets in the north and west of the city were inundated by the River Wensum, which, swollen with rain that had been falling more or less continuously since the beginning of the month, broke its banks. By 1891 the family had moved to 22 Esdelle Street, a new street of terraced housing in the parish of St Augustine. His widowed mother was now employed as a crape dresser. Crape was a type of silk or imitation silk fabric, normally dyed black and therefore much used for mourning attire. Herbert shared his home here with seven of his surviving siblings: Mary, Emily, Jessie, Arthur, Edith, Florence and John. Now aged 12, he had already left school and was working as a grocer's assistant. In 1892 his mother died, aged 47, leaving Herbert an orphan.

How Herbert survived over the next four years isn't known. In 1896, now aged 18, he enlisted in Norwich in the 2nd Battalion, Northamptonshire Regiment. Army life seems to have suited him. In May 1898 he was appointed lance corporal and in June 1899 was promoted to full corporal. That November he sailed with the Regiment for Cape Town to take part in the Boer War. He was clearly a man with considerable leadership abilities as he returned to England in 1904 a full sergeant. In 1908 he was stationed in India with the 2nd Battalion and the following year earned the distinction of being addressed as Colour Sergeant Pitcher. In 1911 he was transferred to the Northamptonshire Regiment's 1st Battalion with

Sergeant Pitcher

the rank of company sergeant major. The Census that year found him resident in the South Raglan Barracks in Devonport.

Following Britain's declaration of war against Germany on 4 August 1914, the 1st Battalion was ordered to France to join the British Expeditionary Force (BEF), arriving at Le Havre on board SS *Galeka* on 13 August. Herbert now held the rank of company quarter-master sergeant, which was technically subordinate to company sergeant major in rank. Presumably, he had taken a step down in rank in order to join the expeditionary force. This was a common occurrence, called 'reversion', as the numbers of each NCO rank allowed to go with a Battalion overseas was strictly limited. In 1914, the 1st Battalion fought at Mons and during the Retreat from Mons, and at the battles of the Marne and the Aisne. In October Herbert was hospitalised in Rouen with a bayonet wound to the leg, which he may have received at Pilckem Ridge on the 22nd during the 1st Battle of Ypres. He returned to active service on 14 November and was Mentioned in Despatches by the Commander-in-Chief, Field Marshall Sir John French, for the first time on 8 October 1914 for his coolness under fire during the Battle of the Aisne where he had taken command of his company after all the officers were either wounded or dead. He would be so honoured on two more occasions.

On 29 January 1915, during the Battle of Cuinchy, Herbert was wounded again. Then in March 1915 he received a battlefield commission as a 2nd lieutenant, becoming, thereby almost certainly the first serviceman from St Augustine's to be promoted from the ranks. He was now posted to front line trenches at Rue de Bois, where on 9 May during the Battle of Aubers Ridge he led a platoon over the top for the first time as its commanding officer. The day was disastrous with the 1st Northamptonshire Regiment losing more than 260 killed in action and 200 wounded or missing. Almost the entire battalion's officer corps was killed or wounded. Herbert was one of only two officers to survive the battle uninjured and for many years afterwards he and the other unscathed officer, Major C. H. Bacon, exchanged telegrams on the anniversary of the battle to commemorate their survival, signed Survivor Number 1 and Survivor Number 2. On 1 January 1916 Herbert was promoted to full lieutenant and was awarded the Military Cross (gazetted on 11 January), for his work in keeping the 1st Battalion's HQ in touch with the Front at Aubers Ridge. On 22 January 1916 the *Norwich Mercury* published his photograph and an account of his award of the MC.

During the war Herbert's home address remained in Norwich, first in Oak Street and then at 2 Chatham Street off Sussex Street. Throughout most of 1917 Herbert was stationed in England, undertaking light duties with the Northamptonshire Regiment's 3rd (Reserve) Battalion while a physical disability barred him from further active service at the Front. On 14 March 1917 he married Miss Julia Hannah Blofield Minister in St Augustine's church, Norwich. Their first child, Marjorie Ivy, was baptised in St Augustine's on 28 November 1917. A son, Herbert, was born in 1920. Interestingly, two Norwich-born boys, presumably godsons, were christened Herbert Flood Pitcher in Norwich in 1908 and 1910.

Herbert was promoted to captain in February 1917. In 1919 he was stationed in Duisdorf in Germany as part of the Army of Occupation. He retired from the Army in 1922, having served with the Northamptonshire Regiment for 25 years. His medals included the Military Cross; the Queen's South Africa Medal (1899–1902) with four clasps (Belmont, Modder River, Orange Free State and

Transvaal); the King's South Africa Medal with the 1901 and 1902 clasps; the 1914 'Mons' Star with Bar; and the British War and Victory medals, the latter with an oak leaf to indicate he had been a mentioned in despatches. After retiring from the Army he settled in Northampton where he became manager of W. & R. Shipman, wine merchants, and a prominent member of the local Freemasons Lodge. He died in 1948. His funeral took place on 7 January 1948 at the Church of the Holy Sepulchre, Northampton.

Captain Pitcher

The 'necessary entracte' –
the life and death of Private John Henry Abigail

St Augustine's Great War roll of honour includes one very unusual commemoration: that of an executed soldier. Such was the stigma attached to what was almost universally regarded as a dishonourable death that the inclusion of an executed man on a war memorial is very rare. The names of the executed were not published in official casualty lists, unless by accident, and they were excluded from civic, national or regimental rolls of honour after the war. Until the mid-1990s it was still a breach of the Official Secrets Act to publish their identities. A request for other examples of executed men on British war memorials, posted by the author on a Great War Forum blog website in 2009, returned less than a dozen other examples and some of these seem not to have been contemporaneous but to have been added in more recent years at the request of relatives.

It is sometimes assumed such deaths were commonplace; in fact they were comparatively rare. It is estimated that just over 300 British and Colonial servicemen were executed during the war for military offences other than murder. More than twice that number won the Victoria Cross. Compared to the figure of almost a million who died on active service, it is a very small number indeed. Why is it then that so statistically insignificant a cause of death continues to fascinate and appal? One reason may be that such stories of individual plight help place the First World War's industrial scale of slaughter on a more comprehensible level. Another reason may be an uneasy feeling that an injustice was done, one that needs to be rectified or at the very least recognised and given adequate explanation. It is often argued that one should not judge the past by the standards of today or allow our modern sensibilities to condemn or excuse those who acted under conditions we can barely imagine. But neither should we withhold our sympathy and understanding from those with whom we share a common humanity, or ignore the inconsistencies and inadequacies in the application of justice where they are found.

John Henry Abigail was born in Thorpe Hamlet, an eastern suburb of Norwich, on 29 April 1897, the fourth child of John James Abigail, a carter and labourer, and Susannah Maria Abigail née

Webb. Abigail is an uncommon surname. It is rarely found in public records outside Norfolk in the 19th century and only 30 males named Abigail or Abigal were recorded in the county in the 1841 Census. The name achieved a brief local notoriety in 1882 when 19-year-old William George Abigail, a hotel waiter, was hanged at Norwich Castle for the murder of his girlfriend, despite the jury having recommended him to mercy on account of his youth. Thirty-five years later John Henry Abigail would also be judicially put to death, aged just a year older than William, his crime not murder but desertion from the British Army.

John's father came from Bacton on the north-east coast of Norfolk. Abigails had lived in this then rather isolated part of the county for generations. John's ancestry has been traced back to his great great grandparents, John and Sarah Abigail, who married in St Andrew's, Bacton, in 1802. A prolific couple, they had at least 13 children, counting only those who lived long enough to be baptised. Successive generations lived lives of rural seclusion until sometime before the taking of the 1881 Census when John's father and widowed grandfather, also named John, moved to Norwich. Like thousands of other affected by the agricultural depression of the 1870s they had probably come to the city to find better paid work and steady employment. Gas Hill, Thorpe Hamlet, where they first settled, is an unusually steep hill for 'flat' Norfolk. As its name suggests it housed a gas works, established in 1830 by the British Gas & Light Company. Next door to them in the row of tiny labourers' cottages that clung to the precipitous hillside above the gas works lived Elizabeth Abigail, John's great grandmother. Born in 1805, her lifetime encompassed the transformation of Thorpe Hamlet from secluded woodland village to semi-industrialised suburb. In 1885 a new, purpose-built prison was built nearby, replacing the Gaol in Norwich Castle where William Abigail had been hanged three years earlier. The following year the Norfolk Regiment's imposing Britannia Barracks was built nearby on the edge of a promontory commanding fine views over the city. Both institutions would feature significantly in John Abigail's short life.

The next known event in the Abigail family story occurred on 6 February 1886, 11 years before John was born, when his father enlisted in the 2nd Eastern Brigade, Royal Field Artillery (Militia

Reserve), also known as The Prince of Wales's Own Norfolk Artillery. Recruits 'attested' their willingness to serve for a fixed term, in John James Abigail's case six years. He signed on for a further six in 1892. After a few months intensive training militiamen were allowed to return to their civilian lives on the understanding they attend a set number of training drills each year and be ready to return to the colours immediately in a national emergency. At the time of enlisting, John James, 18, was a farm labourer lodging in Ketts Hill, Thorpe Hamlet. Five years later the 1891 Census locates him lodging at the William IV pub in Quebec Road, Thorpe Hamlet – his first recorded association with pubs, breweries and alcohol, which were to have such a damaging effect on his family's life. His occupation was now coal labourer. A fellow lodger, Walter Webb, a corn merchant's labourer, would soon become his brother-in-law. On 18 October 1891 John James married Walter's older sister, Susannah Maria Webb, at St Andrew's church in the neighbouring parish of Thorpe-next-Norwich. Both were 23. Susannah's parents, William and Susan, were farm labourers, born and raised, in Great Plumstead about three miles east of Thorpe Hamlet. After marriage, the young couple lived at 10 Gipson's Yard off Camp Road, Thorpe Hamlet. The address no longer exists but seems to have been on high ground overlooking the city between St Leonard's Road and Quebec Road. Here they began a family. First came Ellen Rosina, born 1892, then William Samuel (1894) and Elizabeth Ellen (1895). Curiously, Elizabeth seems to have been the only one of their children to have been baptised, in Thorpe Hamlet's Victorian parish church, St Matthew's. Next came John Henry (1897), the subject of this biography, then Annie Maria (1899).

The Abigails were still in Gipson's Yard at the time of the 1901 Census. John's father was now a carter for Norwich City Corporation. He had purchased his discharge from the Militia in 1895, having risen to the rank of bombardier (equivalent to corporal). He had almost certainly worked with horse teams in the artillery and driving wagons and carts seems to have been a family calling: his grandfather and great grandfather were described as 'common carriers' in Bacton in the 1861 and 1871 censuses respectively. Later in 1901, after the census had been taken, a sixth child, Mary Agnes, was born but died soon after. On 16 October 1904, two more children, twins Percy Edward and Walter Herbert, were born. An eighth child, Florence Ethel (usually known as Ethel), was born in 1908. John would probably have attended Thorpe Hamlet School during these years. It is interesting to note that First World War Victoria Cross winner, Harry Daniels, was also a pupil at this school. School attendance between the ages of 5 and 10 had become compulsory under the 1880 Education Act. This had been extended to 12 in 1899 and non-compulsory, free education was available to 13. John was recorded as still at school in the 1911 Census when he was 13. Unfortunately, the school's attendance registers for this period are lost, so we don't know precisely when John left or what job he went to.

The 1911 Census found the Abigail family still at 10 Gipson's Yard. John's father was a labourer once again, while his mother is described as a laundress. John's older brother, William Samuel, 16, was also working as a labourer, in a 'stone pit', probably in one of the local quarries of the Mousehold Stone Pit Company. His eldest sister, Ellen, was a chocolate packer, perhaps at Caley's Chapel Field factory. Another sister, Elizabeth, was lodging with a widow just across the yard employed as a domestic servant, a common resource for poor families wanting to ease over-crowding in the family home and bring in extra income. Curiously, the family's youngest member, Ethel, 2, is not recorded in the Abigail household or apparently anywhere else. The 1911 Census was the first one in which the head of the household completed the form rather than a paid enumerator. Presumably, John James Abigail forgot to include his youngest child. Later in 1911 John's older brother William followed in his father's footsteps, enlisting in the 1st East Anglian Brigade, Royal Field Artillery; a unit of the new Territorial Force, which had replaced the country's numerous volunteer and yeomanry regiments under Lord Haldane's Army reforms of 1907. Recruits who signed on agreed to attend a week-long summer camp and ten drill sessions per year, usually at weekends, hence their nickname 'Saturday Night Soldiers', but could otherwise continue with their civilian lives. William's Army Service papers from this period note that on enlisting, aged 16, he was just 5ft 4 in height (his father had been 5ft 8 when he had enlisted aged 18), though in good physical condition (all that quarrying) and with good eyesight. Unlike his father, his time as a part-time soldier did not seem to have lasted very long. The last dated entry in his surviving Army Service papers notes he had attended the Brigade's summer camp in 1912. This is followed by an undated note that he had been 'Struck off strength' under Paragraph 268 of the Territorial Force Regulations. The specific reason is not given but failure to attend the requisite number of drills was the most common cause for dismissal.

At some point before 1916 the Abigail family moved closer to the centre of Norwich, taking rented accommodation at 17 Distillery Yard, a small, three-roomed dwelling off Oak Street in the parish of St Miles Coslany. The attendance register of Quay Side Boys School, records that the twins Percy and Walter were admitted from Thorpe School on 5 October 1915, which more or less dates the family's move. Distillery Yard no longer exists, swept away during slum clearances in the interwar years of the 20th century. Unlike Thorpe Hamlet with its mixture of middle-class villas and labourers' cottages, Coslany was an exclusively working-class area where some of Norwich's poorest citizens lived and worked in a labyrinth of overcrowded, insanitary yards, threaded through a noisy, smelly jumble of saw mills, tanneries, dye works, iron foundries and malt houses. Located at the end of a long, narrow alley off Oak Street, Coslany's main thoroughfare, Distillery Yard abutted the River Wensum, then polluted with industrial effluent and sewage. In 1912 the river had inundated low-lying parts of Norwich, including Coslany, and many of the dwelling here were still chronically damp. Distillery Yard and its tenements were the property of G. & R. G. Bagshaw, corn merchants, whose other miscellaneous enterprises included wastepaper, scrap metal and rag & bone collection, game & poultry dealing, fellmongering (i.e. processing those parts of horse and cattle carcases not fit for human consumption) and the manufacture of dog food. Bagshaw's warehouse stood right across the entrance to Distillery Yard next door to the Hot Pressers Arms and opposite another pub, the intriguingly named Greenland Fishery; just two of more than 30 pubs in Oak Street at that time. John's father was now employed as a brewer's carter, probably for Bullard's, whose St Miles Anchor Brewery was located nearby, just north of the river. A few years earlier a man named James Abigail had been Bullard's foreman blacksmith, in charge of looking after the brewery's valuable teams of dray horses. However, by 1911 arthritis had forced him to give up the job. He was in fact John James's cousin, son of his father's older brother, so it is possible it was he who provided John James with a reference

In 1914, before the move from Thorpe Hamlet, the family had found itself with another mouth to feed when eldest daughter Ellen, who was still living at home and unmarried, gave birth to a daughter, Nellie. With so many mouths to feed and very little money coming in, family life now began to spiral out of control, though there is evidence that all had not been well for several years. The National Society for the Prevention of Cruelty to Children (NSPCC), founded in 1884, had begun to take an interest in the welfare of the younger children in 1905 when the twins Percy and Walter were born, Annie was 6 and John 8. Whether matters were then as bad as they later became is not known and it would be 11 years before the NSPCC finally decided that legal action was necessary, having in the meantime issued frequent cautions to the parents that they needed to keep their children clean and respectably clothed. The 1904 Prevention of Cruelty Act enabled the NSPCC's uniformed inspectors to remove children from abusive or neglectful homes with the consent of a Justice of the Peace. Using this authority, on 18 January 1916 Inspector Lycett, accompanied by Dr Laurence B. Mills, an employee of the Norwich Incorporation Workhouse, called at 17 Distillery Yard. What they found there clearly shocked even them, accustomed as they presumably were to scenes of poverty and destitution. Inspector Lycett had previously worked for the NSPCC in the coalfields of South Shields. A newspaper report of 1897 described how he had been called to a house where he found a woman the worse for drink with her baby 'crying piteously', 'unwashed, saturated with filth, stinking and its eyes closed with filth and matter'. The mother was sentenced to six months imprisonment. John and Susannah Abigail were summoned to appear at Norwich Police Court in ten days' time to answer a charge that they were treating their three youngest children, Percy, Walter and Ethel, 'in a manner likely to cause them unnecessary suffering and injury to their health'. On 24 January, before the case came to court, 5-year-old Ethel was removed from home, placed with a foster mother and admitted as a pupil at Wensum View Infants School close to the workhouse in Turner

Road. The twins, Walter and Percy, were taken to the workhouse infirmary in Turner Road, where they were washed, deloused and given clean clothing. This does not appear to have been the twins' first visit. The attendance register for Quay Side Boys School, notes that Walter was sent there on 17 November 1915 followed by Percy on 14 January 1916, just four days before Lycett and Mills decisive visit to Distillery Yard, which suggests that the NSPCC had been visiting the Abigail household regularly for weeks. The twins were subsequently sent to the Norwich Incorporation Workhouse's boys' home in St Faith's Lane near Norwich cathedral and not allowed home again until 21 February 1916

At Norwich Guildhall Police Court (an old term for the magistrates' court) on 28 January 1916 Mr F. A. Bainbridge, representing the NSPCC, stated that 'the case was a very long standing one, and one towards which the society [i.e. the NSPCC] had been far too lenient'. Bainbridge was a prominent Norwich solicitor and a leading figure in the Norfolk Volunteers Regiment during the war. Taking the witness stand, Dr Mills spoke of the filthy conditions under which the children were living, stating that 'it seemed almost impossible that human beings could exist amid such surroundings'. The house was extremely dirty and, in his opinion, not fit for human habitation. The ground-floor was covered in discarded match sticks and the twins' bedding was found to be no more than a pile of revoltingly soiled sacks. The children, although apparently well nourished, were clothed in rags and either wore no shoes or stockings, or boots several sizes too big. Their hair and clothing were infested with lice and fleas, and their bodies were covered with vermin bites. Mrs Abigail told the magistrates, Mr G. Cleverley and Mr F. J. Crotch, that she received 12 shillings out of her husband's weekly wage of 18 shillings to keep the household and feed, clothe and clean herself and the children. Twelve shillings, in the opinion of the Chairman of the Court, Mr Cleverley, was perfectly adequate to maintain a clean, decent home, adding that in any case they should have applied to the Board of Poor Law Guardians if they couldn't manage. Although John and Susannah Abigail pleaded guilty, the charge against Mrs Abigail was dismissed. John James Abigail, however, was sentenced to one month's hard labour at Norwich Prison.

Prisoner 4697 Abigail, J. J. was discharged on 27 February 1916, having served his full sentence without remission. A week later, on 6 March, little Ethel was returned home from her fosterers, having been separated from her mother for six weeks. Whether or not John, who was now 18, was still living in Distillery Yard at this time isn't known, though interestingly, his older brother William, who was now in the Army Reserve, gave it as his home address. Whatever his situation, John's parents' very public shame can hardly have left him unaffected. The case had been reported in all its shocking detail by the local press, including even the names of the children and the family's address. If the family hadn't already been so, there's no doubt it would now have been a topic of considerable gossip and ill-feeling in the neighbourhood. John, however, would soon have other matters on his mind.

On 12 March 1916 John was conscripted. The Military Services Act of January 1916 had come into full effect on 10 February. After the initial patriotic rush in 1914, the number of volunteers had reduced considerably and a compulsory enlistment scheme had to be put into place in order to replace the enormous casualties the Army had suffered on the Western Front and at Gallipoli during 1915. After this date all unmarried men, with a few exceptions, aged between 18 and 41, were regarded as enlisted in His Majesty's Forces, pending any, usually futile, appeal they might wish to make to the local Exemption Board. In May this was extended to married men too. It is possible, though there is no evidence, that John may have volunteered but been rejected as unfit in 1915 when he turned 18 but was found acceptable in 1916 when the increasing demand for men forced the recruiting authorities to lower their standards of height and fitness. The Army might have seemed preferable to the squalor at home and his father and older brother had set him a precedent for 'taking the shilling'. Army medical officers had been shocked by the poor physical condition of many of the working-class men they examined in 1914, the result of generations of poor nourishment and an almost total absence of reliable, affordable health care. Given what is known of John's family circumstances it would not be surprising to find that he was physically and perhaps even mentally underdeveloped. At the Police Court hearing in January Dr Mills had described John's younger brother Walter as 'a not over bright child', a euphemism for some sort of learning disability either congenital or acquired through malnutrition, illness or even physical abuse.

John Henry Abigail's Army Service papers have not survived. The few scraps of information that have come to light pre-dating his court martial tell the following story. After enlisting he was placed in the Norfolk Regiment's 8th Battalion. Known colloquially as the 'Businessman's Battalion', this 'Kitchener' Service battalion was raised in Norwich in September 1914 from men, many of them city clerks and shopkeepers, with little or no military experience – the closest Norfolk came to a 'Pals' battalion. On 19 June 1916 John made his first soldier's will. Soldiers were instructed to complete a basic will form prior to going into the front line. At this period the 8th Norfolks were busy digging trenches at Billon Wood, south of Carnoy, as the British Army prepared for the big push on the Somme designed to relieve pressure on the French at Verdun. The next known fact comes from a ledger known as the Wound Book, preserved today in the Royal Norfolk Regimental Museum in Norwich. In it are listed the names of private and non-commissioned soldiers from the Norfolk Regiment's Regular and Service battalions who were killed in action, died of wounds, disease or accident, or were wounded in action or reported sick between August 1914 and November 1918. An entry against 'Pte 9694 Abigail, J. H.' has the frustratingly brief entry: 'wounded 19/7/1916'. Details of the type of wound or how he received it were not recorded; however, the fact that it doesn't say GSW (gunshot wound) suggests he may have been wounded by a shell or gas. The date of his wounding is significant.

The 8th Norfolks, part of the 53rd Brigade, 18th (Eastern) Division, had suffered heavy casualties during the first two weeks of fighting on the Somme. Another member of the Abigail clan, Private Frederick Abigail from North Walsham, Norfolk, also in the 8th Norfolks and a year older than John, was killed in action on the first day of the battle, 1 July 1916; a day in which the British Army sustained 20,000 casualties. On the 19 July the 8th Norfolks were ordered to attack and seize the southern portion of Delville Wood (known by the Tommies, inevitably, as 'Devil's Wood') near the ruined village of Longueval. By this time there wasn't very much resembling a wood left standing and concealed among its shattered trees, German machine-gunners, snipers and bombers awaited the expected assault behind thick, uncut rows of barbed wire. 'B' Company, John's unit, were placed on the 8th Battalion's left flank and began moving up the valley towards Deville Wood just after dawn at 5.30 a.m. By 9.00 a.m. 'B' Company had penetrated well into the tangled remnants of the wood but had become pinned down by raking machine-gun fire. It remained trapped there, under constant fire for almost three days until relieved by the Gordon Highlanders. The 8th Norfolk's casualties were appalling. According to the Battalion's War Diary three officers and 76 other ranks were killed in action; two other ranks died of wounds soon afterwards; 82 were wounded and 36 were reported missing. *Soldiers Died in the Great War* records the Battalion's losses between 19 and 21 July as 105 officers and men, suggesting that 24 of the missing were subsequently recorded as killed. The dead included a St Augustine's lad, the newly commissioned 2nd Lieutenant Bertie Benn, killed in the opening minutes of the assault, leading a platoon of 'A' Company.

Seven weeks after the 8th Norfolk's costly assault on Delville Wood, John's name appeared in the *Eastern Daily Press* as the first name in a long, alphabetically arranged list of the Norfolk Regiment's recent wounded on the Somme. Although his surname was misspelled 'Abigal', his correct regimental number and initials appear against his name leaving no doubt that the wounded soldier was Private John Henry Abigail. Given his subsequent acts of desertion with their implication of cowardice, it is worth noting that within four months of being conscripted as an untrained civilian, he had taken part in one of the bloodiest battles of the war so far and been wounded in action. John's wound seems to have been sufficiently serious to get him shipped home to 'Blighty'. He was still in England, at the Norfolk Regiment's 3rd (Reserve) Battalion's base in Felixstowe, Suffolk, in December 1916, awaiting redeployment.

While John had been serving King and Country in France the situation at home had not improved, quite the reverse. After his father's conviction and imprisonment for child neglect in January, Inspector Lycett continued to visit the family at regular intervals. Each time he found the younger children clothed in rags and had to warn their mother to keep them clean. The twins, Percy and Walter, were also missing school, for which their parents were being fined, a further drain on the family's meagre resources. On 25 July 1916 a magistrate's order had compelled his parents to admit Percy to Angel Road School. A similar order for Walter followed on 2 October. On his third visit, on Monday 16 October, Lycett found John James Abigail upstairs, still in bed at half past one in the afternoon. On coming down he explained that he was not at work as he had 'overslept himself'. It then emerged, probably from Mrs Abigail, a woman clearly at the end of her tether, that he hadn't been downstairs for two days, telling Lycett in front of her husband that he was a heavy drinker. According to family legend, John James was man of violent temper, often coming home drunk and throwing over the kitchen table. Despite having a criminal conviction and clearly being sometimes too drunk or hung-over to go to work he was still employed at the brewery. Before leaving, Lycett warned John and Susannah that matters must improve or they would face the consequences. On 21 November he called again and was so appalled by the condition of the younger children that he had them removed to the workhouse immediately. The twin's bodies were found to be filthy and the clothes they had received from the workhouse in January were ragged, dirty and infested with lice and fleas. Dr Mills, who later examined them at the workhouse infirmary in Turner Road, went so far as to pronounce their verminous state 'a danger to the community'. The youngest child, Ethel, was found to be slightly cleaner and well-nourished but her clothes were also verminous and her head covered in sores. The proximity of their home to Bagshaw's fellmongers yard, with its piles of rotting hides attracting river rats, probably accounts for the children's infestation and bite marks on their skin. A vivid account of life in 'Bagshaw's Yard' before the First World War by Eric Fowler appeared in the pages of the *Eastern Daily Press* in the 1970s under his pen name 'Jonathan Mardle':

What a place it was! Cobbled and having a drain down the middle of it. It was a common practice for housewives to empty all and sundry of their pots and pans down the drain. Swarming with rats and infested with fleas and bugs, Bagshaw's Yard was the playground of many kids, with their dirty feet and sore eyes and running noses. Bagshaw bought old rags, old bones, old bottles .... As the piles of old bones grew, so did the smell, but nobody seemed to mind. What was it to women who regularly sported black eyes and gave birth to their children in slum attics.

'The Norwich Yards', 10 November 1976.

On 25 November 1916, John and Susannah Abigail came before magistrates Mr W. R. Smith and Mr W. G. Stevens at Norwich Guildhall Police Court. Both pleaded guilty, as they had done at their trial in January. John James, giving what he may have hoped was a mitigating statement, said that he gave his wife £1 a week (8 shillings more than Susannah Abigail had said at their hearing in January) and besides this spent 5 or 6 shilling 'into the house' every week. The twins, he said, would not go to school and he could not afford to keep paying the school fines and clothe the lads too. He asked for an adjournment of the case so that he might try to improve matters. The magistrates refused, found him guilty and sentenced him to six weeks' hard labour at Norwich Prison, two weeks longer than his previous sentence. This time the charge against Susannah Abigail was upheld and she too was sentenced to hard labour, her term to last one month at Norwich Prison. With both of their parents in prison and none of their adult siblings apparently able to take care for them, Percy and Walter were placed under the supervision of Mrs Emma Miller of the Norwich Incorporation Workhouse in Turner Road. Little Ethel had already been put into a foster home. St Miles Coslany Infant School's attendance register tersely notes against her name 'gone in a home 22.11.16'.

John, meanwhile, was in barracks in Felixstowe awaiting deployment. It was from here on 19 December, six days before Christmas Day, that he committed his first recorded military offence. At 9 p.m. he was found to be absent from parade and reported as a deserter. He was arrested in Norwich by a civilian police officer, Sergeant Christie, at 4 p.m. on 27 December 1916. Any excuses he may have given for deserting are not recorded, they seldom were. It would seem a safe assumption, however, that the dire situation at home had played a major part in his decision to run. His parents' second court appearance that year had been widely reported in the local press, not just in Norfolk but in Suffolk too, under shaming headlines such as 'A Dirty Norwich Home' and there had been plenty of time for the news to reach him in Felixstowe. Had he perhaps been denied leave and been anxious about his family, especially his mother, who was due to be released on Christmas Eve, while his father was still in prison and his younger brothers were still in the workhouse and his youngest sister with foster parents?

On the same day as his arrest in Norwich, John appeared at Norwich Guildhall's Police Court on a charge of deserting from the Norfolk Regiment. He appeared before magistrates Mr G. T. Gee (Chairman), Mr John Dodson and Mr W. G. Stevens; the latter had been on the bench during his parents' hearing a month earlier. On 29 December 1916 the *Eastern Daily Press* reported the case under the humiliating headline 'A Deserter':

> *Private John Abigail (20)* [he was in fact 19] *was charged with deserting from the Norfolk Regiment since December 19th. Police-sergeant Christie gave evidence of the arrest, and the accused – who admitted he was a deserter, was ordered to be handed over to the military authorities.*

John's apparent refusal to defend himself or offer excuses, indications perhaps of a streak of stubborn pride and taciturn dignity, would be repeated in even more desperate circumstances in France in 1917.

The day after John's court appearance his father was released from Norwich Prison two weeks early on remission. As one member of the family came out of gaol another went in. Returned to Felixstowe camp John was punished with 168 hours detention in the glass house (military prison) and forfeited nine days' pay. Having offended once, there were no doubt those in authority watching him closely, waiting for him to make his next mistake. They didn't have long to wait. Two weeks into the New Year, on 15 January 1917, John was confined to barracks (CTB) for five days for having a dirty rifle on parade, an offence it was virtually impossible to avoid if the parade officer had it in for you – the merest speck of dust or drop of oil was enough to warrant a charge. A routine punishment for this offence was extra drill or fatigues. Five days CTB seems excessive and as a soldier with ten months' experience in the ranks John may have felt this was unfair and possibly vindictive. Something, perhaps resentment at the way he had been treated over the 'dirty' rifle incident or news of further problems at home, now triggered his second run. On 22 January, two days after the end of this second period of detention, he deserted again. This time he voluntarily handed himself in at Britannia Barracks not far from his childhood home in Thorpe Hamlet at 9.40 p.m. on 27 January, having been on the run for 5 days, 12 hours and 40 minutes, as his charge sheet meticulously records. For this second offence he received 14 days' Field Punishment and forfeited six days' pay.

Two types of Field Punishment (FP) were specified by the Military Manual, No. 1 and No. 2. The Conduct Sheet doesn't specify which one John was subjected to. No. 1 consisted of being kept in irons (leg fetters and handcuffs), usually, though not always, attached to a fixed object such as a post or the wheel of a gun carriage in the open for up to two hours a day for up to three out of every four days and for no more than 21 days in all without court martial. No. 2 was basically the same except the prisoner could not be attached to a fixed object. Although it was forbidden to bind the offender in stress positions, this sometimes happened. In addition to the periods of binding, punishments included long hours of hard labour such as cleaning latrines, breaking rocks and digging ditches, as well as seemingly endless drilling on the square with full pack and rifle, being constantly sworn at, bullied and pushed about by ferocious NCOs. The object was to shame, humiliate or terrorise the offender into more soldierly ways. It had effectively replaced flogging, which had been outlawed in the British Army in the 1880s, though birching was still permitted in the glass house (Army prison).

By early April 1917 John was back in France where the 8th Norfolks were undertaking training in open ground, hand-to-hand combat near Béthune. On the 25th they were shelled and lost seven men and four wounded. In early May they were being held in reserve at Neuville-Vitasse near the Hindenburg Line with the 53rd Brigade while the rest of 18th (Eastern) Division were fighting a losing battle in the Chérisy area. According to the regimental history the 8th Norfolks suffered several more casualties during this period from 'overs', overshot enemy shells intended for the front line that exploded in their reserve position. On 4 May 1917 John's platoon were warned to be ready to move into the trenches that day. The Battalion's War Diary notes that they left Neuville-Vitasse at 9.30

p.m. and took over defence of the Brigade's reserve trenches from the 10th Essex Regiment. It was now that John committed his first military offence to carry a death sentence: deserting in the field while on active service. He was absent without leave for eight days, handing himself in at the 5th Army's Infantry Training School at Étaples, a vast encampment known to the Tommies as 'Eat Apples', on 12 May. The area around Étaples near Boulogne was well known to the Military Police as the first-choice destination for soldiers on the run in northern France. A black market in getting deserters across the English Channel was thought to be engaged in here by local fishermen, though very few are known to have made it over. Those waiting for a passage home could hide here better than in the open countryside. Few of them could speak or understand French and so were unable to pass themselves off as locals. Here they could merge into the general mêlée of British soldiery around Étaples Army camp or even hide in the ancient network of chalk caves and tunnels known as the Sanctuary in the surrounding hills. Presumably, John lacked the resources to buy his passage back to England or simply lost the will to stay in hiding any longer and so decided to face the consequences, knowing full well this might mean death.

John's first Field General Court Martial was held a month later, on 7 June 1917. A transcript of the proceedings has not survived but his conduct sheet records that just two witnesses were called by the prosecution, both NCOs who had presumably been responsible for readying John's platoon to go into the front line: Lance Corporal Bowden (possibly Henry Bowden, later a sergeant in the Bedfordshire Regiment) and Sergeant Henry James Askew, who later won the Distinguished Conduct Medal and was killed in action in April 1918. Although found guilty of desertion in the field, for which he might have been shot, John was sentenced instead to ten years' penal servitude. As was fairly common at this time, his sentence was suspended under the provisions of the Army (Suspension of Sentences) Act 1915. This allowed those convicted to be returned to their units, partly so that they might have an opportunity to exonerate themselves by good conduct but also because trained men, no matter how unreliable, were too valuable a commodity to waste behind bars. The military authorities suspected prison might actually look like a better option than the very good chance of death or mutilation at the

Front. Soldiers under escort, being marched away from the Front to prison, had frequently been observed singing and apparently in good cheer. This state of affairs could not be allowed to continue. John's sentence was therefore suspended by authority of the Second Army's newly appointed commander, General Plumer, on 15 June. John would now have been returned to his company and expected to carry on with his duties.

By the end of July 1917 the 8th Norfolks were in Flanders, held in reserve, awaiting orders in the Comines Canal area, having spent the best part of the previous two months at a support camp at Henin-sur-Cujeul, rebuilding their strength and undertaking training. On 30 July at around 3.45 p.m. John's platoon were warned by their senior NCO, Sergeant Barnes, to be ready to move into the front-line trenches that night. All packs were to be handed in to the quartermaster's store by 6 p.m., a procedure experienced Tommies knew meant they were about to go over the top. July 30 had been designated 'Y' Day, the day prior to the launching of the Third Ypres Offensive, the bitter campaign later branded on the national consciousness as Passchendaele. At zero hour on 'Z' Day, 31 July 1917, 12 British, ANZAC and French infantry divisions went over the top and advanced towards the German entrenchments along an 11-mile front. Heavy rain soon turned the battlefield into a quagmire and by the time the initial attack was called off around 35,000 Allied soldiers had been killed, wounded or were missing. Huge numbers of them had simply disappeared beneath the mud or drowned in the rain-filled shell holes where they had crawled for shelter. The British artillery had begun their barrage of the German's deeply dug defences ten days earlier. An incessant bombardment amounting to more than 4 million shells had been kept up night and day so that those held in the forward areas, like the men of John's platoon, would have had frayed nerves and little chance of sleep before the major battle they knew was imminent. On top of this John had the anxiety of the review of his suspended sentence of ten years' penal servitude hanging over him. In less than a fortnight, if he lived that long, a tribunal would decide what sort of sentence he would have to serve when the war was over. It may very well have been impressed on him now as he waited to go over the top, that if he fought bravely it would go in his favour at the review and if by chance he were to die he would at least have regained his and the regiment's honour. As his comrades prepared themselves for battle a choice of death or dishonour appeared to be all he had left to him. In his desperation, he seems to have panicked and ended up with both.

At around 8 p.m. on 'Y' Day, 30 July, it was noted that Private Abigail had failed to hand in his pack at the quartermaster's store and was nowhere to be found. When he failed to report for duty at 10.50 p.m. as his platoon gathered to proceed to the assembly trenches he was presumed to have deserted. In all the confusion of manpower being moved about the Ypres Salient for the big push, John managed to evade immediate arrest by the squads of military policemen that patrolled the countryside behind the Front. After three days on the run, presumably hungry, wet through, tired and lost, he broke cover and was stopped on the open road about 20 miles south-west of Ypres near the French village of Staple by Mounted Military Policeman Corporal Henry Norman Stallworthy, who asked him if he was on duty. John lied, 'No, I am looking for my battalion, they were billeted near here and I have been out for a walk for 2 hours and when I came back, they were gone'. His explanation did not satisfy Corporal Stallworthy, who promptly arrested him on suspicion he was a deserter. By an odd coincidence Staple was the village in which Victor Silvester, the dance band leader, claimed to have taken part in a botched execution by firing squad when a private in the Argyle and Sutherland Highlanders in 1917.

John was now escorted under armed guard to the 8th Norfolk's Battalion HQ and held there for three weeks awaiting trial. A Field General Court Martial (FGCM) was approved by the Deputy Judge Advocate General, to be held on 22 August 1917. Three officers, who were to act as judge and jury, were appointed to form the FGCM panel. All were from battalions in the same brigade, the 53rd, as the 8th Norfolks. Senior officer and President of the Court was Brevet Lieutenant-Colonel Gerald Victor Wilmot Hill DSO, a Royal Irish Fusiliers officer attached to the 8th Battalion, Suffolk Regiment. By any measure Colonel Hill was an outstanding soldier. By the end of the war he had been wounded twice, awarded two Bars to his Distinguished Service Order (meaning he was awarded the medal three times) and been Mentioned in Despatches on six occasions. He survived the war and in 1933 took command of the Norfolk

Regiment's 1st Battalion and in 1939 was made an aide-de-camp to the king. The second member of the panel was Captain John Noel Richardson MC of the 6th Battalion, Royal Berkshire Regiment. In November 1915 his battalion had had to deal with a private who had attempted suicide and had been tried by court martial as a consequence though not executed. An experienced officer, he had been wounded at Longueval during the Battle of the Somme, coincidentally at around the same time and only a matter of yards from where John had himself been wounded in Delville Wood. He would later be promoted to major and also survived the war, going into the British Colonial Service. The third, most junior member of the panel was 2nd Lieutenant A. D. Whiting, a subaltern in the 10th Battalion, Essex Regiment, on temporary promotion to lieutenant since 1 July. No court martial officer (CMO) seems to have been appointed. A CMO, usually an officer with legal training in civilian life, had been attached to every Army Corps in France since the beginning of 1917. Their role was to see that courts martial were conducted competently and according to military law, but there simply weren't enough of them to go around; there were more than 100 courts martial for offences which attracted the death penalty held on the Western Front in August 1917 alone.

The court martial of Private John Henry Abigail convened on Friday 24 August 1917. The very warm and humid weather of the preceding week had cooled somewhat. A German pre-dawn attack at Inverness Corpse was the only major alarum of the day. It is not known where the trial was held but it would almost certainly have been within sound of the guns. The hearing itself probably lasted less than half an hour; the average time was 20 minutes. The formal charge, read out to the Court at the start of proceedings, was that:

> *When on active Service deserting His Majesty's Service in that he In the Field on the 30th July 1917, absented himself from his Battalion after having been warned for the trenches, and remained absent until apprehended without arms or equipment by the Military Police in a town behind the lines at about 4.30 pm on 2nd August 1917.*

The prosecution in such cases was often conducted by the adjutant of the defendant's battalion, who in this case was Captain Alexander

Tennent Mackintosh Berney Ficklin, a Rugby-educated officer barely two years older than John. Although John pleaded not guilty, he mounted no defence and seems not to have asked for a 'prisoner's friend', normally an officer from the soldier's platoon or company, to help him with his defence, as was his right. In the course of his court martial he did not question any of the four witnesses brought by the prosecution, neither did he bring forward any witnesses of his own or make any statement in his own defence, which he was also entitled to do. John's state of mind, pleading not guilty then making no effort whatsoever to defend himself, can only be guessed at. No medical report, if any was prepared, has survived and no medical evidence was presented at the trial. Shell shock is often cited in these circumstances. A common symptom of this stress-induced psychosis is an inability to think logically or strategically. John's propensity not to defend himself has been noted previously. To this must be added that for a 20-year-old private with only the most rudimentary education to mount his own defence, cross-examine witnesses and challenge the word of the officers prosecuting and trying him is to expect rather more than he or indeed most private soldiers were capable of.

The state of mind of the Court's presiding officers, may also only be guessed at. No account of their private thoughts has been discovered and while there is nothing in the surviving military records to suggest they were anything other than gallant, honest and honourable, it should perhaps be taken into account that the court martial was being held in the midst of a massive, gruelling battle of attrition that was not going well. During the period in which John had absented himself from duty – from the late evening of 30 July to the afternoon of 2 August – casualties in his own unit, the 8th Norfolks, had been fairly light – just nine – though they were to increase dramatically in the weeks that followed. By contrast, the three FGCM officers' battalions had suffered heavy casualties. Over the first three terrible days of the 3rd Ypres Offensive, Colonel Hill's battalion, the 8th Suffolks, had lost two officers and 61 other ranks; Captain Richardson's, the 6th Royal Berkshires, had lost two officers and 71 other ranks; and Lieutenant Whiting's, the 10th Essex, 23 other ranks. Set against these levels of loss suffered by men from their own units, some of whom they would have known personally, the value of the life of one man, a repeat offender who had deserted his own comrades twice in their hour of peril, would not perhaps have counted for very much. Given this, it is difficult to see how a trial conducted in such circumstances could be anything other than prejudiced against the defendant in the broadest sense of the word.

The first three witnesses called to give evidence were men from John's platoon: Corporal Walter Ellwood, Private Cecil Broughton and Private Harry Livings. Corporal Ellwood, like Lance Corporal Askew at John's first court martial, would not survive the war. A Norwich man, born in the parish of St Barnabas, Heigham, married and a father of two, Ellwood was an old soldier, having served as a Regular since 1902. Wounded at the Battle of the Aisne in September 1914 while with the 1st Norfolks, he would be killed in action in March 1918 on the first day of the German Army's spring offensive, the Kaiserschlacht ('Kaiser's battle'). Judging by their Medal Roll Index cards, Privates Broughton and Livings were 1916 conscripts, like John. Ironically, Private Livings would himself be tried and found guilty of desertion in November 1918, receiving as his punishment not death but 112 days detention. As his offence occurred near the end of the war in Felixstowe rather than under fire in France it wasn't regarded as a capital offence by the District Court Martial that tried him.

All three men from John's platoon stated in their spoken evidence that they had seen Private Abigail at the parade in which their senior platoon NCO, Sergeant Barnes, had warned them to be ready to go into the assembly trenches that night. Each stated that Private Abigail had stood close to Sergeant Barnes, within two yards, and so could not have failed to have heard his orders (the deafening barrage upon the German front line was still continuing at this time). John, however, was absent when the platoon marched off that evening. Corporal Ellwood stated that he had instituted a search of the camp at around 8 p.m. after noticing Private Abigail had not handed in his pack but he could not be found (his statement to this effect is underlined in the transcript). Only Private Broughton added something else, something that an alert prisoner's friend, if John had had one to defend him, might have offered to the Court to explain his absence. He stated that Sergeant Barnes had told them to collect firewood for cooking breakfast the next morning. John might perhaps have claimed he had gone out of camp to find kindling and had become lost but he said nothing. Curiously, Sergeant Barnes himself was not called as a witness. He doesn't appear to have been a recent casualty and as the 8th Norfolks were out of the front line at the time of the trial one might have expected him, as the senior NCO involved, to be called to give evidence.

Of the four witnesses called, perhaps the most damning evidence given was by Corporal Stallworthy, the Mounted Military Policeman who had arrested John near the hamlet of Staple. Corporal Stallworthy, aged 26, was from Tongwynlais near Cardiff and a policeman in civilian life. At the end of his evidence he added that when detained Private Abigail was 'without any equipment whatever', a statement that was underlined on the transcript of evidence and expanded to 'without arms or equipment' on the FGCM's Schedule of Proceedings. So, while the principal charge was desertion in the field, a second capital offence, that of casting away arms, had now been entered into evidence supporting the charge that he had been without arms or equipment when arrested.

After considering the evidence, the unanimous verdict of the Court was guilty as charged and the sentence death. Given that John had deserted on active service in the field before and was under a suspended sentence for that offence, the judging panel of officers probably felt they really had no other option. In these circumstances it was the policy of the FGCM to make no statement to the prisoner. Had he been acquitted he would have been told straightaway, so not hearing a verdict meant that he had been found guilty but not what his sentence was. Death sentences were meant to pass up through the Army hierarchy, through the convicted man's battalion, brigade, divisional and corps commanders to the commander-in-chief for confirmation; a process that might take two to three weeks. In John's case the procedure seems to have been curtailed. Documents of the FGCM appear to have were passed to the C-in-C, Field Marshal Douglas Haig via only Brigadier-General H. W. Higginson, CO of 53rd Brigade, who himself reserved judgement. Sixteen days after the trial, Haig gave his decision, writing on the papers: 'Confirmed D. Haig FM [Field Marshall] 9 Sep: 1917'. No more, no less.

It would be interesting to know whether Haig signed what amounted to John Abigail's death warrant before or after reports reached him that serious disturbances had broken out that very day at Étaples, the massive British Army camp near Boulogne. The events of the so-called 'Bull Ring Mutiny' of 9–12 September 1917 were suppressed and denied by the Army and the British Government at the time and for decades after, and only began to gain widespread notoriety when the story of the 'Monocled Mutineer', the deserter Percy Topliss, was published in 1979, followed by a BBC drama series based on the book broadcast in 1986. Riots and mass disobedience had erupted when hundreds of battle-weary Australian, British and New Zealand soldiers had fought with the military police and broken out of camp, incensed beyond endurance by the brutality, hardship and humiliation they were experiencing there, particularly at the hands of the Army's training instructors, known derisively as 'canaries' because of the yellow arm bands they wore. While there is no mention of the events at Étaples in Haig's published diary, there is little doubt that the much more serious and widespread outbreaks of mutiny and desertion in the French, Italian and Russian armies in 1917 was causing considerable anxiety among the higher echelons of the Government and military, fearful that news of these events would damage the morale of British and Colonial troops or even inspire them to do the same. Whether these considerations coloured Haig's judgement it is impossible to say. The plain facts are that John Abigail was a repeat offender, under a suspended sentence, and clemency was always less likely to be exercised if the offence occurred during a period of heightened military activity and peril such as the 3rd Ypres Offensive then in progress.

Sentence of death was 'Promulgated' on 11 September 1917, two days after it had been confirmed by Haig. Promulgation was normally carried out on the day before execution when the prisoner was read the verdict of the court, usually by the battalion adjutant, in front of as many soldiers from the prisoner's company as could be mustered. Execution would be carried out by firing squad the following day at dawn. In many cases this was the first the prisoner knew of his fate. A note at the bottom of the FGCM papers written by the 8th Norfolks' adjutant, Captain A. T. M. Berney Ficklin, states 'Promulgated 7.30 p.m. 11th Sept 1917 and necessary entracte taken'. It is not clear precisely what he meant by 'entracte' in this context. The term *entr'acte* is a theatrical one, meaning an interval, often with singing or dancing, between the acts of a play. To say the least it was a macabre choice of words. If Promulgation was Act One, and execution Act Two, then the 'entracte' was presumably something done in between, as for example selecting the six to twelve men, often chosen by lot or by drawing short straws, who would make up the firing squad; as well as preparing a place of execution and digging a grave. During the night before the execution, the condemned man might be kept company by an Army chaplain. Should the prisoner become hysterical or violent liberal doses of rum or even morphine might be administered to calm him down to a torpid state so that he was virtually unconscious when bound to the execution post or chair, where he was blindfolded by a roll of bandages. A white disc of cloth or paper to act as a target was then pinned to his shirt above his heart as the chaplain intoned 'I am the Resurrection and the Life'. All ready, a silent signal from the officer in charge brought about a volley of shots from the firing squad. Should the execution be botched and the prisoner found to be still alive, it was the gruesome duty of the officer in charge to administer the *coup de grâce* with a shot to the head from his service revolver. After a medical officer had confirmed death, the body was unbound, wrapped in a blanket and placed in a coffin and taken away to be buried immediately in the prepared grave.

A British firing squad

John Henry Abigail was executed by firing squad at dawn on Wednesday 12 September 1917. The sun rose at around 7.15 a.m. in northern France at that time of year but the sky that morning was dull and overcast. His brief life had lasted just 20 years and 136 days. Because of his place of burial, Esquelbecq, it is assumed that he was executed there too but there is no record of the exact location. The small town, with a large church, village square and an attractive chateau, also had a rail head through which many soldiers passed on their way to the Front. No first-hand account of the execution has come to light and the 8th Battalion's War Diary makes no mention of either the court martial or the execution. The village is only a few kilometres north of Rubrouck where the 8th Norfolks were billeted at the time. Bizarrely, the War Diary of the 11th Battalion, Royal Fusiliers, billeted in Esquelbecq at time of the execution, describes almost a holiday atmosphere in the village: improvised fancy dress concert parties on the bandstand, charabanc trips to the seaside for those who had just come out of the trenches and the Battalion's fifes and drums playing in the square in the evening – heard perhaps by John in his condemned cell. Two other executions by firing squad were carried out that morning in other parts of the Western Front, those of Private Charles Button of the 1/5th Battalion, Royal Warwickshire Regiment, and Private William Wycherley of the 2nd Battalion, Manchester Regiment.

The village of Esquelbecq

On 23 September the 8th Norfolks left Rubrouck and marched through Esquelbecq on their way to another part of the Front. Did anyone stop at John's recently dug grave? We shall probably never know.

One additional piece of information about John's last hours did come to light some 97 years after his death. In 2013 thousands of British First World War soldier's wills were digitised and made publically available for the first time. These documents, some of which included personal letters to loved ones, contain what amounts to the soldier's final thoughts as he prepared to go over the top. Private John Henry Abigail's will is unusual in that it is dated twice. The front of the form notes that the enclosed document is the informal will of Private 9694 John H. 'Abagail' or Abigail of the 8th Battalion, Norfolk Regiment. This uncertainty over the spelling of his surname is also found on his Medal Roll Index card, where his surname is spelled 'Abagial' (compare also his listing in the Norfolk Regiment casualty list in 1916). The form is dated 19 June 1916 when the 8th Norfolks were digging trenches at Billon Wood prior to the Battle of the Somme. This, however, has been crossed out and substituted with 12 September 1917, the actual date of John's execution. The will itself consists of a few words almost certainly written by John himself. Written in a schoolchild's hand, perhaps at dictation and omitting some of the words from the standard legal declaration, the lines slope up the page as though he had to write hastily with the paper pressed to a wall.

In the event of death I give the whole / of property and effect to my mother. Mrs Susanah Abigail / 17 Distillery Yd / Oak St / Norwich / Nor

Poignantly, the last, unfinished word, presumably 'Norfolk', ends with a shaky downward stoke. The will is signed 'Pt John Abigail Pt 8 Norfolks' [Private John Abigail Private 8th Norfolks] and dated 'Sept 12.17' in what appears to be the same hand, raising the chilling possibility that John was ordered to write a new will only hours or minutes before his death. Whether a copy of the will ever reached his mother is not known. Almost as though intended as a final insult the authorities managed to mangle the spelling of his name (and age) one last time. In the General Register Office's Army War Dead register John's death is listed under the name 'Henry Abagial', aged 18; the cause of death 'Shot for Desertion'.

John's body was buried in the west corner of Esquelbecq's Communal (i.e. village) Cemetery, one of only two British soldiers buried there. His Commonwealth War Grave Commission headstone, bearing the crest of the Norfolk Regiment but no indication of how he died, stands alongside that of Corporal A. L. Bowring, a signaller in the Royal Engineers who was killed in action on 15 May 1916.

John Abigail's headstone

Why these two isolated graves were not moved after the war to the larger Esquelbecq Military Cemetery is not known. The grave of another executed soldier, Private George Hunter of the 2nd Battalion, Durham Light Infantry, shot for desertion on 2 July 1916, is there so it can hardly be because of scruples about having a 'dishonoured' soldier's grave there. Private Hunter was an even more prolific deserter than John Abigail and was one of the few men who had actually made it back over the Channel. Esquelbecq would later be associated with an infamous war crime. On 28 May 1940, around 80 British soldiers who had been providing cover for the British Expeditionary Force's retreat to Dunkirk, surrendered and were taken prisoner by a unit of the Waffen-SS, who murdered them with machine-guns and grenades at a barn between Esquelbecq and Wormhoudt. The previous day around 90 members of the 2nd Battalion, Royal Norfolk Regiment, who had also surrendered, were murdered by another SS unit at Le Paradis.

Private John Henry Abigail has acquired a certain notoriety in Norfolk as the only member of the county regiment to have been executed during the First World War. 'Nine 'undred of 'is county an' the Regiment's disgrace', as Kipling wrote in his Barrack Room Ballad 'Danny Deaver'. What is less well known is that he was not the only member of the Regiment to have received a death sentence by court martial during the war. In all, 20 members of the Norfolk Regiment, all privates or temporary NCOs, were sentenced to death between August 1915 and December 1918. The catalogue of offences, all of which were punishable by death under the Army Act, were sleeping at their post (8 occasions), desertion (7), insubordination or disobedience (3) and cowardice (2). All but one of them (John's) were reprieved by the British commander in chief (French or Haig) and received instead sentences of between 5 and 15 years penal servitude or shorter terms of hard labour. In every case other than John's the sentences were either permanently suspended or remitted before the Armistice. Two soldiers, Privates W. Ashby and W. Compton, both of the 1st Norfolks, a Regular Army battalion, were in fact sentenced to death twice for desertion in 1918 and yet still avoided execution. Both survived the war, as did most of the others. Only four who returned to the Front under suspended sentences were subsequently killed in action or died of wounds. After the war, their slates were wiped clean and their entitlement to medals reinstated.

Was Private John Henry Abigail unfairly singled out in order to provide an example to others at a time of heightened fear of mutiny and mass desertion or were the circumstances of his case exceptional? It is interesting to note here the case of Private 16087 Jonathan E. Beck who, like John, served in the 8th Norfolks. Private Beck was tried on the same day as John and for the same offence – desertion – most probably by the same panel of officers. Like John, he was found guilty and sentenced to death but for some reason his sentence was not confirmed by Haig and he survived the war. After having his entitlement to the war's three main campaign medals removed in 1918, it was restored in 1919. It would be interesting to know if any mitigating circumstances entered into the decision not to confirm his sentence of death, such as his medical condition, or whether it was pure luck that his papers were returned unsigned by Haig. During 1917 courts martial were instructed to take into account whether the defendant had been wounded on active service. John had been wounded, on the Somme in July 1916, but there is no mention of this fact in his court martial papers.

Attention has been drawn to the intense physical and mental stress placed on those who served at the Front. It is generally accepted, though not necessarily true, that those in authority had little or no understanding of the long-lasting and debilitating effects of combat and fatigue or much sympathy for its sufferers whom they regarded as shirkers. A symptom known as 'shell shock' was recognised quite early on in the war, though it was often treated as a purely physiological rather than a psychological disorder, the result, it was thought, of prolonged exposure of the nervous system to shockwaves from detonated high explosives. However, while it is highly likely that some of those executed were suffering from what might be diagnosed today as traumatic stress disorder, contemporary medical evidence of their state of mind is scarce and unreliable by modern clinical standards.

It is interesting to find that the treatment of officers and men diagnosed with shell shock differed, as did their symptoms. A similar dichotomy in the justice meted out to officers and men found guilty of the same breaches of military law has also been observed. The fact that only two officers, and they both junior ones, were executed for offences other than murder during the war presumably doesn't mean that officers were more disciplined or less prone to cowardice or desertion than non-commissioned men. Numerous officers were indeed found guilty of military offences which attracted a death sentence but the vast majority received sentences of dishonour, such as reduction in rank, imprisonment or cashiering. In addition to concerns about the culpability of men who may or may not have been suffering with mental disorders, and the inconsistencies in the treatment of men of different rank and social and cultural backgrounds, some military and legal historians have also pointed out the unfairness and inadequacies of the Field General Court Martial procedure itself, in which men on trial for capital offences were, as the name implies, hastily tried within sound of the guns, sometimes in the front line itself, by battle-wearied officers called upon to act as both judge and jury with little or no legal training.

It isn't known when John's parents were informed that he had been executed for desertion. During 1917 the War Office changed its procedure for informing the next of kin in these circumstances; the wording of the notification was altered, making it more ambiguous, more open to interpretation that death had occurred in battle. The 1918 Voters Register for Norwich shows that Mr and Mrs Abigail were still living at 17 Distillery Yard, so it has to be assumed that it was one or other or both of them who asked for John's name to be added to St Augustine's roll of honour in 1919. It is interesting to note that the Commonwealth War Graves Commission's Debt of Honour Register records John's parents' names and address, which suggests that one or other of them completed and returned the additional information form, something which the majority of relatives didn't do. Considering the chaotic lives they had led in the past few years this was perhaps a sign that they were sticking together and trying to rebuild their family's pride.

John Henry Abigail is commemorated on the St Augustine's roll of honour and at the Shot at Dawn Arboretum near Lichfield. He was officially pardoned by Her Majesty's Government on 8 November 2006 under the provisions of the Armed Forces Act 2006. His conviction, however, remains. His entitlement to the British War and Victory medals, which was revoked during the war, remains revoked and his Medal Roll Index card notes that he was executed.

After John's older brother William's curtailed foray into the Territorials before the war when he was a teenager, he joined the Army Reserve in December 1915, presumably as a Derby Recruit (a voluntary enlistment scheme in which mobilisation was postponed, often for many months, depending on one's circumstances). He was eventually transferred to the Royal Naval Division (RND), in June 1917. As befits a Norfolk man he served in the RND's Nelson Battalion, first going over to France in October 1917 (the RND mainly fought on land as infantry). On 30 December he was wounded by a bullet, which grazed his face, presumably at a battle known as the Action of the Welsh Ridge in which German storm troopers, dressed in white snow camouflage, launched a surprise attack on the British line. On 24 March 1918, during the Battle of Bapaume, he was declared missing in action and it would be June before news reached home that he was still alive and had been taken prisoner. He saw out the rest of the war in a German POW camp at Limburg. He had been married in Bournemouth in 1917 to Amy Louisa Light. They had three children. After the war they settled in the West Country where William became a farmer. John's mother, Susannah, outlived John by little more than six years, dying in 1923, aged 55, of a strangulated femoral hernia; this was an operable condition requiring emergency surgery, which she clearly did not receive before it led to gangrene and death. His father, John James, lived until 1927, still at 17 Distillery Yard, dying at the age of 59 with chronic bronchitis. John James's cousin, James Abigail, after arthritis forced him to give up being a blacksmith at Bullard's brewery seems to have turned his back on alcohol, running a Temperance coffee stall for tram workers at the terminus in Orford Place. He later became secretary of the Norwich Medical Institute, a free clinic providing healthcare to poor members of friendly societies. One of James's sons, Sydney, rose from private in the Grenadier Guards during the war to become a lieutenant in the Norfolk Regiment, possibly with the 12th (Yeomanry) Battalion. On 15 July 1920 he resigned his commission (he was then in the 5th Battalion) and was granted the honorary rank of captain. It is interesting to contrast the military careers of these second cousins. Had either been born and raised in the other's circumstances, who knows how their lives might have turned out. 'There but for the grace…'

Private Abigail's memorial on the St Augustine's screen

Primary sources

American Battle Monuments Commission Honor Roll (www.abmc.gov)
Australian War Memorial (www.awm.gov.au)
Aviva Group Archive, Norwich (formerly Norwich Union Archive)
Benn family documents (used with permission)
Births, marriages and deaths (http://freebmd.rootsweb.com)
British Army First World War Service Documents – (National Archive ref. WO363)
British Army Medal Rolls Index cards, 1914–1920
Census of England & Wales, 1841–1911
Canadian Great War Project (www.canadiangreatwarproject.com)
Canadian Virtual War Memorial (www.veterans.gc.ca)
Canadian War Memorials on the World Wide Web (www.cdli.ca)
Carrow Works Magazine (Norfolk Heritage Centre, Norwich Library)
Commonwealth War Graves Commission's Debt of Honour Register (www.cwgc.org)
Eastern Daily Press, Eastern Evening News, Evening News and *Norwich Mercury* (Norfolk Heritage Centre, Norwich Library)
Ellis Island (Immigration) Records, New York, USA (www.ellisisland.org)
Fox family documents (used with permission)
Grenadier Guards Archive, Regimental HQ, Wellington Barracks, London
Hall family documents (used with permission)
Ireland's Memorial Records 1914–1918 (The Committee of the Irish National War Memorial, 1923)
Jarrold's Norwich Directory (various years)
Jode family documents (used with permission)
London Gazette, 1914–1920 (www.gazettes-online.co.uk)
National Archives, Kew (www.nationalarchives.gov.uk)
National Archive of Australia (www.naa.gov.au)
National Archive of Canada (www.collectionscanada.gc.ca)
National Library of Australia (http://nla.gov.au)
Norfolk Libraries' online Picture Norfolk collection (picture.norfolk.gov.uk)
Norfolk Public Houses: A listing (www.norfolkpubs.co.uk)
Norfolk Record Office, Norwich (www.archives.norfolk.gov.uk)
Norfolk Regiment's Wound Book, Royal Norfolk Regimental Museum
Norfolk Roll of Honour 1914–18. List of men from Norfolk Parishes who fell in the Great War (Norfolk News Company, Norwich, 1920, reissued by Gliddon Books, Norwich, 1988)
Northampton Museum & Art Gallery

Norwich Absent Voters Registers for 1918–20 (Norfolk Heritage Centre, Norwich Library)

Norwich Birth & Death Returns (Norfolk Heritage Centre, Norwich Library)

Norwich Electoral Registers for 1913/14, 1914/15 and 1918 (Norfolk Heritage Centre, Norwich Library)

Norwich Prison nominal roll (Norfolk Heritage Centre, Norwich Library)

Norwich Roll of Honour of Citizens Who Fell in the Great War, 1914–19 (Norwich Corporation, Norwich, 1924)

Norwich schools' log books and attendance registers (Norfolk Heritage Centre, Norwich Library)

Ontario County Records and Archives Center, New York State, USA

Pardon for Soldiers of the Great War, Bill 87 (TSO, London, 2005)

Rosary Cemetery Monumental Inscriptions, transcribed by P. E. Hamlin (*Norfolk Genealogy*, Norwich, Vol. XVIII, 1986)

Rosary Cemetery (Norwich) burial register (Norfolk Heritage Centre, Norwich Library)

St Andrew's church (Thorpe St Andrew) marriage register (Norfolk Heritage Centre, Norwich Library)

St Augustine's church, Norwich, Great War Roll of Honour chancel screen and other war memorials (with permission of The Churches Conservation Trust)

St Augustine's church, Norwich, baptismal and marriage registers (Norfolk Heritage Centre, Norwich Library)

St Augustine and St Mary Coslany Parish Magazine, various years (Norfolk Heritage Centre, Norwich Library)

St Miles Coslany's church, Norwich, baptismal register (Norfolk Heritage Centre, Norwich Library)

St Matthew's church, Thorpe Hamlet, Norwich, baptismal and marriage register (Norfolk Heritage Centre, Norwich Library)

St Paul's church, Norwich, marriage register (Norfolk Heritage Centre, Norwich Library)

Saskatchewan Virtual War Memorial (http://svwm.ca)

Silver War Badge record of awards

Soldiers Died in the Great War 1914–19 (CD-ROM edition, Version 2.0, published by Naval & Military Press, 2004)

Soldiers of the Great War, compiled by W. M. Haulsee, F. G. Howe and A. C. Doyle (Washington, D.C., Soldiers Record Publishing Association, 1920)

Soldiers' wills, HM Courts & Tribunal Service (probatesearch.service.gov.uk)

The Alderman Norman's Claimants Unity (www.normanfoundation.org)

The Lovelace Trust (www.lovelacetrust.org.uk)
The Norwich Union Magazine (Norfolk Heritage Centre, Norwich Library)
The Royal Norfolk Regimental Museum, Castle Museum, Norwich
Victor, New York State, USA – town website (www.victorny.org)
War Diaries of British and Canadian battalions, brigades and divisions
(various sources)

Bibliography

American Battle Monuments Commission, *American Armies and Battlefields in Europe. A History, Guide and Reference Book* (US Government Printing Office, Washington, D.C., 1938; 1995 reprint)

Babington, Anthony, *For the Sake of Example. Capital Courts Martial 1914–18, the truth* (Leo Cooper, London, 1983)

Bastin, Jeremy, *The Norfolk Yeomanry in Peace and War* (The Iceni Press, Fakenham, 1986)

Bull, William Perkins, *From Brock to Currie: the military development and exploits of Canadians in general and of the men of Peel in particular, 1791 to 1930 (The Perkins Bull Foundation, Toronto, 1935)*

Corns, Cathryn and John Hughes-Wilson, *Blindfold and Alone. British Military Executions in the Great War* (Cassell, London, 2001)

Coxford, Ronald, *A Half Crown Holy Boy. The Story of the 2/6 (Cyclist) Battalion Norfolk Regiment and the letters of one young soldier in the 1st World War* (self-published, 2007)

Gliddon, Gerald, *The Battle of the Somme. A Topographical History* (Allan Sutton Publishing, Stroud, 1994)

Gliddon, Gerald (ed.), *Norfolk and Suffolk in the Great War* (Gliddon Books, Norwich, 1988)

Gray, Edward, *A Damned Un-English Weapon. The story of submarine warfare 1914–1918* (Seeley, Service, London, 1971)

Rachael M. Hawkey, 'Vernon Griffiths (1894–1985). His Life and Philosophy of Music Education', PhD thesis (University of Canterbury, New Zealand, 1993)

Holden, Wendy, *Shell Shock: The Psychological Impact of War* (Channel 4 Books, London, 1998)

Holmes, Frances and Michael, *The Story of the Norwich Boot and Shoe Trade* (Norwich Heritage Projects, Norwich, 2013)

Holmes, Richard, *Tommy. The British Soldier on the Western Front 1914–1918* (HarperCollins, London, 2004)

Leeds, Herbert (ed.), *Peace Souvenir: Norwich War Record* (Jarrold & Sons, Norwich, no date [published *c.*1918])

Long, J. V. A., *An Introduction to Shoemaking* (The Shoe & Leather News, London, no date)

Mansfield, Nicholas, 'Volunteers and Recruiting', *Norfolk and Suffolk in the Great War* (Gliddon Books, Norwich, 1988)

McCarthy, Chris, *The Third Ypres. Passchendaele. The Day-By-Day Account* (Arms & Armour Press, London, 1995)

McLaren, Stuart, 'Death in the dawn's early light', *Norfolk Roots*, 8, November 2005, pp 20–3

Meeres, Frank, *Norfolk in the First World War* (Phillimore, Chichester, 2004)

O'Neill, H. C., *The Royal Fusiliers in the Great War* (London, 1922)

Oram, Gerard, *Death sentences passed by military courts of the British Army 1914–1924* (Francis Boutle Publishers, London, 1998)

Petre, F. Lorraine, *The History of the Norfolk Regiment, Volume II, 4th August 1914 to 31st December 1918* (Jarrold & Sons, Norwich, 1924; Naval & Military Press reprint)

Putowski, Julian and Sykes, Julian, *Shot at Dawn* (Leo Cooper, Barnsley, 1998)

Rainsford, W. Kerr, *From Upton to the Meuse with the 307th Infantry* (D. Appleton & Co, New York and London, 1920)

Smith, R. J. and R. G. Harris, *The Yeomanry Cavalry of Norfolk* (Picton, Chippenham, 1991)

Wavell, Colonel A.P., *The Palestine Campaigns*, 3rd edn (Constable, London, 1935)

Westlake, Ray, *British Battalions in France and Belgium 1914* (Leo Cooper, Barnsley, 1997)

Westlake, Ray, *British Battalions on the Somme* (Leo Cooper, Barnsley, 1994)

Young, Michael, *Army Service Corps 1902–1918* (Leo Cooper, Barnsley, 2000)

Roll of Honour by Military Unit
at Time of Death

American Expeditionary Force: Cooke, J

Army Service Corps: Copland, A W; Sizer, E J

Australian Imperial Force: Neasham, C F

Bedfordshire: Hardy, J; Wiseman, G A

Cambridgeshire: Ralph, W

Cameronians (Scottish Rifles): Springall, C W

Canadian Expeditionary Force: Allen, A R; Clarke, F C; Crosskill, T S; Howell, A J; Howell, G W;

Devonshire: Bovill, W R

Durham Light Infantry: Bailey, G

East Yorkshire: Fox, F G

Essex: Carriage, R H; Gant, R V; Willsea, W S

Gloucestershire: Fuller, R

Grenadier Guards: Attridge, G S

Hampshire: Purdy, H

King's Own Royal (Lancaster): Gooch, H F

King's Own Scottish Borderers: Hudson, W A; Jolly, E G

King's Own Yorkshire Light Infantry: Park, W B

King's Royal Rifle Corps: Spooner, W

Labour Corps: Brown, R; Pye, G; Stocks, W

Lincolnshire: Lundy, F

London (Post Office Rifles): Halfacre, E C

Machine Gun Corps: Clarke, E

Norfolk (1st Battalion): Cannell, A; Cartwright, H; Clarke, H H; Cossey, A M; Denham, E; Forster, H; Grady, A; Hardy, G; Lince, A; Loome, E H; Mitchell, R; Plunkett, E E; Scott, G R; Simpson, F; Swann, W;

Want, A; Woodcock, W

Norfolk (2nd Battalion): Bearman, E; Cropp, A; Fulcher, A

Norfolk (4th Battalion): Cushion, B C; Fox, A; Mason, W H; Skipper, G W; Wiseman, E P

Norfolk (5th Battalion): Baker, S E L; Clarke, E H

Norfolk (7th Battalion): Benn, W H; Carey, C E; Elsegood, T; Gayton, F; Middleton, F J; Whittaker, S

Norfolk (8th Battalion): Abigail, J H; Benn, B W; Brightwell, W; Mason, A W; Meadows, H; Youngs, A S

Norfolk (9th Battalion): Meachen, A; Miller, H A V; Scott, S J; Stocks, J W; Wilson, W

Norfolk (12th Battalion): Jode, G R L

Northumberland Fusiliers: Coxford, W; Lake, A; Lundy, A J

Rifle Brigade: Barber, E H; Palmer, S; Pert, L H

Royal Air Force: Brighty, F G

Royal Army Medical Corps: Hall, F H

Royal Dublin Fusiliers: Mutton, S A W

Royal Engineers: Lake, A N; Plunkett, W

Royal Field Artillery: Powell, H R

Royal Fusiliers (City of London): Fuller, J J

Royal Horse Artillery: Hewitt, P

Royal Sussex: Howard, S; Shorten, J D

Suffolk: Betts, E G

The Queen's (West Surrey): Fevyer, H E; Marshall, A C; Mason, J E

Welsh: Warminger, J H

West Yorkshire: Dennis, E H; Madgett, S

Wiltshire: Crosskill, B G

York and Lancaster: Tidd, W

Index